Women's Human Rights

Women's Human Rights

Seeking Gender Justice in a Globalizing Age

NIAMH REILLY

polity

The right of Niamh Reilly to be identified as Author of this Work has been asserted in accordance with the UK Copyright, Designs and Patents Act 1988.

First published in 2009 by Polity Press

Polity Press
65 Bridge Street
Cambridge CB2 1UR, UK.

Polity Press
350 Main Street
Malden, MA 02148, USA

ISBN-13: 978-0-7456-3699-3
ISBN-13: 978-0-7456-3700-6 (paperback)

A catalogue record for this book is available from the British Library.

Typeset in 11.25/13 pt Dante
by Servis Filmsetting Ltd, Stockport, Cheshire
Printed and bound by MPG Books Group, UK

The publisher has used its best endeavours to ensure that the URLs for external websites referred to in this book are correct and active at the time of going to press. However, the publisher has no responsibility for the websites and can make no guarantee that a site will remain live or that the content is or will remain appropriate.

Every effort has been made to trace all copyright holders, but if any have been inadvertently overlooked the publishers will be pleased to include any necessary credits in any subsequent reprint or edition.

For further information on Polity, visit our website: www.politybooks.com

For Ed

Contents

Acknowledgements   viii

List of acronyms and abbreviations   x

1   Women's Human Rights Advocacy   1

2   Human Rights, Gender and Contested Meanings   22

3   Women's Human Rights as Equality and Non-Discrimination   44

4   Violence and Reproductive Health as Human Rights Issues   69

5   Women's Human Rights in Conflict and Post-Conflict
    Transformation   93

6   Development, Globalization and Women's Human Rights   116

7   Fundamentalisms and Women's Human Rights   140

8   Conclusion   160

Notes   167

Bibliography   176

Index   194

Acknowledgements

The immediate impetus to write this book was the two years that I spent at the University of Limerick (UL) as a postdoctoral fellow in Women's Studies in 2003–5. I am especially grateful to Breda Gray at UL for her encouragement to get this project off the ground and for her ongoing support and intellectual engagement in bringing it to fruition. My preoccupation with its subject matter, however, goes back to an earlier time in 1990 when I first started to work at the Center for Women's Global Leadership at Rutgers University, while also pursuing my doctorate in Politics there. I was privileged to be part of a small group of staff and students who worked with Charlotte Bunch to build the Center from an idea into a substantial international organization at the heart of a new global women's human rights movement. During the 1990s, mainly in my role as coordinator of two popular tribunals on women's human rights in Vienna (1993) and Beijing (1995), and as coordinator of the '16 Days of Action Against Gender Violence' in its first years, I had the remarkable opportunity of working with dozens of activists and emerging thinkers and scholars from every region of the world, whose pioneering contributions continue to define the ever-evolving field of women's human rights. I owe an enormous debt to these women and men, too numerous to mention, whose dedication to the pursuit of gender justice and women's equality, at the UN and in disparate locations from Algeria, Chile and Brazil to India, Ireland, Sudan, Uganda and the United States, continues to inspire me. More specifically, this book owes much to Charlotte Bunch and to the many colleagues and friends who shaped the Center's activities in its early years, including Roxana Carrillo and Susana Fried. In particular, Charlotte's early and now commonsense understanding of 'global feminism' as a perspective that relies on building political solidarities among women across difference, and not on misplaced aspirations to women's sameness, underpins this book.

While different and more expansive in scope, this book builds firmly on my doctoral research. In this regard, I am pleased to acknowledge erstwhile mentors during my time at Rutgers – Stephen Bronner, Sue Carroll, Alice Kessler-Harris, Jacqueline Pitanguy and Linda Zerilli – whose faith in my research interests and capacities at critical moments was invaluable. In particular, the influence of Steve Bronner's persuasive defence of the radical promise of Enlightenment principles of reason, the rule of law, and democracy – while always contesting oppressive interpretations of these values – is evident throughout the book. More recently, a number of colleagues generously gave their time to comment on early drafts of my work, including Christine Bell, Fionnuala Ní Aoláin and Didi Hermann. I am also extremely grateful to two anonymous readers of the manuscript whose constructive comments helped me enormously in refining and streamlining the book. In addition, I greatly appreciate the collegial environment that I currently enjoy – within the Global Women's Studies Programme and School of Political Science and Sociology at the National University of Ireland, Galway – which buoyed my efforts to finalize this book. I also thank the staff at Polity for all of the assistance and support they have afforded toward the completion of this project.

Finally, because writing a book is often a tedious and drawn-out undertaking, quietly supportive friends and family have played a greater role than they know in seeing me over the finish line – most notably Ursula Barry, Mary Fitzpatrick, Maryann and Ed Hatton, Christine Kelly, Boni Luna, Díóg O'Connell, Anne Smith, Walt Jimenez, my siblings Ronan, Grace, Barry and Michael, our sister Mary, who is always missed, and my sons Donagh, Cian and Naoise. I am also grateful to my mother, Pat, who first sparked and encouraged my abiding interest in politics and social justice and whose own life and times (1924–90) in deeply conservative and patriarchal Ireland form an important subtext of this book. Above all, I thank Ed Hatton whose constant and unfailing support made it possible for me to write and revise amidst the many competing demands of our daily life.

Acronyms and abbreviations

AI	Amnesty International
APWLD	Asia Pacific Forum on Women, Law and Development
AWID	Association for Women's Rights in Development
BPA	Beijing Platform for Action (1995)
CAFRA	Caribbean Association for Feminist Research and Action
CEDAW	UN Convention on the Elimination of All Forms of Discrimination Against Women (1979)
CESCR	UN Committee on Economic, Social and Cultural Rights
CLT	cultural legitimacy thesis
CPD	UN Commission on Population and Development
CRLP	Center for Reproductive Law and Policy
CRR	Center for Reproductive Rights
CSW	UN Commission on the Status of Women
CWGL	Center for Women's Global Leadership
DAWN	Development Alternatives with Women for a New Era
DEVAW	UN Declaration on the Elimination of Violence against Women (1993)
ECOSOC	UN Economic and Social Council
EGI	Realizing Rights: The Ethical Globalization Initiative
ESCR-Net	Economic, Social and Cultural Rights Network
EU	European Union
FLS	Nairobi Forward-looking Strategies for the Advancement of Women (1985)
FWCW	Fourth World Conference on Women (Beijing, 1995)
GAD	gender and development
HERA	Health, Empowerment, Rights, and Accountability network
HRC	UN Human Rights Council
ICASC	International Campaign on Abortion, Sterilisation and Contraception
ICC	International Criminal Court

ICCPR	International Covenant on Civil and Political Rights (1966)
ICERD	International Convention on the Elimination of All Forms of Racial Discrimination (1965)
ICESCR	International Covenant on Economic, Social and Cultural Rights (1966)
ICPD	International Conference on Population and Development (Cairo, 1994)
ICTFY	International Criminal Tribunal for the Former Yugoslavia
ICTJ	International Center for Transitional Justice
ICTR	International Criminal Tribunal for Rwanda
ILO	International Labour Organization
IMTFE	International Military Tribunal for the Far East
INSTRAW	UN International Research and Training Institute for the Advancement of Women
IPC	International Preparatory Committee
IPU	Inter-Parliamentary Union
ISRRC	International Sexual and Reproductive Rights Coalition
IWHC	International Women's Health Coalition
IWRAW	International Women's Rights Action Watch
IWRAW Asia Pacific	International Women's Rights Action Watch Asia Pacific
IWTC	International Women's Tribune Center
IWY	International Women's Year (1975)
LGBT	lesbian, gay, bi-sexual and trans-gendered
MDGs	UN Millennium Development Goals
NIEO	New International Economic Order
NGO	non-governmental organization
OIC	Organisation of the Islamic Conference
POA	ICPD Programme of Action (Cairo, 1994)
RBA	rights-based approaches to development
RSH	reproductive and sexual health
SAP	structural adjustment programme
SCR 1325	Security Council Resolution 1325 (2000)
SRVAW	UN Special Rapporteur on Violence against Women
TFA	transnational feminist advocacy
Tokyo Tribunal	Women's International War Crimes Tribunal on Japan's Military Sexual Slavery (2000)
UDHR	Universal Declaration of Human Rights (1948)

UN	United Nations
UNCHR	UN Commission on Human Rights
UNDW	UN Decade for Women (1976–85)
UNESCO	UN Educational, Scientific and Cultural Organisation
UNGASS	UN General Assembly Special Session
UNIFEM	UN Development Fund for Women
VAW	violence against women
VDPA	Vienna Declaration and Programme of Action (1993)
WCAR	World Conference Against Racism, Racial Discrimination, Xenophobia and Related Forms of Intolerance (Durban, 2001)
WEDO	Women's Environment and Development Organization
WGLI	Women's Global Leadership Institute
WGNRR	Women's Global Network for Reproductive Rights
WHR	women's human rights
WID	women in development
WiLDAF	Women in Law and Development in Africa
WILPF	Women's International League for Peace and Freedom
WIN	Women's International Network
WLUML	Women Living under Muslim Laws
WSF	World Social Forum

1

Women's Human Rights Advocacy

Introduction

Since the late 1970s, a new wave of transnational feminist advocacy (TFA) has highlighted and contested the gendered impacts of an array of global issues. The UN Decade for Women (UNDW) (1976–85) and the post-Cold War revival of interest in more comprehensive visions of human rights provided particular impetus to these developments. Hence, from the early 1990s, transnational feminist networks and non-governmental organizations (NGOs) began to engage systematically across the different entities of the United Nations (UN) involved in defining global agendas on human rights, conflict and security, the environment, development and economic policy. In this context, actors from women's movements of the global South, as well as the North moved into transnational forums in unprecedented numbers and with an exceptional level of coordination. They collaborated effectively – across disparate standpoints and identities – in a targeted effort to ensure the inclusion of women's perspectives and gender analyses in a wide range of global norm-setting and policy processes. This book spotlights this TFA and, drawing on examples from particular campaigns and initiatives, explores its origins, concepts, issues, practice and theoretical significance. My purpose here is to make visible, thematize, and highlight the transformative potential of TFA in a context of globalization, a potential that is rooted in critical, bottom-up understandings of human rights as universal and indivisible.

Why is this book important? What are the particular events and conceptual challenges to which it is responding? My answer has four interrelated parts. First, this book seeks to highlight the gendered dynamics of global issues and forces and to explore ways of responding to their detrimental impact in the lives of women and girls. In particular, feminist scholars and advocates around the world have problematized gender-specific experiences of widening inequalities in a context of neo-liberal globalization; global health crises and disease pandemics; organized crime, including trafficking; rising fundamentalisms across all regions and religions; and contemporary forms of militarism and conflict, including the 'war on terror'. Moreover, a very large literature now exists recognizing violence against women (VAW) as a pervasive global concern that is implicated in each of these issues and beyond.

In mainstream discourse, however, 'global issues' – whether conflict and security, Third World poverty, macroeconomics, climate change or disease pandemics – are rarely understood fundamentally as 'gender issues' and 'local issues'. That is, their immediate impacts and meanings are inevitably experienced, negotiated and contested in the everyday lives of women, men and children in contexts of *unequal gender power relations* in intimate relationships, families and communities. This insight suggests that generating effective responses to contemporary challenges and crises 'as if women matter' requires that all such issues are viewed through a gender lens that is centrally concerned with validating women's concrete experiences and with promoting and protecting women's human rights (WHR), broadly defined.

Second, this book aims to illustrate and defend the ongoing importance of developing and applying critical gender analyses to contemporary human rights thinking and practice and of keeping such transformed understandings of human rights at the heart of feminist projects. Given the many political and intellectual challenges that currently threaten the legitimacy of human rights, however, this is not a straightforward undertaking. The growth and success of WHR advocacy throughout the 1990s has been met with major political resistance, especially in the form of new fundamentalist projects *across all religions and regions*. These explicitly contest commitments to women's equality and human rights claims more generally as 'Western', a threat to national sovereignty, individualistic and/or 'anti-family'. Similarly, the 'war on terror', as well as high-profile conflicts and crises in Iraq, Israel/Palestine, Sudan, Zimbabwe and elsewhere, have eroded greatly the credibility of international human rights and humanitarian paradigms in the early twenty-first century. These developments, especially under conditions of persistent, unequal global power dynamics, democratic deficits throughout the UN and the cynical use/abuse of international law by dominant powers, make it exceptionally difficult for progressive voices to defend and promote the emancipatory and transformative potential of international human rights and global governance.

At the same time, however, it can be argued that highly visible failures in human rights protection and implementation serve only to underline the imperative of retaining and re-energizing global political commitment to upholding the principle of 'all human rights for all' and of the international community providing the necessary resources to back that commitment. From this normative standpoint, I suggest that the kinds of TFA explored throughout this book have a key role to play in promoting a critical vision of human rights and, more specifically, in ensuring the formulation of meaningful gender-conscious norms and practical strategies in the process. Most importantly, drawing on concrete examples, this book highlights the conditions under which TFA can serve emancipatory and counter-hegemonic purposes, especially vis-à-vis unequal and gendered North–South power relations.

Third, this book brings an advocacy-oriented perspective to a number of long-running debates in feminist political and social theory that raise fundamental questions about the prospects for ending gender-based oppressions within a human rights paradigm. Particularly relevant are debates around the ostensible chasm between 'universalist' feminist positions on the one hand and identity-based, multiculturalist and postmodern feminist positions on the other. Simply put, anti-universalist feminist critics across the philosophical spectrum challenge dominant Western-centric, neo-liberal, male-defined and otherwise biased interpretations of supposedly universal norms (human rights, equality, rule of law, etc.) and their role in perpetuating practices that systematically disadvantage women and marginalized groups in society. This includes, for example, a public–private divide that conceals private abuses of power; atomistic individualism that privileges rights to private property and profit-making over rights to development, health, welfare and so on; failures to recognize and address inequalities flowing from structural disadvantage and oppression, including global inequalities; 'impartialist reasoning' that often serves male-defined interests (e.g. failures of justice systems in rape cases); and cultural and political processes of false universalization wherein the perspectives of a hegemonic grouping become *the* particular worldview from which universal norms are formulated and imposed on less dominant groups in society, including women and minorities. Postmodern and post-structural thinkers are particularly trenchant in their rejection of universal norms – viewing them as modernist, totalizing narratives that are deeply implicated in a complex of dominating and oppressive practices.

In response, emancipatory cosmopolitan feminist positions (exemplified by this book) hold that, notwithstanding the negative impact of false universalization, critically re-interpreted 'universal' norms remain an indispensable point of departure in contesting all forms of oppression and discrimination. Without doubt, there are many well-documented failures in the interpretation and application of universal norms of equality, human rights, the rule of law, etc. A core contention of this book, however, is that such failures and exclusions should not be viewed as inevitabilities of failed modernist and Enlightenment paradigms. Rather, they reflect contestable disparities in and abuses of power that can and should be challenged through emancipatory political projects. Indeed, such projects – exemplified by WHR movements and other rights-based movements the world over – are pivotal to non-oppressive modes of universalization. Rather than eschew universal norms as inherently regressive, therefore, the conceptual challenge is to identify and thematize the conditions of their substantive realization and transformative potential.

Finally, this book reflects a situated analysis and a commitment to praxis. That is, it is shaped by my own experience as a participant in UN-oriented TFA for WHR during the 1990s (Bunch and Reilly 1994), and my interest in applying the insights gleaned in this context to a wider critical inquiry into the prospects for 'the feminist project' in a globalizing age. In this sense, it re-engages with the notion that there is a normative relationship between feminist theory and scholarship on the one hand and transformative practice on the other. A significant effect of the postmodern intellectual movement has been to make this distinction within feminism and its original orientation toward traditional activism appear naïve. Within this intellectual milieu, much recent feminist scholarship is characterized by an immersion in radical deconstructive analyses of discursive practices with little or no reference to concrete sites of struggle. In the meantime, 'old-style' political feminist practice – which retains a commitment to collective action and improving the conditions of women's lives, often through a primary orientation to states – is rarely viewed as relevant to cutting-edge feminist theorizing even though it is generally accepted as well intentioned and perhaps strategically necessary.

In contrast, this book highlights the continuing need to explore the role of women's movements and feminist advocacy vis-à-vis the state, law, policy and global governance as sites of contestation *and* potentially transformative action in a globalizing age. In particular, I endorse an emancipatory cosmopolitan feminist perspective that addresses the dangers of false universalization, the intersectionality of subject positions and the gendered dynamics of globalization and global forces. Understood in this way, the account of emancipatory cosmopolitan feminism elaborated in the following sections forms the normative and analytical framework for the rest of the book.

What is cosmopolitanism?

While cosmopolitan thinking takes many forms, Carol Gould's distinction between moral and political cosmopolitanism is a useful one (2004, 166). Moral cosmopolitanism refers to accounts that retain a commitment to treating all human beings with equal concern within a global frame. This is most cogently expressed in the idea of universal human rights, which underpin human freedom (variously defined) and are independent of legal or political status (Habermas 2001, Okin 2000, Nussbaum 1999). Kant was the principal originator of cosmopolitanism in modern Western political thought. Most notably, in his essay 'Perpetual Peace', he advanced cosmopolitanism to promote peace among nations and foster mutual respect among individuals by virtue of their common humanity. This includes the idea of 'cosmopolitan right' resonant in contemporary cosmopolitan visions that embrace some form of discourse ethics (Held 2002, Linklater 1998). Cosmopolitan right entails a universal entitlement *and* a duty to engage in free and open dialogue with others from different cultures and contexts, enabled by the human capacity to 'present oneself and be heard within and across political communities' (Held 2002, 310). Such Kantian cosmopolitan values flow from the idea that all persons are equal moral, reasoning and autonomous beings. Consequently, every person is entitled to be treated with equal concern and not as means to ends and, by the same token, everyone has a duty to treat others in the same way. This grounding of cosmopolitan claims in a particular form of human rationality is clearly questionable. Nonetheless, a moral assertion of the equality of all human beings and the idea that the well-being of persons is paramount in the pursuit of justice remain at the heart of all contemporary cosmopolitan positions, including the account of cosmopolitan feminism that informs this book.

Proponents of political cosmopolitanism (building on moral cosmopolitanism) are generally concerned with specifying the legal, political and institutional loci of cosmopolitan political practice (Held 2002, Archibugi 2003, Falk 2004). David Held, for example, defines cosmopolitanism as 'the ethical and political space which sets out the terms of reference for the recognition of people's equal moral worth, their active agency, and what is required for their autonomy and development' (2002, 313). Advocates of political cosmopolitanism often argue that international law and organizations are already primary loci for cosmopolitan governance, while nonetheless underlining the need to build democratic legitimacy and deepen democratic practice at the global level. In particular, they point to international human rights law (Beetham 1999, Pogge 2005) and the International Criminal Court (ICC) (Held 2002, Falk 2004) as important ingredients in formulating global governance that is more accountable. Most ambitiously, some envisage a form of world government, under-pinned by international law (Held 1995, Falk 2004). In tandem with discussions of cosmopolitan democracy, others explore evolving modes of global citizenship, often with particular reference to the role of social movements and NGOs in cosmopolitan practice (Edwards and Gaventa 2001, Khagram et al. 2002).

In contrast, sceptics flag the many democratic deficits and problems of legitimacy associated with such 'cosmopolitical' visions. These include the potential emergence of a tyrannical world power (Urbinati 2003); the threat of erasure of cultural plurality and global imposition of Western liberal values (An-Na'im 1992, Matua 2002); the absence of democratic, participatory and bottom-up channels of decision-making (Gould 2004, 170); the problematic ways in which the composition of global civil society mirrors wider political, economic, cultural and gender power imbalances (Robinson 2003, 169); and the impossibility of facilitating 'the ethical-political self-understanding of citizens of a particular democratic life' in a 'community of world citizens' supported by a relatively weak 'cosmopoli-tan solidarity' (Habermas 2001, 107). These are all very valid concerns, and in the absence of a global, broad-based movement I am deeply sceptical about cosmopolitan proposals for a constitutional world government. However, I agree with proponents of political cosmopolitanism that human rights law and UN forums – if approached from a critical, bottom-up perspective – are vital elements in the realization of emancipatory cosmopolitanism.

Cosmopolitan feminism

A commitment to cosmopolitan tenets is present in the work of a variety of feminist political thinkers. It is most evident in recent discussions of global feminist projects under the banner 'women's rights are human rights' (Okin 2000, Ackerly and Okin 1999, Jaggar 2000, Nussbaum 1999). This global turn, however, is relatively new. Until the 1990s, most feminist political theorists assumed a territorially bounded, Western, liberal, 'devel-oped' state as its empirical frame of reference and focused on problematizing gender blindness within these parameters. A number of factors combined to prompt these and other theorists to take account of the global arena and to investigate the prospects for feminist solidarity and gender justice across women's differences and beyond the liberal democratic state. These included the proliferation of compelling Third World, postcolonial and anti-racist feminist critiques of established feminist discourses, which hitherto had reflected predominantly white, Western and otherwise privileged perspectives (for example, hooks 1984, Spelman 1988, Spivak 1988, Mohanty 1988); the surge in transnational feminist organizing, including unprecedented levels of participation by women from the 'developing world' sparked by the UN Decade for Women (1976–85) and extended throughout the 1990s to the present (Antrobus 2002 and 2004a, Fraser and Tinker 2004, Moghadam 2005, Winslow 1995); and more recently, a growing recognition across different feminist circles of the need to address the gendered impacts of globalization and to refocus attention on the interplay between economic, social and political arenas (Mohanty 2003, Moghadam 2005, Petchesky 2003).

My account of cosmopolitan feminism builds on an evolving body of feminist political theorizing that continues to engage with the transformative promise of universal norms in ways that respond to well-founded anti-universalist critiques including work by Ackerly and Okin, Benhabib, Nussbaum, Phillips and Jaggar. At a minimum this means the following: (1) recognizing that patriarchal power relations persist globally, albeit expressed and experienced differently by differently situated women; and (2) retaining a critical commitment to upholding 'universal' norms in contesting gender-based and other forms of oppression. Equally, I build on anti-relativist currents in postcolonial feminist writing.[1] Uma Narayan, for example, warns that the anti-Western, anti-universalist logic of much postcolonial writing feeds into a 'cultural essentialism' that 'plays a powerful ongoing role in political movements that are inimical to women's interests in the Third World' (Narayan 2000, 85). Similarly, Arati Rao notes that 'no social group has suffered greater violation of its human rights in the name of culture than women' (Rao 1995, 169). She is concerned that WHR cannot be realized as long as 'falsely rigid, ahistorical, and selectively chosen' definitions of culture persist in human rights thinking and practice (p. 174). Illustrating this point, Sharon Hom (1992) highlights female infanticide and son preference as harmful 'traditional and modern practices of Chinese culture' that evade critical scrutiny in the name of respect for cultural diversity. Similarly, Hom notes how relativist rights arguments have allowed the Chinese government to claim that the collective right of economic development justifies coercive population control policies that deny Chinese women reproductive health and autonomy. For Hom, such visions of human rights are no better than the 'Western individualist model', which claims to be gender neutral. Both approaches, she argues, 'reflect the decisions and priorities of predominantly male leaderships who define both the political sphere and collective interests'. Thus, she continues, 'situating a rights vision in a relativist perspective, which accepts the legitimacy of prioritising the collective interest over "individual" interests is deadly for women in the context of a collectivity dominated and defined by men' (p. 293).

Support for an emancipatory cosmopolitan feminism is also implicit in Chandra Mohanty's influential essay 'Under Western Eyes: Feminist Scholarship and Colonial Discourses' (1988), even though it is most often read as a quintessentially postmodern, anti-universalist and postcolonial feminist text. While acknowledging the influence of Foucault in developing her analysis, Mohanty challenges these readings:

> I did not write 'Under Western Eyes' as a testament to the impossibility of egalitarian and non-colonizing cross-cultural scholarship, nor did I define 'Western' and 'Third World" feminism in such oppositional ways that there would be no possibility of solidarity between Western and Third World Feminists. . ... In 1986 I wrote mainly to challenge the false universality of Eurocentric discourses and perhaps was not sufficiently critical of the valorisation of difference over commonality in postmodern discourse. Now, I find myself writing to reemphasize the connections between the local and the universal. . . . The challenge is to see how . . . specifying difference allows us to theorize universal concerns more fully. (Mohanty 2003, 224–6)

Problematizing identity politics and emphasizing that Third World women are not a monolithic category, Mohanty argues that it is possible to identify coherent Third World feminist struggles based on 'common differences'. That is, even as different women in the Third World experience oppression differently, they do so in relation to common systems of power and domination that affect all Third World women. This perspective resonates with Charlotte Bunch's definition of 'global feminism', which she defines as a 'transformational feminist politics that is global in perspective [and where] . . . the particular issues and forms of struggle for women in different locations will vary [and activists] . . . strive to understand and expand the commonality and solidarity of that struggle' (Bunch 1987, 303).

Following the same logic, this book advocates a non-oppressive understanding of global feminism that is not based on the premise that all women are oppressed, or oppressed in the same way, or that they automatically share common values and agendas. It does recognize, however, that there are persistent structural forces at work worldwide that disadvantage women and girls in gender-specific ways, particularly those who are also marginalized vis-à-vis class, ethnicity, 'race', sexual orientation, disability and so on, as well as location in the global economy. This recognition opens up the possibility for feminist dialogue, solidarity and collective action across multiple boundaries. Feminist economist Bina Agarwal (1994) captures some of the complexities involved in positing global feminism under these conditions:

> When I position myself . . . as a woman challenging patriarchy . . . especially in relation to body politics, I can stand with Western feminist[s]. . . . But when I position myself as a Third World Woman, I find myself on a different side of the platform, questioning the often ethnocentric preoccupations of First World feminist academia with its economic and intellectual privilege. And finally, when I position myself as a privileged Third World woman academic in my own culture, I stand vulnerable to interrogation by my less privileged sisters and seek to build bridges with them. (p. 255)

In the early 1980s, Bunch suggested that an emerging global feminist movement was discernible but had not yet 'given birth to a common language and analysis' (Bunch 1987, 281). Arguably, the feminist transformation of human rights discourse and practice that defined much of Bunch's work – especially in the 1990s – offers such a 'common language and analysis'. More recently, Nira Yuval-Davis affirms this idea when she argues that 'transversal politics' is integral to non-oppressive feminism where 'women's rights are human rights' is the discursive framework in which transversal political activists often work (2006, 283). Understood as 'an alternative to assimilationist "universalistic" politics . . . and to identity politics' (p. 281), Yuval-Davis argues that emancipatory 'transversal feminist politics depend on decentred, non-West-centric, non-racialised, and an as comprehensive as possible dialogic approach' (p. 289). Moreover, she notes that: 'The highest feminist achievement of the last twenty years [is that] so much of the 1970s inherent ethnocentric, West-centric, and often even racist constructions have been rejected and that such a wide, often Southern-led dialogue has contributed to the determination of global feminist agendas' (p. 289). This characterization is consistent with my observations of the Global Campaign for Women's Human Rights and informs my understanding of cosmopolitan feminism as process-oriented and dialogic feminist practice in a globalizing age. However, while agreeing with Yuval-Davis on the need to problematize the limitations of established human rights discourse (legalistic, top-down, civil and political bias, etc.), her account of transversal feminist politics understates the centrality of human rights discourse in making such politics possible in the first place. In contrast, I argue that retaining a critical commitment to the legal *and* substantive realization of universal human rights norms (i.e. equality and non-discrimination across political, economic, social and cultural realms) *is* a constitutive moment of non-oppressive global feminism rather than simply a complementary mode of advocacy. Moreover, the term 'cosmopolitan feminism' is most appropriate to emphasize both the transnational nature of the feminist solidarity involved and its grounding in a commitment to the bottom-up, critical (re)interpretations of universal norms, especially human rights.

Cosmopolitan feminism as emancipatory human rights practice

In this section, I set out the main features of the emancipatory framework of cosmopolitan feminism that shapes this book.[2] In doing so, I highlight the conditions of emancipatory feminist projects that are grounded in 'universal' human rights but reject the imposition of Western-centric, gender-biased and other exclusionary interpretations of rights. Towards this end, I posit five mutually constitutive moments of cosmopolitan feminism. Taken together, these form a coherent conceptual and practical framework for transformative, non-oppressive transnational feminist action in a context of globalization:

1 a critical engagement with public international law, especially human rights;
2 a global feminist consciousness that contests patriarchal, neo-liberal/capitalist and racist power dynamics;
3 cross-boundaries dialogue and networking that recognize the intersectionality of forms of oppression;
4 collaborative transnational advocacy and action around concrete issues;
5 utilization of global forums as sites of feminist cosmopolitan solidarity and civic action.

A critical engagement with public international law

In keeping with other articulations of cosmopolitanism, cosmopolitan feminism expresses a commitment to public international law,[3] particularly human rights norms and law. In doing so, however, it challenges the limitations of established international law as a 'progressive narrative' and a 'liberal conception' with a 'state-centric focus' (Crawford and Marks 1998). A critique of established human rights is set out in more detail in the following chapter. Briefly, mainstream approaches understand human rights primarily as a top-down body of international law that is interpreted by experts or a system of intergovernmental institutions charged with formulating and monitoring the implementation of human rights standards. In contrast, cosmopolitan feminist engagement with human rights challenges this legalist bias and seeks instead to integrate the moral, legal and political elements of human rights into a framework of critical, bottom-up action to achieve what Charlotte Bunch calls the 'feminist transformation of human rights' (1990). Importantly, it also entails a radical critique of public–private configurations in international law. The act of claiming rights, therefore, is central to this conception in which international human rights ideas and standards are subject to ongoing processes of contestation, (re)interpretation and (re)definition. This is very different, however, from saying that the content of human rights is decided in a relativist vacuum because the struggle to contest the meaning of human rights is always with reference to established human rights standards (Bronner 2004, 147). Consequently, a participative, dialogic process – grounded in the idea that the content of universal human rights must resonate with the concerns of, and be defined by and with, concrete, situated women – is integral to advancing WHR claims.

The Global Campaign for Women's Human Rights is a particularly strong example of this approach. In the late 1980s, there was a growing recognition within and across women's movements that violence against women was a universal phenomenon that affected women in every region, even though the form it took differed from place to place (Carrillo 1991). This was pivotal in the emergence of a far-reaching feminist challenge to mainstream human rights concepts and practice. When plans for a UN world conference on human rights were underway in the early 1990s, many questioned the failure of international human rights standards and advocacy to address women's experiences. This meant asking why abuses affecting women primarily – such as domestic violence, trafficking or forced pregnancy – had not been taken seriously as human rights issues (Bunch 1990).

With the exception of the Convention on the Elimination of All Forms of Discrimination Against Women (CEDAW) (1979), which attempted to deepen the definition and scope of sex-based discrimination as a human rights issue (see chapter 3), women's rights had been viewed very narrowly in terms of legal equality with men and were generally invisible or marginalized within the wider human rights machinery. The Global Campaign for Women's Human Rights (discussed in chapter 4) highlighted the gendered ways in which traditional approaches to human rights privileged male-defined aspects of civil and political rights in situations where violations are carried out by the state. Especially through the use of popular tribunals organized alongside major UN forums, the campaign demonstrated how this gender bias served to deny the human rights dimensions of harmful and often fatal forms of gender-based violence because they occur in 'private' contexts of family or community and are generally perpetrated by non-state actors such as spouses and family members (Bunch and Reilly 1994).

As will be discussed in chapter 4, the Global Campaign resulted in the adoption of a raft of significant new international human rights standards and mechanisms. For example, violence against women was recognized as a violation of human rights in the Vienna Declaration and Programme of Action (VDPA) (1993) and in the UN General Assembly Declaration on the Elimination of Violence against Women (DEVAW) (1993). In 1994, a UN Special Rapporteur on Violence against Women (SRVAW) was appointed to investigate the issue and to encourage effective governmental, regional and UN remedial measures. The Beijing Platform for Action (BPA), which is still considered by many to be a comprehensive 'blueprint' for WHR, was adopted by 189 countries in 1995. Above all else, therefore, the 'women's rights as human rights' movement of the 1990s is associated with achieving recognition of VAW as a global, human rights issue.

More recent examples of cosmopolitan feminist engagement with international law build on this recognition. The ICC NGO Women's Caucus for Gender Justice effectively mobilized the support of women's networks internationally in its campaign to ensure the gender sensitivity of the 1998 Rome Statute of the ICC. For the first time in international law, the ICC criminalized sexual and gender violence as war crimes and crimes against humanity. Another example is the PeaceWomen project, which links NGOs around the world focusing on 'women, peace and security issues'. This initiative, which secured the adoption of Security Council Resolution 1325 (2000),[4] continues to coordinate NGO efforts to ensure its implementation. Resolution 1325 is significant because it signalled the first time that the Security Council turned its 'full attention' to the subject of women and conflict situations. Both of these examples are explored in more detail in chapter 5.

A global feminist consciousness

A global feminist consciousness that challenges the systemic interplay of oppressive patriarchal, capitalist and racist power relations is integral to contesting false universalization and neo-imperialist manifestations of supposedly cosmopolitan values. This is similar to Mohanty's Third World feminist consciousness noted above – a critical perspective that focuses on contesting structural power without assuming homogeneity of gender identity or experience or even an ongoing consensus among women across a range of issues. From this perspective, the global arena is understood to be shaped by interconnected unequal and contested power relations across lines of geo-politics and geo-economics as well as gender, 'race', class and other social positions. In particular, a global feminist consciousness challenges the false dichotomies that pervade understanding of the international arena – especially in the Western, 'developed' world. Hence, the powerful hierarchical binaries of North/South, Christianity/ Islam, secular/fundamentalist, First World / Third World, freedom/ authoritarianism, etc., are implicated in the construction of harmful stereotypes and the invisibility of inequalities across lines of gender, race and class. For example, poverty and inequality are major features of the so-called First World; Islam is not synonymous with fundamentalism, terrorism and anti-democratic values; forms of Christian fundamentalism – which is pervasive in many regions – also undermine democratic values and potentially promote terrorism (e.g. attacks on abortion clinics and practitioners); and free-market privatization is not equivalent to democratization.

More concretely, a global feminist consciousness brings the gendered dimensions of globalization and related global issues sharply into focus and underlines the necessity of bringing feminist analyses to bear in the formulation of remedial responses. For example, roughly half of the 40 million people living with HIV/AIDS are women in the Third World, and the rate of female infection is rapidly exceeding that for males (Amnesty International 2004). This is explained by the continued prevalence of various forms of VAW, sex-based discrimination, women's disproportionate poverty and the marginalization of Third World countries on the global stage. Similarly, at least half of the world's 80 million migrants (International Labour Organization (ILO) 2002) are women, and in some parts of Asia this percentage is as high as 70 per cent. While migration is inextricably linked to profound economic disparities between countries, women experience migration in gender-specific, racialized ways that leave them more vulnerable than male counterparts and non-migrant women to violence and exploitative employment, including high-risk work in the sex industry.

More generally, there is a growing recognition of the unequal, gendered impact of globalization (Streeten 2001). On balance, globalization has made most women more vulnerable to poverty, involuntary migration, economic and sexual exploitation and related forms of VAW. While proponents of cosmopolitanism have argued persuasively that current global problems demand a cosmopolitan and not simply an international approach, women's experiences equally underscore the need for a feminist cosmopolitan response to global issues. More positively, a global feminist consciousness also recognizes new opportunities for collaboration among groups and individuals in seeking to advance social justice internationally. The model of emancipatory cosmopolitan feminism posited here reflects such an optimistic response.

Intersectionality, cross-boundaries dialogue and networking

Emancipatory cosmopolitan feminism has as its driving process a commitment to action-oriented dialogue and networking among women across boundaries of class, 'race', ethnicity, religious and cultural identity, sexual orientation and so on – both within states and across geo-political divides. More than three decades of second-wave feminist critiques have driven home the message that any contemporary feminist project, activist or academic, cannot be based on an assumption of women as a monolithic group with a 'natural' common agenda. Moreover, cosmopolitan feminism fully recognizes that, within and beyond women's movements, differences inevitably give rise to tensions and conflict, especially when there is a failure to acknowledge power differentials that map on to these differences. This demands a strongly anti-essentialist standpoint – one which recognizes that, even as gendered power dynamics generally work to the disadvantage of women and girls, gendered disadvantage is experienced differently according to other aspects of identity and location, especially with respect to class, 'race', sexual orientation, (dis)ability and so on. This recognition of the intersectionality of women's experiences and identities (Crenshaw 1997, 2000; Collins 2000) means that feminist practice must be alert to new and shifting forms of 'multiple discrimination'.[5] For example, regarding the challenges of addressing the interplay of gender, race and ethnicity within a women's human rights framework, Crenshaw argues that:

> Ensuring that all women will be served by the expanded scope of gender-based human rights protections requires attention to the various ways that gender intersects with a range of other identities, and the way these intersections contribute to the unique vulnerability of different groups of women. Because the specific experiences of ethnically or racially defined women are often obscured within broader categories of race or gender, the full scope of their intersectional vulnerability cannot be known and must, in the final analysis, be built from the ground up. (Crenshaw 2000)

Building on this understanding of intersectionality, it follows that the priorities of emancipatory cosmopolitan feminist projects can only be determined in the context of genuine, ongoing cross-boundaries dialogue and networking. While there are always gaps between principle and practice, evidence of a feminist cosmopolitan commitment to cross-boundaries networking is found in various global feminist networks in the form of inclusive organizing strategies, participative membership or representative organizational structures.[6]

Collaborative transnational advocacy around concrete issues

Cosmopolitan feminism is ultimately an account of emancipatory feminist practice – it only becomes coherent in the context of struggles linked to concrete issues and events. As already noted, in the case of the Global Campaign for Women's Human Rights, VAW emerged as a pivotal unifying issue that galvanized a far-reaching cosmopolitan feminist project. Similarly, the TFA to address gender justice in the ICC statute was linked directly to wider mobilization of women's movements against war rapes in the Balkans conflict of the 1990s, and a longer-running campaign for recognition of the human rights of 200,000 'comfort women' who were subjected to sexual slavery by the Japanese military during World War II.

In the late 1980s, the reality or threat of violence in women's lives came into focus as a global concern, and a growing body of research demonstrated that it cut across all socioeconomic and cultural categories (Pietilä and Vickers 1990, 142–8). While women in North America and Europe set up refuges and shelters for victims of battery, in Africa they challenged customary practices that permitted the dispossession of widows or the practice of female genital mutilation. In Asia, groups organized against female infanticide, dowry-related abuse and killings, and trafficking in women. As the Global Campaign for Women's Human Rights took shape in the early 1990s, the issue of VAW was a natural focus, given the vitality of organizing on the issue in every region of the world. An important aspect of VAW was that no region could claim immunity and 'developed' Western countries could not evade the issue as one that only occurred in 'less developed' countries. This recognition of VAW as a global phenomenon that takes different forms in different contexts was crucial in underpinning a call for accountability to human rights standards across all regions and cultural contexts, and rejecting any defence of such violence on the basis of cultural differences.

The emergence of VAW as a unifying issue at a global level, therefore, reflected the priorities of grassroots organizations and networks. Importantly, as campaign participants collaborated to develop global campaign strategies, they did so on the understanding that local strategies to counter domestic violence, dowry abuse, female infanticide, female genital mutilation and so on would be context-specific (see chapter 4). This standpoint accommodates a wide range of experiences of VAW. It includes, for example, male violence in the home as well as harmful traditional practices that other women perform. This context-sensitive approach contrasts with previous North–South feminist encounters, for example at world conferences during the UNDW. During this period, efforts by some US and European feminists to single out female genital mutilation for particular condemnation were perceived (generally correctly) as neo-imperialist and prompted some African women to defend the practice in cultural relativist terms (Joachim 1999, 145).

Utilization of global forums as sites of feminist cosmopolitan solidarity and action

A substantial body of scholarship argues that patterns of increased NGO activity around UN forums over recent decades signalled the emergence of a global civil society and a shift away from the nation-state as the primary locus of political power. Women's transnational NGO networks are frequently cited as playing a pivotal role in this process (Dickensen 1997, Keck and Sikkink 1998, Joachim 1999, Thompson 2002). Illustrating this argument, the Global Campaign for Women's Human Rights targeted a series of UN world conferences, beginning with the World Conference on Human Rights (Vienna, 1993) and culminating with the Fourth World Conference on Women (FWCW) (Beijing, 1995). The campaign utilized these global forums to promote public awareness, develop the campaign and secure concrete commitments to WHR. Through a combination of strategies that create opportunities for bottom-up participation (popular tribunals, petition drives and so on), the Global Campaign and similar cosmopolitan projects also fostered intensive lobbying of policy- and lawmakers at local, national and regional levels. In doing so, participants acquired the knowledge and skills needed to be active 'global citizens' and participate in multilevel governance processes. The new WHR measures achieved in the 1990s, therefore, attest to the success of TFA and the pos- sibility of local NGO actors playing an increasingly visible and effective role in shaping international law and policy.

Addressing women's transnational organizing around the Beijing women's conference, Dickensen suggested it marked a 'global feminist transformation of liberal democracy', wherein the 'possibilities of self- determination, long denied at the nation-state level, may be realised by circumventing the nation-state from above or below' (1997, 110). Since the September 11, 2001, attacks on the World Trade Center and the Pentagon in the USA, however, such optimistic accounts of the prospects for cosmo- politan citizenship are less evident and the focus on the rule of law has intensified. David Held, for example, expresses concern that the post- World War II 'rule-based multilateral order' is 'fragile, vulnerable and full of limitations' (Held 2005, 15). He talks less about new forms of cosmo- politan political participation and more about the importance of sustaining progress towards a 'truly internationalist or cosmopolitan framework of global law' (p. 10). This emphasis on top-down law reflects an understand- able sense of urgency that egregious acts of international terrorism should not be accompanied by a retreat into national particularism or security policies that potentially erode the foundations of human rights and democ- racy.

It is important, however, to consider the gender implications of this 'backslide' of support for bottom-up, civic engagement with international law and global governance (Charlesworth and Chinkin 2002). Well before the September 11 attacks, WHR gains had become the subject of intense backlash in UN, regional and national policy as conservative governments and NGOs mobilized to contest such gains.[7] This backlash is linked to the rising influence of fundamentalist projects and a burgeoning neo-liberal resistance to rights-based approaches, which are viewed as a threat to the expansion of a 'free-market' global economy. Moreover, following September 11, the resurgence of a macho military security paradigm at the expense of critical human security and human rights discourses has also made it more difficult to maintain a focus on WHR concerns. Once more, they appear trivial in comparison to the challenges of the global 'war on terror'. In this climate, advocates have expended much energy since the mid-1990s keeping women's human rights on key UN agendas (e.g.

vis-à-vis the Millennium Development Goals (MDGs)) instead of advancing implementation of hard-won global agreements. These events, explored in more detail below, particularly in chapter 6, underline the critical importance of sustained cosmopolitan feminist practice that engages with global political, legal and economic arenas in the struggle to keep a focus on WHR issues at the macro as well as micro levels.

In sum, informed by examples of UN-focused feminist engagement, which are explored in detail in subsequent chapters, I have offered an account of cosmopolitan feminism, understood as a framework of emancipatory practice in a globalizing age. In particular, I argue that critically (re)interpreted human rights are indispensable to such practice. In making this argument, however, I fully recognize that the false universalization of human rights – from male, neo-liberal, Western, state-centric and other privileged perspectives – continues to undermine the radical promise of human rights. At the same time, all feminist projects must take fully into account the intersectionality of different forms of oppression, across economic, social, cultural and political domains. Ultimately, however, problems of false universalization and exclusion are political ones and need to be tackled through emancipatory political projects that expose previously hidden abuses of power and give expression to previously excluded and marginalized voices. The chapters in this book highlight key examples and chart the evolution of such emancipatory, cosmopolitan feminist practice.

Chapter outlines

Most of the chapters of this book focus on a particular issue, or set of issues, around which significant TFA has been galvanized since the late 1970s, generally under the banner of claiming WHR. Chapter 2 is an exception in that it offers a broad overview of the philosophical and historical context out of which current human rights ideas have arisen, and highlights some of the key features of human rights institutionalization and practice within the United Nations. The chapter further develops the book's overarching framework by offering a comprehensive critique of mainstream human rights from a feminist, advocacy-oriented perspective. Specifically, I provide thematic discussions of five interrelated modes of hierarchical binary thinking (legalism, civil–political rights bias, sovereignty, etc.) that pervade human rights discourse and define its boundaries, inclusions and exclusions. In doing so, I introduce recurring themes that I revisit and elaborate in subsequent chapters in the context of TRA around concrete issues and campaigns.

Chapter 3 reviews efforts to develop international equality and non-discrimination norms – largely driven by governmental delegates and UN officials, many of whom came from national women's movements. Hence, the chapter explores key events since the establishment of the UN and the adoption of the Universal Declaration of Human Rights (UDHR) (1948), which laid the foundations for contemporary WHR movements. I suggest that these early decades of UN-focused feminist advocacy can be understood primarily as the liberal feminist phase of the WHR movement and are characterized by a focus on enshrining women's equality in law, especially securing equal civil and political rights. At the same time, however, this phase culminated in the Convention on the Elimination of All Forms of Discrimination Against Women (CEDAW) (1979), which sowed the seeds for pursuing a more radical vision of rights and for extending the concept of discrimination to structural and indirect forms of discrimination, including poverty and VAW. In particular, I consider the impact of the UNDW (1976–85) in sparking the proliferation of women's organizations and networks globally and in setting the stage for the emergence of the Global Campaign for Women's Human Rights in the late 1980s and throughout the 1990s.

Events that occurred from 1985 to 1995 provide the primary focus of chapter 4. This decade of transnational WHR advocacy is marked by a strong challenge to the public–private dichotomy in human rights discourse, which entailed shining a spotlight on violations that are perpetrated in private and 'privatized' contexts by private actors (e.g. domestic abuse, VAW in the name of religious belief or cultural practice, denials of reproductive and sexual rights, etc.). In doing so, TFA initiated a fundamental departure in human rights thinking and practice, which heretofore focused on violations of 'public' civil and political rights perpetrated by state actors. The first part of the chapter traces the rising importance of VAW as the primary unifying issue for the far-reaching Global Campaign for Women's Human Rights in the early 1990s, and the impact of this campaign on mainstream human rights discourse and bottom-up access to modes of human rights accountability. In this chapter, I also discuss the activities and achievements of the closely linked transnational movement for reproductive and sexual health as human rights. In doing so, I highlight the uniqueness of this phase of TFA in galvanizing broad-based support for, and grassroots participation in, the WHR movement in the 1990s – especially through greater NGO involvement in UN conferences such as the International Conference on Population and Development (ICPD) (Cairo, 1994) and the FWCW (Beijing, 1995).

Chapter 5 addresses women's experiences of conflict and post-conflict situations. In particular, I critically examine the prospects for achieving gender justice and WHR in post-conflict transitions. The chapter is divided into three main sections. The first reviews the gendered limits of mainstream approaches to transitional justice and highlights gender biases in related discourses that shape how conflict and post-conflict transitions are understood and enacted to the detriment of women. The second examines the benefits and limitations of efforts to ensure gender-sensitive approaches to wartime criminal justice, with particular reference to the International Criminal Court. The third section considers the prospects for a more comprehensive approach to gender justice that shifts the emphasis from 'women as victims' of conflict to women as agents of transformation, through an examination of the significance of Security Council Resolution 1325. Ultimately, I argue that achieving gender justice in post-conflict transitions is inextricably tied to wider bottom-up efforts by women's movements to realize a comprehensive vision of WHR within a framework of critically interpreted, universal, indivisible human rights.

Chapter 6 highlights the gendered dimensions of neo-liberal economic policies (privatization, restructuring, etc.) and the mainstream development paradigm, and the difficulties both pose for advancing WHR. I consider the benefits of closer integration of development and human rights paradigms with a particular focus on linking 'women's human rights' and 'gender and development' analyses and actions. In doing so, I identify ongoing conceptual and political obstacles to forging links between these two key arenas of advocacy and what is required to bridge them. From the 'women's human rights' strand, this requires more explicit, critical engagement with the limits and failures of the neo-liberal macroeconomic and development paradigms. From the 'gender and development' side, this means further constructive engagement with existing human rights standards to strengthen human-rights-based approaches to development and underpin efforts to challenge economic, social and cultural marginalization of women and girls. These themes and issues are explored with particular reference to the millennium development initiative and implementation of the MDGs. Ultimately, I argue the importance of developing feminist understandings of the indivisibility of human rights in efforts to achieve the Goals, wherein the interdependence of social, economic, cultural, civil and political rights in women's lives is fully recognized. Conceptually, the chapter highlights the tensions between Third World, socialist and liberal feminist paradigms and posits a feminist, human-rights-based approach to development and economic justice that builds on the radical tenets of each of these perspectives.

Finally, in chapter 7, I consider the growing threats to WHR posed by expanding fundamentalist and traditionalist political projects. I consider specific examples of the impact of these movements on WHR across the spectrum of political, civil, economic, social, cultural and bodily integrity rights. Focusing on the period from 1995 to 2005, the chapter identifies key features of the global backlash against WHR and its relationship to rising religious fundamentalisms. These developments are reviewed in the context of specific UN forums and processes, especially reviews of governmental actions to implement the Beijing Platform for Action (BPA) (1995) and the ICPD Programme of Action (POA) (Cairo, 1994). In particular, I highlight the ways in which fundamentalist movements have organized politically to oppose WHR agendas at every level – UN, national and local. Drawing especially on the analyses and actions of members of the Women Living under Muslim Laws (WLUML) network, I explore the principles, actions and institutional safeguards that are necessary to challenge the political power of fundamentalist movements. In doing so, I highlight the pivotal role of women's movements in every region, historically and currently, in contesting fundamentalist movements. Importantly, I argue that effective resistance to these movements necessarily entails retention of a commitment to critically reinterpreted 'universal values' within a feminist human rights framework.

2

Human Rights, Gender and Contested Meanings

Introduction

Most theorizing and debate around human rights, especially beyond the field of law, has revolved around questions of foundations and justifications. There is no shortage of trenchant critiques of human rights from diverse intellectual perspectives – communitarian, cultural relativist, socialist and postmodern, as well as feminist. While writers in all traditions raise important questions about the nature of human rights, by and large the literature has failed to explain and thematize the continued centrality of human rights ideas and processes in emancipatory political practice. This book responds to this deficit from a gender perspective.

The present chapter sketches the historical origins and key philosophical debates that have shaped contemporary human rights discourse.[1] Specifically, I highlight how gendered ideas and practices affect the ways in which women's experiences have been included (or not) in mainstream conceptualizations of human rights and in the formulation and implementation of legal/quasi-legal human rights standards. In particular, I consider how different forms of hierarchical binary thinking have operated to close off consideration and limit the articulation of substantive, transformative and emancipatory approaches to human rights. In doing so, I am not suggesting that making human rights a reality is simply a question of 'thinking differently' or deconstructing binary thinking in an abstract way. Hierarchical binary thinking in human rights discourse is widely institutionalized and its effects are very real; everyday denials of human rights are explicitly or implicitly condoned and concealed by privileging the 'public' over the 'private' sphere; 'civil and political rights' over 'economic and social rights'; and the interests of the 'developed' North over the 'developing' South. The exclusions and forms of discrimination that come into focus when traditional ways of thinking about human rights are questioned, therefore, must also be challenged concretely through targeted initiatives aimed at bringing about fundamental change in political, legal, social, economic and cultural realms.

The 1990s Global Campaign for Women's Human Rights, which is the focus of chapter 4, is an important example of this kind of praxis. Its success hinged on effectively challenging the failure of the international human rights community to recognize the gravity of abuses like sexual or domestic violence and to address them meaningfully in global human rights agendas. Successfully contesting such 'private' abuses as violations of human rights has initiated a paradigmatic shift in human rights discourse. A core theme running through this book is that such shifts are both imperative and attainable, but they can be achieved only through sustained emancipatory human rights praxis. This means making visible previously invisible violations and sustaining pressure for changes in the ways that human rights are conceptualized, institutionalized and implemented. Further, I argue that such praxis demands the participation of broad-based movements (grounded in bottom-up, democratic values), which play a pivotal role in the dialectical relationship between political and legal theorizing, human rights law and practice, and institutional and policy change.

The remainder of this chapter is divided into two parts. The first provides an overview of the philosophical and institutional context that has shaped how contemporary human rights ideas and practice operate. Here I highlight key aspects of the Kantian philosophical tradition that continue to shape contemporary human rights concepts and debates, and provide a brief discussion of the conceptualization and institutionalization of contemporary human rights within the United Nations. The second part of the chapter closely examines contemporary human rights discourse and identifies five dominant modes of thinking that must be unpacked and contested if we are to build more transformative approaches to human rights. In both parts, I foreground the gendered implications and challenges posed to advancing women's human rights (WHR).

Philosophical context and the institutionalization of human rights

Kantian ethics and justice

Contemporary conceptions of human rights are shaped significantly by the radical tenets of Kantian ethics. They also reflect the biases of a deeply gendered liberal framework, which Kant was also instrumental in defining. Efforts to realize the transformative potential of human rights, including feminist initiatives, entail critical engagement with both aspects of the Kantian legacy. Consequently, it is useful to review the main elements of that legacy and its contemporary expression. Kant argued that individuals have certain 'natural' (or human) rights that cannot be overridden by the 'positive' laws of states. This apparently sensible but contested claim is at the heart of all external challenges to institutionalized discrimination and persecution in situations ranging from Hitler's Germany to the racially segregated USA before the 1960s, apartheid South Africa and contemporary Israel/Palestine. Legal positivists, in contrast, recognize only 'legal obligation' and adopt a relativist position on 'moral obligation', which is constructed as outside the scope of the law. In Kantian ethics, however, there is only one kind of obligation: the categorical imperative.

This ultimate moral principle flows from the premise that all persons are equal moral and autonomous beings entitled to be treated – and obliged to treat others – with equal concern. As discussed in the previous chapter, Kant's ideas of cosmopolitanism and cosmopolitan right are also key in constructing an understanding of human rights as a framework for bottom-up, transnational advocacy. Kant's radical ideas about the equality and freedom of all individuals, coupled with his understanding of everyone's obligation and duty towards others – both within and beyond states and nations – helped to shape the claims of revolutionary movements in eighteenth-century Europe and North America.

The transformative potential of Kant's cosmopolitan ethics, however, is hugely undermined by the gender and class biases of his liberal theory of justice, which are equally deeply entrenched in contemporary human rights. Kant equated human 'freedom' with the capacity to be an autonomous (albeit morally constrained) decision-maker and agent. This led him to formulate a theory of justice comprised of three fundamental liberal principles. First, everyone has a right to freedom of expression and freedom of action. Second, everyone is entitled to enjoy 'equality with all as subjects', that is, legal equality vis-à-vis the state. And, third, 'active citizens' have a right to democratic participation in the creation of legislation that governs them (Reiss 1970, 75).

Kant's account of justice, however, works against the transformative potential of his ethics on various levels. First, he defines women as passive citizens and condones their exclusion from the exercise of public power. In doing so, his influential writings are implicated in perpetuating the patriarchal public–private divide and normalizing the gender inequalities in public and private life that have been contested by WHR movements everywhere. Second, Kant's theory of justice pointedly excludes economic equality. Reflecting the de facto situation in most contemporary liberal democracies, he argues that civil and political equality is consistent with the 'utmost inequalities in the mass and degree of possessions' (Reiss 1970, 75). Kant's endorsement of gender- and class-based inequalities as compatible with 'justice' typified the burgeoning bourgeois liberalism of his day. The tensions between the expansive promise of Kantian ethics and the limits of classical liberalism continue to play out in contemporary human rights discourse. How these tensions are negotiated has major implications for what we understand human rights issues to be in the first instance, and for who or what entity is held accountable when violations occur.

Human rights at the United Nations

The articulation of universal human rights in the mid twentieth century reflected a revival of Kantian ethics and a departure from dominant instrumental and legalist understandings of rights. Prompted by abhorrence at atrocities committed during two world wars, especially the genocides perpetrated under Nazism, the 1948 Universal Declaration of Human Rights (UDHR) asserted the idea that, simply by virtue of being human, people everywhere and under all circumstances possessed certain inalienable rights. Contrary to some popular perceptions, however, it is inaccurate to characterize the UDHR as an amalgam of imposed 'Western' values. The UDHR was a politically negotiated and carefully worded document that reflected the international consensus of the day – however tentative. It was drafted jointly by representatives from eight countries – Australia, Chile, China, France, Lebanon, the United States, the United Kingdom, and the USSR. It was examined and revised in detail by the eighteen-member Commission on Human Rights, was the subject of 81 meetings and 168 amendments of the Third Committee of the General Assembly, and, finally, was adopted by the General Assembly – forty-eight votes for, zero against, and eight abstentions (Robertson and Merrills 1996, 28).

The preamble of the UDHR asserts the 'inherent dignity and the equal and inalienable rights of all members of the human family [as] the foundation of freedom, justice and peace in the world'. Furthermore, it pronounces that 'the advent of a world in which human beings shall enjoy freedom of speech and belief, and freedom from fear and want, has been proclaimed as the highest aspiration of the common people'. As a declaration and not a binding treaty, states were more inclined to endorse its expansive vision. Nonetheless, by explicitly linking economic, social and cultural rights to political and civil rights, under an overarching right not to suffer discrimination (Article 2), the UDHR pushed at the boundaries of traditional liberalism. Alongside the right to 'life, liberty and security of person'

(Article 3), the right to freedom of opinion and expression (Article 19), the right to vote and to take part in government (Article 21), and the right to due process and to equal treatment before the law (Article 10 and Article 11), the UDHR equally asserts a number of substantial economic and social rights 'indispensable for . . . dignity and the free development of . . . personality' (Article 22). These include the right to work, to receive fair remuneration and social protection, and to form and join trade unions (Article 23), as well as the 'right to a standard of living adequate for . . . health and well-being . . . including food, clothing, housing, and medical care' (Article 25).

The UDHR represents the first instance of the international recognition of economic and social rights as human rights (and not merely as a subset of other rights, for example, of labour rights). This suggested the possibility of a new consensus that might expand the meaning of human rights beyond the confines of classic liberal civil and political rights. The tentative shift in global understanding, however, was short-lived. Cold War power politics subsequently dominated the international arena and militated against further progress towards promoting an indivisible framework that prioritized all human rights equally. During this time, while always subject to contestation, Western powers dominated efforts to define and interpret human rights. Hence, limited models of representative democracy, the non-commission of egregious violations by states and free-market capital-ism were constructed as *the* international human rights agenda. More generally, institutionalization of the new international human rights regime proceeded extremely slowly and was marked by state resistance both to strengthening substantive social and economic rights and establish-ing thorough international monitoring mechanisms.

After four years of contentious debate on whether economic, social and cultural rights should be included alongside political and civil rights in a single legally binding agreement, in 1952 the UN General Assembly stepped back from the indivisibility ideal expressed in the UDHR and decided to sponsor two separate treaties.[2] This underpinned a trajectory of prioritization of civil and political rights over economic, social and cultural rights in the coming decades. At the same time, despite calls and proposals for intensive monitoring mechanisms from different countries, the United Kingdom and the United States in the end backed minimal monitoring by ad hoc committees. Moreover, the Soviet Union opposed all monitoring arrangements on the grounds that they would violate state sovereignty. Ultimately, a permanent Human Rights Committee was narrowly approved solely to adjudicate interstate disputes, and all proposals for individual or group complaints procedures were firmly rejected (Robertson and Merrills 1996, 31).

Draft texts of the International Covenant on Civil and Political Rights (ICCPR) and the International Covenant on Economic, Social and Cultural Rights (ICESCR) were first circulated in 1954 but were not completed until 1966. While the slow pace of progress reflected the low priority accorded the draft treaties by dominant state players, the twelve-year gap also provided a valuable window for emerging postcolonial nations to shape the content of the treaties. In particular, during that time there was renewed discussion around the 'right to self-determination', which appears in both covenants and reflects the importance of this right from the perspective of new Third World states. Overall, however, negotiations on the nature and scope of the rights in each covenant put civil and political rights on a firmer footing than social and economic rights. For example, rather than stating 'everyone has the right to work' and 'everyone has a right to join trade unions', the ICESCR declares that states 'recognize the right to work' and 'undertake to ensure the right of everyone to . . . join trade unions'. This contrasts with the rights asserted more unconditionally in the ICCPR, including 'Everyone shall have the right to recognition everywhere as a person before the law' and 'No one shall be subjected to torture, or to cruel, inhuman or degrading treatment or punishment.'

There was also much debate about whether the obligations contained in the covenants must be met immediately or progressively. Ultimately, a standard of progressive realization was agreed for social and economic rights while civil and political rights were understood to demand immediate compliance. Similar discrepancies arose around the issue of treaty monitoring. The Human Rights Committee evolved into the ICCPR monitoring body, and by 1966 an 'optional protocol' was in place allowing individuals to bring complaints against a state in cases of violation of civil and political rights. States that signed and ratified the treaties (States Parties) had to submit periodic reports under both covenants, but the procedures for monitoring the ICESCR were vague and resources were inadequate. It was 1985 before a dedicated ICESCR Committee, similar to the Human Rights Committee, was established to oversee implementation of the covenant.[3]

This secondary standing of the ICESCR vis-à-vis the ICCPR reflected the ideological and political divides of Cold War politics and the marginalization of the interests of Third World states therein. The United States and other developed Western powers pushed for a narrowly liberal interpretation of human rights, emphasizing the individual freedoms needed to underpin a capitalist economy – 'freedom to innovate and to invest time, capital and resources in the processes of production and exchange' (Evans 1997, 135). In contrast, the East European states, rhetorically at least, cast human rights as a 'point of departure towards a new world order that sought to deliver economic and social justice' (p. 135). Third World leaders also emphasized social and economic justice issues, but viewed them through a global rather than state-centric lens. From this perspective, they sought recognition for the 'right to development' and related obligations on the part of developed countries to realize that right. Further, stressing the limited resources of developing states, Third World leaders supported the idea that social and economic rights should be progressively achieved and not defined as immediate obligations.

In tandem with the marginalization of economic, social and cultural rights, women and gender perspectives were also sidelined in the evolving human rights regime. Initially, the Commission on the Status of Women (CSW)[4] and the Commission on Human Rights (UNCHR)[5] were both established with a mandate to promote and protect 'human rights'. As will be discussed in chapter 3, establishing the CSW was championed by feminists at the UN to ensure the inclusion of women's concerns in mainstream human rights agendas *and* their treatment as a distinct category of human rights as necessary. Despite this vision, a huge disparity emerged, both in the status and in allocation of resources, between the CSW and the UNCHR. The administration of the CSW was isolated and underfunded in Vienna, while the rest of the human rights machinery developed in the key UN cities of Geneva and New York. Prior to the 1990s, there was no connection between the work of the two bodies and the area of 'women's rights' was seen as independent of and less important than the more serious terrain of 'human rights'. This failure to take women's right seriously as 'human rights' is also reflected by the fact the UN Women's Convention continues to have the most reservations of all the human rights treaties – whereby states reserve the right to be 'exempt' from certain articles of the treaty – usually to do with women's role in the family and cultural or religious practices.

The fall of the Berlin Wall and the end of apartheid in South Africa were dramatic turning points in world history that revitalized interest in the potential of human rights as a global ethical framework. For many, given the ideological vacuum created by the end of the Cold War, it was an obvious framework to turn to because it was capable of articulating the cause of economic, social *and* political justice in an integrated and action-oriented framework. Plans were soon underway for a second World Conference on Human Rights (Vienna, 1993).[6] Mobilizing around the proposed event, a well-organized and extensive network of human rights advocates, NGOs and social movements emerged to challenge the political and conceptual deficiencies that had stymied human rights implementation to date.

At the forefront of this drive, women's organizations and networks around the world seized the opportunity to launch a sustained campaign for the recognition of 'women's rights as human rights' and the substantive realization of human rights in women's lives (see chapter 4). The resulting Vienna Declaration and Programme of Action (VDPA) was widely recognized at the time as a much-needed reaffirmation of the UDHR and as a blueprint for implementing human rights in a post-Cold War era (Boyle 1995). In addition to its extensive treatment of women's rights as human rights, the Vienna Declaration sought to break the stalemate around the traditional civil/political versus economic/social/cultural divide and reaffirm the 'indivisibility and interdependence' of all human rights (Boyle 1995). In particular, it declared that 'democracy, development and respect for fundamental freedoms are interdependent and mutually reinforcing' (Paragraph 8).

The mini renaissance of human rights fostered by the Vienna conference encouraged unprecedented growth in the engagement of social movements and NGOs with international human rights rhetoric and standards. Notwithstanding the many successes of such bottom-up human rights initiatives, huge gaps persist between the rhetoric of Vienna and human rights practice. Neo-liberal globalization continues to exacerbate global inequalities and to leave the most vulnerable sections of many societies at much greater risk of extreme poverty, disease, displacement and trafficking. The rise of fundamentalist movements and contemporary forms of conflict, including the 'war on terror', are also straining the credibility of international and regional human rights systems. Yet a core objective of this book is to demonstrate the indispensable role of critically reinterpreted human rights discourse in seeking gender justice in a globalizing age. To understand better the conditions under which such a transformative model of human rights might be achieved, I now turn to examine more closely the limitations and radical potential of contemporary human rights discourse.

Building transformative approaches to human rights

Building bottom-up, transformative approaches to human rights – especially from a gender perspective – requires the deconstruction and redefinition of several entrenched modes of thinking and practice that perpetuate the exclusions of mainstream human rights discourse. In the following subsections, I explore five specific modes of hierarchical binary thinking:

- gendered configurations of the public–private divide
- prioritization of civil and political rights
- Western hegemony and cultural relativism
- legalism
- state sovereignty and state-centric human rights

These five are key sites of contested meaning that must be engaged in efforts to promote substantive and integrated visions of human rights in women's lives.

Gendered configurations of the public–private divide

The role of the liberal public–private divide in perpetuating gender inequalities and undermining WHR is well documented. In defining the 'private sphere' as beyond public accountability, domestic abuse often goes unrecognized and perpetrators go unpunished. The usual invisibility of gender-specific abuses in the private sphere is exacerbated in traditional human rights discourse by a state-centric bias that focuses primarily on state-sponsored violations. Critiquing this state of affairs, Susan Okin notes:

> The Universal Declaration of Human Rights . . . is frequently referred to as being addressed exclusively to governments as potential violators of human rights, and not at all to individual persons. . . . [T]he Declaration by no means [has as] its sole intent to warn governments against their own potential for violation. To the contrary, besides hardly mentioning governments at all, it suggests strongly that at least some of the obligations correlative to the rights it pronounces fall on individuals as well as on states. (Okin 1981, 239)

The global movement for WHR has challenged especially the invisibility of abuses in 'private' contexts of family and intimate relationships and the failure of the international human rights community to name different forms of violence against women (VAW) as violations of human rights. Most notably, for the first time, physical and sexual violence, usually perpetrated by men against women in the 'private sphere', was brought into focus as a global human rights issue (Bunch 1990). In doing so, women's movements exposed the limitations of a human rights regime that prioritized direct state abuses, and sparked new debate about the nature of a state's human rights obligations. In particular, if VAW was to be taken seriously as a human rights concern, it was clearly necessary to examine acts of omission as well as commission by states and ask what they were doing to prevent such violence and to hold non-state or private perpetrators accountable for their actions.

The effects of the gendered public–private divide, however, are not limited to the failure to recognize abuses by private actors in clearly demarcated 'private spaces'. Public–private configurations also operate to 'privatize' or conceal gender-specific violations, even in situations that are already understood to be sites of serious human rights violation. For example, when mainstream human rights organizations initially responded to calls from women's movements to address gender-based human rights abuse, they did so by documenting gender-based forms of torture such as rape and sexual violence occurring in police or military detentions (Amnesty International 1991). Similarly, sexual violence and sexual slavery are now widely recognized aspects of militarization and the conduct of war. Prior to the international mobilization of women's groups to ensure a gender-sensitive International Criminal Court statute in 1998 (the Rome Statute), however, such violations were usually regarded as 'natural' and implicitly 'private' side effects of war and, consequently, were downplayed in international humanitarian law and international legal responses to war crimes. (These examples are revisited in more detail in chapter 5.)

Public–private configurations that structure the relationship between the state and the economy also have gender-specific implications for how human rights issues are defined and prioritized. Implicit in the debate about the relative importance of 'civil and political' versus 'economic, social, and cultural rights' are ideologically driven assumptions about the role the state ought to play in managing a state's resources, ensuring a population's welfare and generally structuring the opportunities for self-realization and development available to individuals and groups in a given society. Those who equate 'human rights' with basic 'civil and political rights' and view the achievement of social and economic rights as 'unrealistic' (for various reasons) generally accept uncritically the imperatives of neo-liberal, free-market economics. This includes a drive towards deregulation, privatization and a minimal state on the assumption that it is more 'efficient' if 'goods and services' (including healthcare, education, transport and so on) are provided by private, profit-driven agents rather than the state. More generally, in a climate of deference to the 'free market', trade union activity, social welfare programmes and any expansion of workers' entitlements (e.g. maternity and parental benefits, etc.) are viewed with suspicion because they distort the 'true' (market-determined) value of labour and potentially inhibit economic growth by making an economy 'uncompetitive' in relation to other economies where lesser protections might apply.

The material effects of this ideological position are not gender neutral. Where public–private lines get drawn in the state–economy relation has real implications for the realization (or not) of WHR.[7] In most societies women are still expected to carry the responsibility of caring for dependent family members (children, elderly, people with disabilities, etc.) and accessing basic goods and services on behalf of the family, including food, water, accommodation, healthcare, education, etc. The privatization of basic goods and services makes them unaffordable to many and increases the pressures on women to work longer hours in order to earn more income and/or absorb a greater burden of unpaid social care. Further, reduced public and social spending exacerbates female poverty and makes girls and women particularly vulnerable to forced migration, forced prostitution, trafficking and a wide range of related abuses.

More generally, privatization processes construct 'private' spaces in which inequalities are cast in terms of 'personal choices' rather than infringements on human rights. Hence women 'choose' flexible (i.e. insecure, low-paid) jobs because they enable women to combine paid work with family responsibilities; women 'choose' to migrate (often unwittingly in cooperation with traffickers); or they 'choose' to work in prostitution, and so on. Throughout this book, I problematize different mainstream configurations of the public–private divide and consider how they hinder progress in advancing substantive visions of human rights in women's lives.

Prioritization of civil and political rights

In mainstream human rights discourse, the prioritization of civil and political rights reflects the hierarchy of 'public' over 'private' in the traditional liberal public–private dichotomy. While not dismissing the importance of contesting state-sponsored abuses like denials of freedom of expression or torture in detention, feminist human rights scholars have argued that this hierarchical binary is deeply gendered insofar as it defines human rights priorities according to the criterion of 'what men fear will happen to them' in their relationship with the state, society and other men (Charlesworth 1994, 71). In mainstream human rights practice, this bias is evident in the mandate of Amnesty International (AI), for example, which has been hugely influential in establishing popular understandings of what constitutes a human rights issue. While considerable change has taken place within AI in recent years, the organization is most strongly associated with efforts to challenge states' practices, such as arbitrary detention or the mistreatment of prisoners, especially where the 'crime' has been to speak out, or mobilize others to act, against a repressive state. The right and ability to oppose government policy without fear is undoubtedly an important condition of human freedom. The problem is, however, that, at least through the early 1990s, this view of what constituted 'human rights' came to be viewed by the international human rights community as the most important, if not the only, locus of serious human rights concern.

Feminist critiques of established human rights entail close scrutiny of the gender dynamics and impact of this prioritization of civil and political rights and the consequent marginalization of economic and social rights, within mainstream human rights thinking. In everyday social relations, the most significant potential threats to men's physical security and well-being are repressive state actors and other men who act violently. By and large, family life and intimate relationships are not arenas where adult men fear violence or abuse. Further, for those men who belong to dominant social groupings (majority, educated, middle-class and so on), minimal liberal democratic conditions and the 'rule of law' are generally conducive to their interests and welfare. Even under such 'normal' conditions, however, women (and men in marginalized or discriminated-against communities) often experience their relationship with the state very differently. For example, a woman who has experienced rape or domestic violence might be unwilling to report it to the police for a variety of well-grounded reasons. She could fear further violence from the perpetrator, or expect that she will not be believed or taken seriously by the authorities, or simply not want to face an adversarial court case. Importantly, if she and/or the perpetrator belong to a marginalized/minority community, she could also fear the repercussions of involving police who could act with prejudice against members of her community. In contrast, a state that is uniformly repressive directly threatens the lives, freedom and welfare of *everyone* subject to its power – including men who occupy hegemonic positions under 'normal' conditions of the 'rule of law'. Hence, putting the prevention of this particular form of the abuse of power – arbitrary state power – at the top of a society's priority list reflects class, gender and 'race' biases.

Once it is recognized that differently situated people have varied relationships to the state, it also becomes clear that an exclusive focus on securing civil and political rights against the state constitutes a very partial human rights agenda. For those who are more vulnerable to violations in 'private' contexts of family or intimate relationships, or as members of discriminated-against minority communities, therefore, a narrow definition of human rights protection as the absence of direct state abuses of civil and political rights only partially addresses their experiences of human rights abuse. In order to ensure that human rights are protected and promoted in these situations and in the lives of marginalized groups more generally, the substantive rules about what constitute human rights must change along with the understanding of human rights accountability and implementation.

Western hegemony and cultural relativism

Debates about the meaning of the universality of human rights and whether human rights simply express Western hegemony and, therefore, are fundamentally at odds with respect for cultural diversity and integrity are a major feature of contemporary human rights discourse. In chapter 1, I highlighted some feminist responses to these arguments articulated by Western and non-Western commentators. Here, I explore in more detail some of the debates surrounding the universalist–relativist binary. While strong cultural relativism in human rights discourse is incompatible with the advancement of WHR, equally any feminist defence of the 'universality' of human rights demands a comprehensive critique of top-down universalist approaches. In this section, I outline influential relativist, universalist and intervening positions in mainstream human rights scholarship and locate cosmopolitan feminist engagement with human rights in relation to these debates.

The work of Muslim human rights scholar Abdullahi Ahmed An-Na'im is a well-regarded example of moderate cultural relativism. He holds that a 'lack or insufficiency of cultural legitimacy of human rights standards' is a primary cause of violations of human rights around the world (An-Na'im 1992, 19). An-Na'im affirms existing international human rights standards, but he argues the need to 'enhance their cultural legitimacy', primarily through internal dialogue aimed at developing interpretations of human rights in light of local norms and values. From this perspective, 'adequate legitimacy' achieved 'within each tradition' is a precondition for building 'cross-cultural legitimacy' and agreement on the 'meaning, scope and method of implementing human rights' (p. 21). Ultimately, therefore, the 'interpretation and practical application' of human rights in any society 'must be determined by the moral standards of that society' (p. 37).

On the face of it, An-Na'im's 'cultural legitimacy thesis' (CLT) has much appeal as a dialogic framework that eschews both traditional cultural relativism and rejects the external imposition of the 'human rights' agendas of dominant powers. But it also presents threats to WHR along the lines highlighted by feminist critics such as Hom, Rao, Narayan and others. The 'cross-cultural dialogue' element of An-Na'im's account, for example, relies on a hierarchical scenario wherein the understanding of what is (or is not) a human rights concern in a given cultural context is brokered by the elites in that culture, according to their judgment of how a particular practice is comprehended by (and affects) the 'average' member of that culture. The difficulty is that, unless all affected individuals are willing participants in the prevailing cultural mores and are able to 'opt out' if they so choose, we cannot be sure that the human rights of individuals or subgroups within a community will be protected in a communitarian dialogue that is dominated by privileged male elites. This is especially a concern for women, who invariably constitute the primary locus of enforcement of cultural mores and identity, especially with regard to sexuality, marriage and reproduction (Yuval-Davis 1997).

Further, An Na'im's rigid delineation between 'internal discourse' and 'cross-cultural dialogue' belies contemporary patterns of globalization. Similarly, his insistence on the idea of 'authenticity' of cultural values is at odds with his own fluid and expansive definition of culture as continuous and mutable (p. 27). Furthermore, in asserting that 'disadvantaged individuals and groups' should use 'internal cultural discourse' to seek support for their interests, An-Na'im underestimates the many obstacles to articulating such positions – from cultural norms that severely restrict women's public presence to active state repression of opposition voices. Ultimately, therefore, in an overarching concern to combat the 'cultural imperialism' of international human rights discourse, An-Na'im's framework pays insufficient attention to intra-cultural inequalities and conflict and their detrimental impacts on women in particular.

At the other end of the spectrum, Jack Donnelly's work best captures a mainstream universalist stance on human rights. He rejects radical cultural relativism on the one side, which holds that 'culture is the sole source of the validity of a moral right', and radical universalism on the other, which asserts that 'culture is irrelevant to the validity of moral rights' (Donnelly 1989, 110–12). However, like most mainstream universalists, Donnelly gives too little space to local agency and context in determining the meaning and content of human rights. This flows primarily from an analytical framework that is embedded in an uncritical modernization narrative. Most notably, he explicitly equates the growing de facto acceptance of human rights standards around the world with a linear process of Western modernization, which, for better or worse, is being accelerated by globalization. There is no doubt that traditional cultural relativist arguments are increasingly undermined by globalization; increasingly integrated networks of communication, transport, economic and financial activity, and political organization are altering local realities and calling into question the notion of clearly demarcated boundaries. It is inaccurate, however, to present globalization as a one-way process of homogenization, Westernization and global moral convergence that renders the relativist–universalist debate obsolete.

Equating the 'universalization' of human rights with Westernization and modernization reinforces a false hierarchical divide between 'the West and the rest'. This narrative relies on notions of a dynamic 'West', holding the key to transcendent 'truth and justice', while the 'backward' developing world is mired down in the particularities of culture and tradition, until globalization whittles away the distinctions to create a homogenized, Westernized 'global culture'. As Arati Rao notes, this version of events is deeply flawed because it fails to recognize that the 'concept of human rights itself is a historically circumscribed and context-bound phenomenon' (Rao 1995, 168). This failure, Rao argues, generates an 'overly simple notion of the relationship between culture and human rights in our world of differences . . . with universalists falling on one side and relativists on the other' (p. 168). The result is a false oppositional dichotomy in which geopolitical boundaries are erased and a multitude of cultures are collapsed into two falsely unified packages, one bearing the stamp 'human rights' and the other lacking it.

In contrast, a basic premise of this book is that the relation between 'the universal' and 'the particular' is better understood as an ongoing, multilevel process of negotiation, and not a fixed and polarized binary. Richard Wilson (1997), for example, argues that the traditional cultural-relativist stance closes off recognition and analysis of the ways in which human rights thinking and practice have in fact been adopted and transformed by many marginalized groups for whom it was once foreign and supposedly oppressive. He cites, for example, indigenous groups in Guatemala, Panama, Canada and South Africa who have actively engaged in negotiating the particular content of their 'universal' human rights. That is, the bottom-up, dialogic process of negotiating the meaning of human rights in a specific context necessarily consists, simultaneously, of universal and particular moments.

Wilson's critical anthropological perspective is very useful in articulating a non-oppressive understanding of the universal moment in human rights thinking and practice. In particular, he notes that, in a context of deepening globalization, 'moral differences are not reliant on enclosed systems as before, but are more fragmented and susceptible to transnational flows of moral values' (p. 12). As a result, the 'universality of human rights . . . becomes a question of context, necessitating a situational analysis' (p. 12). Importantly, such contextualization does not inevitably amount to a relativist stance or one-way Western imposition because increasingly, local and global 'contexts are linked in a variety of processes' (p. 12). This could include, for example, participation in UN human rights treaty monitoring processes or in world conferences, or more recently, in the Millennium Development Goals (MDGs) initiative. In attempting to understand the way in which human rights are 'universal', therefore, the question of whether and in what ways human rights standards map onto customary codes of traditional societies is not the right one. Instead, we should, as Wilson suggests, consider how moral and legal values 'traverse contexts' and are interpreted, enacted and owned in contexts different from those in which they originate. In terms of human rights, therefore, we might ask how human rights law 'frames and shapes localised normative orders and how they in turn resist and appropriate international law', as well as 'how social actors develop distinct ways of using transnational law in national courts to construct a case as a human rights case' (p. 13).

In an age of globalization, it is imperative to find ways of negotiating the relationship between context and cultural particularity on the one side, and a cosmopolitan commitment to human rights on the other, without invoking crude dichotomies or untenable notions of cultural authenticity. In practice, the value and meaning of human rights ideals have always been and will continue to be the subject of contestation and reinterpretation, across different regions and cultural contexts, inside and outside of UN forums. Recognition of this reality entails a rejection of approaches to human rights that treat them as static, 'Western values' that are being imposed on non-Western countries through international law. Human rights values are not fixed or determined by the particular historical moment or geo-political context of their first articulation. Instead, they must be understood as continually contested and (re)constituted through concrete, bottom-up struggles in local–global nexuses where the universal and the particular meet, recognition of the indivisibility of human rights is paramount and the invisibility of human rights abuses in the private contexts is not tolerated. This is the vision of universal human rights at the heart of this book, which I believe is demonstrated by the examples of innovative cosmopolitan WHR thinking and practice explored in the remaining chapters.

Legalism

The promotion of transformative and substantive visions of human rights implies a critique of legalism. Simply stated, legalism views the law as an objective set of principles and rules that structure and regulate society and social relations from on high, while remaining independent of that society. This form of positivist thinking fosters static and conservative readings of the role of the law. As Franz Neumann noted, 'All traditional legal conceptions are negative ones. They limit activities but do not shape them' (1957, 17). This is evident, for example, when compliance with human rights treaties by states is equated with formal ratification (along with the non-commission of egregious abuses). Legal positivism also underpins the commonly made argument that there is a 'real' (i.e. legally enforceable) obligation on the part of states to implement formal 'political and civil rights' but not 'social and economic rights' because the former are 'justiciable'[8] while the latter are not. Regardless of the technical-legal merits of this argument, the focus on 'justiciability' per se is an example of narrow legalism. It closes off discussion of alternative, norm-based methods of monitoring, measuring and assessing how any human rights – civil, political, social, economic or cultural – are protected and substantively realized in a given context.

Moreover, legalist perspectives are deeply flawed on an epistemological level. They promote deference to the authority of legal experts who are constructed as objective interpreters of the 'Truth' of the law. In contrast, feminist, postmodern and critical theorists have argued that 'the law' can never be fully objective, neutral or independent from the exercise of power. In doing so, they have highlighted male bias in the definition of legal subjects and operation of adversarial legal processes, underlined the limits of formal legal equality in addressing structural inequalities, and exposed repressive uses of the law in the name of upholding the 'rule of law'. From such critical perspectives, legalist approaches to human rights that focus solely on technical and formal aspects of the law are inadequate because they fail to confront the ways in which the definition, meaning, interpretation and implementation of the law are inextricably tied to the exercise of political, economic, cultural and social power.

The challenge for human rights advocates is to reclaim the radical promise of the 'rule of law' – that is, to foreground its role as a cornerstone of democratic political engagement and a transparent, rule-based process for deterring, calling to account, and punishing abuses of human rights. This necessarily entails contesting misuses of the 'rule of law', which perversely facilitate abuses of human rights in the name of establishing or restoring 'order', 'peace', 'democracy' and so on.[9] The rehabilitation of the 'rule of law', however, cannot be achieved through top-down or coercive means. Instead, this book brings attention to examples of WHR advocacy that illustrate the process of reclaiming and reconstructing the 'rule of law' within a wider transformative human rights framework. This discussion is taken up in more detail in chapter 7, which examines the ways in which women's movements and feminist scholars have articulated responses to rising fundamentalisms. In contrast to traditional, narrowly liberal and legalistic definitions of the rule of law, this involves a greater role for broad-based movements and transnational civil-society actors as they endeavour to shape international human rights standards and seek their implementation at all levels from the local to the global.

State sovereignty and state-centric human rights

Although the current international human rights system was conceived as a restraint on state sovereignty in situations of state-sponsored human rights abuse, the contest between seeking accountability for such abuses and deferring to state sovereignty often sees the latter winning out (Picciotto 1997). The Westphalian world order in the mid seventeenth century first articulated the principle of state sovereignty, which is intertwined with notions of territoriality, autonomy and legality (McGrew 1997, 3). The sovereignty principle constructs the state as the ultimate source of legal and political authority, while the idea that each state is autonomous – and therefore the best judge of how to conduct its own internal and external affairs – reinforces the imperviousness of states to external accountability. From the perspective of those who pioneered the UN Declaration of Human Rights, the genocides and other heinous acts perpetrated by states during World War II were the product of the primacy of state sovereignty and a failure to ensure that human rights were fundamental in nation building.

Following World War II, there was renewed international political will to establish greater international accountability on the part of states, so that they could never again trample the human rights of individuals and groups with such impunity. In this sense, the UDHR (1948) and the establishment of a United Nations Commission on Human Rights signalled a significant attempt to shift the balance of core principles in international politics away from state sovereignty and towards respect for human rights. More than four centuries of state-centric tradition, however, would not be transformed so easily and territorial state sovereignty remained a basic principle in the formation of the United Nations. Most notably, Article 2 of the UN Charter asserts that the UN Organization is 'based upon the principle of the sovereign equality of all its members', and that 'nothing contained in the . . . Charter shall authorize the United Nations to intervene in matters which are essentially within the domestic jurisdiction of any State' (Brownlie 1992, 4). Hence, states are subject to international human rights law by consent only – that is, by signing and ratifying particular human rights treaties. This principle is trumped by a 'higher law' (*jus cogens*) only in situations where states perpetrate egregious violations such as apartheid, genocide or slavery. This is illustrated in a comprehensive report on racism in South Africa: 'The United Nations is unquestionably justified in deciding that a matter is outside the essentially domestic jurisdiction of a State when it involves systematic violations of the Charter's principles concerning human rights, and more especially that of non-discrimination, above all when such actions affect millions of human beings, and have provoked grave international alarm' (UN 1953). In practice, however, as the situation in Darfur most recently illustrates, *realpolitik* and the logic of state sovereignty often militate against the international community making declarations of *jus cogens* and sanctioning remedial actions.

More generally, the principle of state sovereignty, exacerbated by legalism, legal dualism[10] and narrow liberalism, has enabled states to take a minimalist or 'negative' approach to the implementation of their human rights obligations domestically. As sovereign entities, states are the signatories of human rights treaties and, therefore, the primary duty bearer in meeting a treaty's provisions. By and large, however, the scope of these duties has been defined in narrow liberal terms: establishing formal legal equality and refraining from violating civil and political rights have been viewed as end goals rather than points of departure in the implementation of human rights obligations. To proponents of substantive and transformative visions of human rights, the combination of state-centric bias and minimal/legalistic definitions of compliance with human rights obligations poses challenges on at least three levels. First, it has fostered a human rights system that, until very recently, ignored abuses of human rights by non-state actors (whether spouses or transnational corporations). Second, the prioritization of liberal rights has meant that mechanisms to encourage substantive implementation of the full spectrum of human rights at national and global level are very underdeveloped. Third, in an unequal world, the construction of states as atomistic duty bearers fails to address the duty of third parties – other states, UN bodies, the World Trade Organization, etc. – in respecting, protecting and fulfilling human rights everywhere, particularly in the Third World.

These limitations are being challenged on several fronts. More broadly, it is increasingly recognized that neo-liberal globalization and the growing influence of unaccountable non-state actors, as well as global issues like extreme poverty, disease pandemics, climate change and international crime, are testing the de facto sovereignty of territorial states. Despite uni-lateralist rhetoric and posturing on the part of some hegemonic powers, the vast majority of governments participate in international organizations and standard setting in addressing an ever-expanding array of global policy agendas. In this context, it is both necessary and desirable to reconsider the role of the state in implementing human rights and to develop ways of holding accountable non-state actors for the human rights implications of their actions. In the absence of a world government, however, states will necessarily continue to play a key role in all of these processes. The challenge, rather, is to develop more nuanced understandings of the state's duty not only to respect (i.e. refrain from violating) rights but actively to protect and fulfil the full range of rights – economic, social, cultural, as well as civil and political.

State-centric definitions of human rights reinforce prioritization of 'civil and political' rights because refraining from directly violating these rights is clearly recognized as an immediate and direct responsibility of state actors. Protecting and promoting social and economic rights, on the other hand, is generally understood to require a more expansive vision of a state's role in implementing human rights.[11] It demands that, in addition to commissions of violations by state actors, we also look at omissions that indirectly violate human rights and ask whether or not a state has done enough (i.e. exercised 'due diligence') to prevent and remedy such viola-tions and to hold non-state actors accountable for abuses they commit. This means, for example, assessing whether there are adequate supports and services in place to meet the needs of victims of domestic abuse and to ensure the prosecution and appropriate punishment of perpetrators. It might also include documenting deaths and other dire human rights consequences that result from inequitable access to healthcare, especially in wealthy countries. Moreover, in efforts to realize a more holistic and indivisible vision of human rights, global inequalities must be taken into account and more attention must be paid to specify the collective duty of the international community in realizing rights, particularly in countries that are less well-off. These themes are considered in more detail in chapter 6, which addresses the ongoing struggle to reconcile human rights and development paradigms from a gender perspective.

In addition to rethinking basic assumptions about the role of states and the nature of their duty to implement human rights, a bottom-up, transformative vision of human rights requires more nuanced understandings of accountability processes and mechanisms. Formal quasi-legal accountability mechanisms can and should play a key role in promoting human rights. It is also important, however, that seeking accountability vis-à-vis human rights standards is understood not only as a legal or quasi-legal process but also as a structured opportunity for bottom-up participation in monitoring compliance with human rights and defining the meaning of human rights implementation in a given context.

Some human rights accountability mechanisms are more amenable to bottom-up engagement than others. For example, all states that have signed and ratified a human rights treaty are required to submit regular, publicly evaluated reports to the relevant UN treaty-monitoring body detailing how they are implementing their commitments domestically. In particular, because this process is more transparent and less legalistic than formal complaints procedures, for example, it offers enormous potential for bottom-up participation in human rights monitoring. Moreover, within the constraints of state sovereignty, the effectiveness of the human rights system in getting states to 'respect, protect and fulfill' their human rights commitments is very reliant on the capacity of human rights campaigners to persuade their governments to take action. In particular, active participation by locally based NGOs and grassroots organizations is vital in focusing the attention of governments and treaty bodies on the specific requirement of substantive implementation of human rights provisions on the ground. However, while rhetorically encouraged at UN level, the important monitoring role of NGOs and other human rights advocates at the local and national level is largely undeveloped and under-resourced.

Participation in bottom-up, civil-society actions is the most common point of entry into human rights discourse for women and women's organizations. From this perspective, overcoming barriers to meaningful, broad-based, civil-society participation in human rights is a feminist issue. Currently, the state is the only body formally required to submit periodic reports and come before the monitoring committee to answer questions on its implementation of a given treaty. Informally, however, most treaty-monitoring bodies rely heavily on submissions from NGOs and quasi-independent agencies to inform their critical questioning of states. But this is not a requirement and country reviews often take place in the absence of such independent 'shadow' reports. In a welcome development, in recent decades NGOs in every region have been increasingly active in efforts to hold governments accountable for implementing the provisions of the human rights treaties they have signed. This is an important trend and an example of how state-centric human rights thinking and practice are being contested by civil-society actors seeking the substantive realization of human rights.

In the following chapters, I revisit the limiting effects of traditional, legalistic, liberal and state-centric accounts of human rights, for example, in historical failures to address violence against women, the gendered dimensions of war and conflict, or the gender-specific impact of neo-liberal globalization. In doing so, however, I also highlight ongoing efforts to expand and deepen the understanding of what is meant by human rights and to strengthen accountability and monitoring processes in ways that promote compliance with human rights obligations across the board, by state and non-state actors alike.

3

Women's Human Rights as Equality and Non-Discrimination

This chapter explores key moments in the emergence of the women's human rights (WHR) movement since the establishment of the UN and the adoption of the Universal Declaration of Human Rights (UDHR) (1948). Focusing on feminist advocacy during the first four decades of the UN, I highlight the most important gains secured during this time. These are primarily concerned with creating new international legal standards to underpin women's equality and to promote the norm of non-discrimination on the basis of sex. The Convention on the Elimination of All Forms of Discrimination Against Women (CEDAW) represents the pinnacle of this formative phase of feminist advocacy at the UN. It is often presumed that this phase of feminist engagement with the UN was a Western-driven phenomenon and ultimately concerned with advancing a narrow liberal feminist agenda aimed at achieving an 'equality' between privileged men and women. However, while it can be acknowledged that feminist advocacy during this period was limited insofar as it was 'elite' or 'expert' led and occurred largely before the emergence of a broad-based global women's movement in the 1980s, it is inaccurate to infer from this that the evolving feminist agenda was simply 'Western' or that it focused on issues that affected middle-class, Western women only.

In fact, many of the most radical provisions secured through feminist engagement were initiated by women from the South or by cross-regional groups of women. Further, because the changes that were being sought often had far-reaching implications for the prevailing social order in many societies, they were often strenuously contested by states in the various UN forums in which they were debated. This is evidenced, for example, by the ongoing resistance of states to the full implementation of CEDAW. Furthermore, critics of feminist activism in the global South – and Western-based commentators who espouse strongly relativist positions – often dismiss the claims of indigenous feminist groups by arguing that non-Western women who pursue 'Western feminist agendas' have been 'Westernized' and, therefore, do not represent 'authentic' Southern women.

This binary reasoning is highly problematic since it denies the possibility of oppositional subject positions in non-Western settings where women contest both Western imperialism *and* repressive traditionalism.

More generally, the account offered here highlights the radical moments of the feminist praxis that culminated in CEDAW. I argue that the first phase of feminist advocacy at the UN succeeded in pushing the concept of sex-based, legal equality in human rights law to new limits, especially in relation to the interconnection between women's civil, political and economic rights and their marital and family status. For example, while CEDAW undoubtedly embodies liberal feminist, legally focused currents in transnational feminist advocacy (TFA), its reach goes well beyond women's claim to formal equality in the public sphere – important as this is. The convention is unique among human rights treaties in giving full attention to economic and social rights alongside civil, political and legal rights. In this way, CEDAW challenges the wider, Western-driven agenda to institutionalize the prioritization of civil and political rights over economic and social rights. In doing so, it specifies the conditions for achieving substantive, gender-based equality in all spheres of life in ways that other human rights treaties do not. As such, CEDAW offers a solid bridge to the sections of the global women's movement that emphasize structural inequalities and related gender-specific human rights issues in economic, social and cultural spheres. Viewed in this way – that is, as a transformative tool at the disposal of civil-society actors – CEDAW has the potential to play a very significant role in addressing widening global inequalities and the gender-specific impacts of unchallenged neo-liberal globalization.

In the present chapter, I explore the singular impact of the UN Decade for Women (UNDW) (1976–85) in sparking the proliferation of women's organizations and networks globally and, ultimately, in shaping the contemporary transnational movements for WHR. It is widely recognized that the UNDW changed the tenor of TFA in the context of the UN. It set the stage for the emergence of a broad-based and regionally representative global women's movement with strong links to national and local organizations around the world. In this sense, the Decade presaged the surge in the 1990s in transnational civil society and ensured that many women's groups were well positioned to participate effectively in some of the most transformative campaigns of that period. In effect, it fostered a more diverse and multifaceted global women's movement – one that was challenged to accommodate different feminist and gender perspectives across multiple boundaries of location, identity and ideology, as well as professional divides (women's and human rights non-governmental organizations, (NGOs), service provision, law, media, academia, UN officials, etc.). As will be discussed below, these changes were also accompanied by a reduced focus on the law, traditionally defined, as the primary route to women's equality. Ironically, however, the Decade simultaneously laid the foundation for the emergence of a 'bottom-up' critical approach to the law as a transformative tool in civil-society-led projects. Hence, while transnational, the emerging global women's movement of the 1970s and 1980s was relatively disengaged from and disenchanted with the law. This changed quite dramatically in the early 1990s with the rise of the Global Campaign for Women's Human Rights and the 'feminist transformation of international human rights' (Bunch 1990).

The story of CEDAW

The UN Convention on the Elimination of All Forms of Discrimination Against Women (CEDAW) was first offered for government signatures at the second UN World Conference on Women in Copenhagen in 1980. Even though it reflected the culmination of more than thirty years of feminist advocacy within the UN system, Arvonne Fraser notes that 'on the whole the convention received little attention' as the 'newer women's groups were now concentrating on women in development or single issues such as health care or employment' (Fraser 2001, 55). The fact that the adoption and ratification of a comprehensive WHR instrument was greeted as a non-event by the burgeoning global women's movement is telling and calls for some explanation. CEDAW was an ambitious attempt to enshrine in international law a global commitment to women's equality in all spheres of life, public and private. Yet, the ascendant global women's movement was dismissive. In part, this response reflected the growing influence in international forums of 'second-wave' feminist thinking, which, in the absence of radical social transformation, was highly critical of the limits of individually focused, formal legal equality, especially in relation to the family and personal relationships. It also reflected the increasingly vocal presence of Third World feminists[1] who were more concerned with challenging the exclusion of women from the new UN development programmes of the 1960s and 1970s and/or exposing the exploitive, gendered dimensions of the nascent neo-liberal economic agenda behind them.

The launching of CEDAW at the Copenhagen conference marked the midpoint in the UNDW. As noted, the Decade was pivotal in facilitating the emergence of a more inclusive and critical global WHR movement. As the Decade progressed, the influence of Third World, socialist and radical feminist ideas began to permeate international feminist discourse and displace more traditional liberal feminist tenets, including the latter's commitment to law as the primary tool of feminist advocacy. At the heart of the traditional liberal feminist project is a belief in the idea that equal treatment in the law is the principal mode of achieving equal treatment in society, with a particular focus on public life and employment. In contrast, Third World, socialist and radical tenets entail profound scepticism about the capacity of Western, middle-class, male-biased, liberal law to address inequality and injustice in the (global) economy, in the home and in family or intimate relationships.

On the macro level, Third World and socialist feminist analyses highlight the ways in which (global) capitalism, colonial/postcolonial relations of power, and patriarchal structures interact to perpetuate the subordination of women, often in ways underpinned by liberal legal frameworks. During the Decade, while legal equality was a significant focus of some feminist initiatives in the South, many were sceptical about its transformative value. The top priorities for most Southern feminists continued to be issues of global inequality, poverty and the failures of economic development – especially the exclusion of women from development planning and programming. At the same time, the core message of the US and European women's liberation movements of the 1970s – 'the personal is political' – began to make its presence felt in international feminist gatherings during the Decade. The result was to focus attention on the politics of home and family life. In particular, this radical feminist perspective sought to expose how the socially constructed private sphere conceals abuses, such as violence against women (VAW) and denials of reproductive and sexual autonomy, and allows abusers to act with impunity. More generally, prevalent critiques of liberal feminism highlighted how liberal feminist politics and strategies had failed to address the particular experiences of working-class, minority and lesbian women. Against this backdrop, where the hegemony of liberal feminism was being challenged on various fronts, the CEDAW initiative suffered by association. In 1980, therefore, CEDAW was viewed as a liberal feminist tool with a narrow focus on individual rights and equality between some men and some women in public life and employment. While this critique of traditional liberal feminism is well grounded, its automatic extension to the processes that produced CEDAW belies the convention's radical origins and, perhaps more importantly, its transformative potential.

Broadly speaking, the story of CEDAW begins with women's participation at the founding conference of the United Nations in San Francisco,

California, in 1945. In particular, Margaret Bruce notes that the Latin American delegates – Bertha Lutz from Brazil and Minerva Bernardino from the Dominican Republic – successfully argued that the UN Charter should contain a specific commitment to 'equal rights of men and women' and explicitly prohibit discrimination on grounds of sex (Bruce 1998). This laid the legal foundation for the subsequent creation of a women's sub-commission under the new Human Rights Commission in 1946 and, within a year, the establishment of a full Commission on the Status of Women (Morsink 1991, 230). Each of these steps set the stage for further lobbying by feminist advocates within the new UN to ensure that the Universal Declaration of Human Rights would be understood as applying to the lives of women and men equally.

The Universal Declaration of Human Rights

Drafting a 'bill of human rights' was the first priority of the UN Human Rights Commission, which was established in 1946 with former US first lady Eleanor Roosevelt serving as its chairperson. The form such a bill should take was a highly contentious issue. The Soviet Union resisted the idea of a legally binding convention that would intrude on state sovereignty and/or impose Western principles of law in non-Western countries. And the USA effectively reinforced this position by arguing for 'short articles enunciating general principles' instead of the more detailed convention language proposed by the UK (Humphrey 1983, 414–16). While it was anticipated that the commission would ultimately deliver a legally binding bill of rights with effective implementation mechanisms, in 1947 it was the task of crafting a broadly acceptable declaration of human rights that gathered momentum as an achievable project.

Critics often view the UDHR as an expression of Western biases and hegemonic power. While examples of destructive Western dominance in global politics and economics abound, unreflective narratives of Western hegemony are problematic and render invisible the ways in which such domination can be challenged and successfully resisted. Records of the process to draft and agree the declaration demonstrate that delegates from Asia, Latin America and the Soviet bloc countries in particular – in addition to European and American delegates – were deeply involved in contesting and shaping the substantive content of the declaration (Morsink 1991, Humphrey 1983, Glendon 2001). While often ignored, this reality is reflected in the content of the UDHR. The declaration clearly delineates a range of important 'Western' civil and political rights, such as freedom from torture and arbitrary detention, equality before the law and so on. At the same time, however, it contains several articles that set out numerous economic and social rights (22 to 26), prohibit servitude and slavery (4), and protect the right to own property – both individually and collectively (17). Further, Article 27 lays the foundation to address questions of global inequalities by recognizing every person's right to 'a social and international order in which the rights and freedoms set forth in this Declaration can be fully realised'.

Furthermore, as will be addressed below, without numerous interventions by feminist advocates and supporters, often driven by women from the global South, the UDHR would not express the degree of gender sensitivity that it does, which opens the door to further elaboration of the ways in which it applies to women's lives. While the UDHR may be invoked in processes to impose 'Western values' or as a crude instrument of Euro–US *realpolitik*, this should not discount the origins of the declaration in a cross-regional process of contestation, debate and compromise. As such, the UDHR reflects a working 'global consensus' that most states acknowledge – even as they conceal abuses and dispute the meaning and prioritization of the rights it purports to promote. Further, this global consensus is also evident in the fact that human rights language continues to frame and inspire bottom-up social and political justice movements in every region, around issues ranging from VAW and sexual abuse to agrarian reform and the rights of indigenous peoples and other minorities.

The declaration-drafting process, therefore, was shaped by the political, economic and cultural debates and the differences of the time – many of which continue to define human rights discourse to the present. Charles Malik, an influential member of the drafting committee from Lebanon, for example, strenuously argued for the centrality of the 'human person' and personal freedom within a framework of 'natural law'.[2] In contrast, Soviet delegates pushed for the priority of collective rights over individualism and stressed employment and welfare rights over civil and political rights vis-à-vis the state (Lash 1972, 53). At the same time, Peng-chun Chang of China is credited with effectively representing 'the Asian perspective' and in doing so helped to resolve many 'stalemates in the negotiation process by employing . . . Confucian doctrine to reach compromise between conflicting ideological factions'.[3] Within this milieu, therefore, it is unsurprising that political and ideological differences around how to address women's rights and equality were also a major feature of negotiations and debate throughout the drafting process.

Initial drafts of the proposed declaration began with the wording 'all men'. This prompted much debate among the drafters and other contributors to the process. Bodil Begtrup (Denmark), for example, as chairperson of the new Commission on the Status of Women (CSW), was particularly concerned that gender bias in the language of the draft declaration should be recognized and addressed (Morsink 1991, 233–6; Fraser 2001, 45). Margaret Bruce, who acted as secretary to the declaration-drafting committee, also recalls CSW members Minerva Bernardino (Dominican Republic), who first proposed the establishment of a women's subcommission of the UN Commission on Human Rights (UNCHR), and Marie-Hélène Lefaucheux (France) as two 'distinguished women' who 'worked hard to ensure that women's rights were not overlooked' in the drafting process (Bruce 1998). In wider deliberations on the emerging draft, Hansa Mehta (India) consistently raised the issue of gender, with strong support from Soviet delegates. As a direct result of these interventions, the recurring terms 'everyone' and 'no one' replaced 'all men' and 'no man'. Similarly, early drafts of Article 1 of the Declaration failed to repeat the Charter's explicit commitment to the 'equal rights of men and women'. This was successfully challenged by Minerva Bernardino and Lakhsmi Menon (India). They argued that the gender-neutral use of 'everyone' and 'no one' throughout the declaration was insufficient to underpin women's equality. They pointed out that in many countries the term 'everyone' was readily used in relation to processes such as voting, from which women were excluded in practice (Morsink 1991, 232). Menon further noted that the omission might seem deliberate and even encourage sex-based discrimination on the part of some governments (p. 232).

The CSW also contributed to debates on Article 16 and Article 25, which address rights in relation to marriage and family status. However, it did not directly challenge the idea of the heterosexual, patriarchal family as 'natural and fundamental'. Nor is there any evidence of a concern among feminist advocates at the time (or any other participants in the process) about the rights of gays or lesbians in relation to family life. In this regard, the CSW did not take the opportunities that arose in debates on these articles to call for less prescriptive language on the family. Even on a more basic level, it didn't seek to change the use of the term 'his family', which served to reinforce the prevailing assumption of male-headed households (Morsink 1991, 242). These blind spots partly reflected the limits of a pre 'second-wave' liberal feminist analysis that left intact the 'private' sphere of the family (and especially sexuality) and sought to address the inequalities that arise in these contexts by securing women's equal status in public life vis-à-vis the state. There is no doubt that this approach is inherently limited. However, it is also important to highlight that, at this time, members of the CSW were very concerned about the ways in which marital status – no less than race or religion – was used to deny women's civil rights to own property, retain a nationality, make contracts, etc.[4] Against this backdrop, CSW members, supported by Soviet delegates and Shaista Ikramullah representing Pakistan, effectively challenged conservative Christian governments and NGOs to secure the unprecedented recognition in international law of women's 'equal rights as to marriage, during marriage and at its dissolution' (Article 16).

Setting international legal standards on women's equality

Following the adoption of the UDHR, the CSW turned its attention to establishing legally binding international standards to promote women's equality. In 1945 more than half of the original fifty-one Member States of the United Nations denied women the right to vote. Later, in 1950, some twenty-two countries still had not extended equal rights to women to vote and to hold office. In this context, it is unsurprising that political rights were highlighted as a CSW priority from its inception. Inspired by an earlier Inter-American convention,[5] the Convention on the Political Rights of Women (1952) targeted these inequalities. It asserted women's rights to vote in elections, to be elected to any public office and to carry out all related functions on a basis of equality with men. Debates surrounding the adoption of the convention were contentious with just under one-fifth of states abstaining (eleven out of forty-six). Further, more than forty states reserved the right not to comply with some of the convention's provisions. The resistance to endorsing women's political rights in such an international policy forum in 1952 is striking and is a measure of the radical nature of the agenda for women's political equality at that time.[6]

In addition to its work on political rights, the CSW continued to focus on marital status as an impediment to women's civil rights. In particular, building on the guarantee in the UDHR of the 'right to a nationality' (Article 15), the commission drafted the Convention on the Nationality of Married Women, which was adopted by the General Assembly in 1957. This responded to specific concerns that laws in many countries were drafted on the basis that nationality was determined or conferred by the male 'head of family'. This meant that a woman who married a man of a different nationality could be deprived of her own nationality and, in some circumstances, such as divorce, rendered 'stateless'. Significantly, the nationality convention also met with steep opposition from governments that argued that the principle of equality should not be allowed to override a state's sovereign interests in determining how it regulates nationality and citizenship. As a result, at the General Assembly vote to adopt the convention, a remarkable one-third of states (twenty-four) abstained, while two voted against its adoption (UN 2000).

The CSW was also responsible for the Convention on the Consent to Marriage, Minimum Age for Marriage and Registration of Marriages, adopted in 1962. This initiative grew out of debates surrounding the drafting of the UN 1956 Supplementary Convention on the Abolition of Slavery, which addressed the issue of women and girls being sold into marriage. Some States Parties to this convention wanted stronger measures to underpin the principle of free consent of both parties to marriage. In response, the CSW undertook a major study of the issue (UN 2000). The findings revealed that the practice of child marriages was pervasive and prompted the CSW to commence work on the consent to marriage convention, which prohibits marriages where the 'full and free consent of both parties' has not been given. Later in 1965, the CSW issued a recommendation that fifteen years should be observed as the universal minimum age of consent to marriage (UN 2000).

While the CSW focused primarily on establishing the legal standards of equality in the first two decades of its operation, it also made efforts to bridge the divide between civil/political and social/economic rights that structured evolving mainstream human rights discourse. Notably, it worked with the International Labour Organization (ILO) in the development of its 1951 convention and its recommendation of an 'equal remuneration of work of equal value', which inscribed in international law the idea that pay rates should be determined by the specifications of the job and not the sex of the employee. The ILO continued to promote women's economic equality through the introduction of several important international standards, including, for example, the ILO Maternity Protection Convention (1952) and the Convention Concerning Discrimination in Respect of Employment and Occupation (1960).[7] Further, recognizing the links between education opportunities and advancing gender equality, the CSW also cooperated with UNESCO on its Convention Against Discrimination in Education (1960).

The UN Decade for Women: 1976–1985

The first UN Development Decade (1960–69) brought changes in thinking within the UN about how best to achieve advancement for women. Tensions surfaced between those who emphasized the importance of the law and legal reform to transform gender-based inequalities and those who focused on promoting development. The latter emphasized the need for concrete programmes to meet basic needs and to provide services, education and training in order to empower marginalized women (Fraser 2001, 47). In 1963, the UN produced a report on the 'world social situation', which substantially addressed issues such as housing, health, education and so on for the first time. In the same year, the appointment of a UN Special Rapporteur on Family Planning also signalled a new departure – one that encompassed the 'social' sphere. Also in 1963, Chile introduced a General Assembly resolution on the 'participation of women in national and economic development' that called for the inclusion of women in national development plans and directed the CSW to move beyond its legal focus to consider the role of women in economic and social development. During the decade, the CSW oversaw the drafting of the UN Declaration on the Elimination of Discrimination against Women (1967). Overall, however, the development of new legal standards received less attention and resources than before. The new emphasis on integrating women into development received further affirmation with the adoption by the General Assembly of its Programme of Concerted International Action for the Advancement of Women (1970).

In 1972, against a backdrop of increasingly visible, national-level, second-wave women's movements, the General Assembly agreed to convene a world conference on women in 1975 – something that the CSW had sought since its inception. In addition, 1975 was designated International Women's Year (IWY). These steps marked the beginnings of a new era in women's transnational organizing and solidarity. They laid the foundation for fundamental shifts in policy and thinking in the 1990s that would see women's rights and gender issues move from the margins to the centre of key UN agendas. The IWY had a significant impact. More than eighty countries created national commissions, committees or centres and organized promotional events (Allan et al. 1995, 31). More generally, the IWY raised awareness about the UN as a site of global deliberation and policy-making among an ever-widening network of women's organizations globally, and it fostered greater recognition of women's marginalized position, especially in developing countries.

The first UN World Conference on Women took place in Mexico City (June 1975). According to the UN Division for the Advancement of Women (UNDAW), the event was a turning point wherein 'the campaign for the advancement of women [that] had begun as a struggle for [formal] equality . . . evolved to encompass the role of women in society and especially in economic development' (UN 2000). Others argue along similar lines that it 'marked the beginning of the bringing together of two distinct agendas: the women's agenda defined and developed by . . . [the] CSW over thirty years, and the larger political agenda of the UN, articulated within its major political bodies' (Allan et al. 1995, 29). In this sense, the conference was an early step in the emergence of a 'bottom-up', civil-society-driven process to integrate women's concerns and gender perspectives throughout all major UN agendas. Furthermore, the wider programmatic approach to 'women's issues' was evident in the three-part conference agenda addressing the following: the involvement of women in strengthening international peace and eliminating various forms of racial discrimination and (neo)colonialism; gender stereotypes and other obstacles to achieving equal rights, opportunities and responsibilities; and the integration of women in development.

The Mexico City conference was the first major intergovernmental conference dedicated to addressing women's role and status in societies everywhere. It was attended by 1,200 governmental delegates from 133 states. Women made up 73 per cent of all delegates and 113 delegations were headed by women. In addition, members from 114 accredited NGOs attended the conference.[8] A parallel NGO forum, the International Women's Year Tribune, attracted approximately 4000 participants (5WWC n.d.). The governmental proceedings, however, were dominated by heated political debates. Developing countries used the conference to push forward the promised 'New International Economic Order', which had also been declared by the UN in 1975. Eastern European delegations called for decolonization and disarmament, while the USA argued that all of these issues were distractions from the primary concern of equality (Allan et al. 1995, 32). Nonetheless, other observers noted that many delegates who were 'passionate on women's issues, tried to find common ground on which to formulate political and economic strategies' (UN 2000). Fraser also comments that while 'contentious divisions between developing world and industrialised countries surfaced . . . and were energetically reported by the world's media . . . the atmosphere in Mexico City appeared more tense than it actually was' (Fraser 2001, 50).

The more constructive moments of the event were captured in the Mexico City World Plan of Action, which was agreed by delegates by consensus at the close of the conference. It provided comprehensive guidelines to further women's equality and inclusion in peace and development initiatives over the next decade. The Plan included targets to be met by 1980, including the following: equal access to all levels of education and training; legislation to underpin women's political participation; increased employment opportunities; and improvements in health services, sanitation, housing, nutrition and family planning. The targets also addressed issues affecting particular groups of women, including migrant women, female prisoners and trafficked women. Further, the conference called on the UN to continue working towards a comprehensive convention on the elimination of discrimination against women, with effective implementation procedures. Importantly, it also urged the UN to designate 1976 to 1985 as the UNDW and recommended that another world conference on women be held in 1980. In addition, the Mexico City conference led to the establishment of the UN International Research and Training Institute for the Advancement of Women (INSTRAW) and endorsed the creation of a UN voluntary fund for the Decade for Women (which later became the United Nations Development Fund for Women, or UNIFEM). Many significant NGO initiatives also originated in Mexico City, in particular the International Women's Tribune Center (IWTC), which played a key role in subsequent years in extending the reach of the new global feminism that emerged around the conference.

Despite the commitments made at the Mexico City conference, in subsequent years governmental reports on the implementation of the World Plan of Action revealed very slow progress in achieving the Decade goals (UN 2000). In part, this reflected the rising influence of neo-liberal thinking and structural adjustment policies, which militated against securing the resources necessary to improve the situation of women. Ironically, despite the programmatic focus of the Decade, Mexico City had provided a much-needed boost to the process to establish a legally binding women's convention. In 1976 the CSW completed a draft Convention on the Elimination of All Forms of Discrimination Against Women, which was later adopted in 1979. A second World Conference on Women was held in Copenhagen (July 1980) to review progress in implementing the Mexico City plan and to update it for the second half of the Decade. Delegates agreed that there had been some advancement since the Mexico City conference, including the adoption of CEDAW, new national anti-discrimination programmes, improved UN data collection and a higher level of awareness of women's issues throughout the UN machinery. Reflecting the belief that the prospects for implementing the Decade goals would be improved by identifying specific action objectives in concrete policy areas, the Copenhagen agenda was narrowed down to three core areas of concern: employment, health and education.

As in Mexico City, however, intergovernmental deliberations reflected wider divides in international politics. There were major confrontations between North and South delegates on issues of Zionism and racism. While delegations from the North argued that women's marginalization was the result of discrimination within their own societies, delegations from the South emphasized the role of international economic exploitation and the legacy of colonialism in subordinating women. Eastern European countries argued that socialism had already delivered equality between women and men and now called for women's participation in promoting peace and disarmament. At the same time there were some areas of growing consensus, for example, in recognition of the need to address VAW and to support grassroots organizations in their efforts to empower women. Amidst protracted debate and dissent, the conference finally adopted a Programme of Action – by vote rather than consensus. While ninety-four delegates voted to adopt the action programme, twenty-two abstained and four voted against – Australia, Canada, the United States and Israel (Tinker 1981). The Copenhagen Programme of Action is notable in that it called on states to underpin women's equal treatment in relation to property ownership and access, inheritance, child custody and nationality. It also stressed the need to combat stereotypical attitudes about women as major obstacles to implementing the Decade's goals. Further, it called for a world survey on the status of women and a third conference in 1985 to take stock of the achievements of the Decade and to set new guidelines for 1985–2000.

Following in the tradition of the NGO activities at the Mexico City conference, an NGO Forum also took place over two weeks, parallel to the Copenhagen governmental conference. Hundreds of panels and workshops addressed the official themes of equality, development and peace, and health, education and employment, as well as issues such as apartheid, racism, trafficking and the situation of migrant and refugee women. As in the case of the International Women's Year Tribune at the Mexico City conference, wider political divisions evident at the governmental conference also played out in the NGO Forum. Overall, Western women focused on equality, while women from developing countries highlighted development issues and those from Eastern Europe pursued questions of international peace. There were intense confrontations around the situation of Palestine, and Iranian women supporters of the Khomeini regime clashed with Iranian women exiles (Tinker 1981).

Nonetheless, the Forum was a significant step forward in the development of a more active role for transnational civil society at UN forums. There were tensions between the Forum and the governmental conference because organizers of the latter treated the Forum as a completely separate event and did not facilitate Forum participants' access to the governmental deliberations.[9] Despite the lack of direct access, however, many unaccredited NGOs arranged regular meetings with governmental delegates in order to brief them on specific issues and, in this way, served as an informal conduit between the Forum and the conference (UN 2000). At the Forum itself, there were approximately 8,000 participants from 187 countries. However, while somewhat more international than the Mexico City Tribune, regional representation was very skewed towards Europe and the USA, which inevitably led to legitimate protests from participants from developing countries that their voices were not being heard.[10] Further, most of the participants were primarily from professional women's organizations. The newer international networks with significant grassroots links, which would come to dominate at similar global forums throughout the 1990s, were just beginning to form. Both the Mexico City Tribune and the Copenhagen NGO Forum played important roles in fostering the emergence of such networks. At Copenhagen, for example, new regional and international networks were formed in the areas of female sexual slavery, women in the media and women's studies as an academic project.

The third and final governmental conference of the Decade took place in Nairobi in 1985. A draft document, Nairobi Forward-looking Strategies for the Advancement of Women (FLS), was the focus of deliberations. Reflecting a process that was considerably less fraught than that in Copenhagen, the FLS was adopted by consensus after a number of contentious issues were diffused (especially around the links made between Zionism and racism). Charlotte Bunch attributes this to the fact that that vast majority of the governmental delegates were women who demonstrated 'great determination that something constructive should emerge from this conference' and, in doing so, 'created a climate of compromise' (Bunch 1987, 347). The result was a more expansive and woman-centred plan aimed at transforming women's lives. It targeted three arenas for concerted action at the national level: constitutional and legal measures, social participation, and political participation and decision-making. Under this rubric, it recommended specific measures in a wide range of policy areas from employment, health, education, housing and social services to community development, transport and the environment. In addition, the FLS included guidelines for promoting women's participation in peace initiatives and explicitly addressed the situation of women in Palestine, under apartheid and in armed conflicts. Prefiguring later debates around 'intersectionality', the FLS continued the trend of recognizing the diversity of women's situations and experiences. It highlighted, in particular, the need for specific measures to address the experiences of women migrants and refugees, minority and indigenous women, women with disabilities, and women heads of households, as well as women affected by drought, urban poverty, trafficking and forced prostitution, and women in prison.

Arguably, however, the Nairobi NGO Forum created the most enduring imprint on the shape and direction of the emerging global women's movement. Exceeding all expectations, between 13,000 and 15,000 people attended the Forum, which involved more than 1,000 meetings over two weeks. It is widely agreed that this gathering marked a dramatic turning point in achieving greater regional balance and giving more space to the perspectives of women from the South. Bunch notes that 'not only were Third World women . . . present in large numbers, but also they were taking the initiative in many areas' (1987, 348). Many influential women's networks of ongoing importance were established or significantly shaped by the Nairobi Forum. The research and advocacy network, Development Alternatives with Women for a New Era (DAWN), for example, originated in Nairobi. The DAWN perspective captured the spirit of the new global women's movement, which increasingly rejected the false ghettoization of 'women's issues' and insisted on the need for integrated feminist analyses and action across all issues and all spheres from the local to the global level. In addition, the International Women's Rights Action Watch (IWRAW), dedicated to monitoring implementation of CEDAW, was launched at Nairobi. The Forum was also a critical event in the development of the Latin American regional women's communications network – ISIS International (Portugal 2004, 108). According to one UN source 'the end-of-Decade meeting produced a new feeling of solidarity among women from all over the world, and participants went back to their respective countries with the sense of having joined a truly international women's movement' (UN 2000).

The Convention on the Elimination of All Forms of Discrimination Against Women

Well before the UN Decade for Women, the process to create a comprehensive convention on WHR was put in train in 1963 when a General Assembly resolution, sponsored by developing and Soviet bloc countries, called for a UN declaration on the elimination of discrimination against women (Fraser 2001, 46). In 1965, drawing on inputs from representatives from Poland, Ghana and Mexico, the CSW commenced work on the UN Declaration on the Elimination of Discrimination against Women. It addressed discrimination under the law and in political life, education, employment, marriage and the family, and traditional customs and practices. Such an expansive approach went beyond mainstream understandings of state-sponsored discrimination that prioritized legal equality. In doing so, it laid the foundations for pursuing an integrated approach to civil, political, economic, social and cultural rights.

Because the proposed declaration challenged deeply held beliefs about the role of women in societies everywhere, meetings of the Economic and Social Council (ECOSOC) of the United Nations to review it involved contentious debates, especially around Article 3 and Article 10 (Fraser 2001, 48). The former, calling for the 'abolition of customary . . . practices which are based on the idea of the inferiority of women', was strongly contested as an infringement on cultural integrity. Discussion of Article 10, addressing issues around 'protecting' women workers, also provoked much debate as women's rights advocates sought to ensure that the concept of protection would be limited to very specific conditions (primarily in relation to reproductive health) and could not be interpreted to bolster exclusionary employment practices. The declaration was finally adopted by the General Assembly in November 1967 and soon afterwards the CSW delegate from Poland proposed that it should form the basis of a legally binding convention on the elimination of discrimination against women (p. 49).

Given the new emphasis within the UN on development-oriented programmatic initiatives, progress on the treaty was very slow. In 1972, a working group, consisting of CSW representatives from the Dominican Republic, Hungary and Egypt, commenced work on the basis of an initial draft provided by the Philippines delegate. The Mexico City conference gave the CSW a renewed mandate to finalize and adopt the convention, which the commission aimed to achieve before the mid-Decade conference in 1980. Influenced by the new attention given to women in development issues, new articles were now added on access to health services (including family planning) and rural women (Fraser 2001, 54). As the draft convention moved through ECOSOC and General Assembly reviews, a number of articles that directly challenged existing national legal systems were the subjects of intense debate. This included Article 15 and Article 16, stipulating full equality under the law and in marriage, and Article 9, ensuring women's right to convey their nationality to their children (p. 54). Nonetheless, buoyed by the energy of the momentum generated by the UNDW, the CSW achieved its goal and the convention was adopted by the General Assembly in December 1979.

As noted earlier, the convention was first presented for states' signatures at the mid-Decade conference in Copenhagen in 1980. CEDAW entered into force just over one year later, more quickly than all previous human rights treaties. It remains the second-most ratified international human rights treaty (after the Convention on the Rights of the Child). Despite not being greeted with widespread enthusiasm by the burgeoning global women's movement at the time, this is remarkable, and testifies to the impact of the Decade in making it difficult for states to be seen to oppose women's rights. However, it also conceals another less encouraging statistic – that CEDAW is the international human rights treaty with the greatest number of reservations attached to state ratifications. Many of these reservations allow states to avoid some of the most basic requirements of the convention. Most often these are objections to amending existing family law codes in keeping with Article 16. They also contest articles calling on states to pursue proactive measures to eliminate discrimination and to ensure equality before the law and with regard to nationality. The large number, substance and persistence of these reservations continue to underline the fact that many states simply are not committed to some of the treaty's core principles.[11]

The Convention on the Elimination of All Forms of Discrimination Against Women is unique in a number of ways. It is the first international instrument to provide a comprehensive definition of discrimination against women. Borrowing from the 1965 International Convention on the Elimination of All Forms of Racial Discrimination (ICERD), it defines discrimination as: '*any distinction, exclusion or restriction* made on the basis of sex which has the *effect or purpose* of impairing or nullifying the recognition, enjoyment or exercise by women, irrespective of their marital status, on a basis of equality of men and women, of human rights and fundamental freedoms in the political, economic, social, cultural, civil or *any other field*' (Article 1) (my emphasis). Significantly, it departs from ICERD by replacing the phrase 'any other field of public life' with 'any other field' and, in doing so, signals the intended application of this treaty to all spheres of public and private life – from the law and politics, to the economy, community and the family.

More generally, the definition of discrimination enshrined in CEDAW contests the automatic hierarchical ordering of rights in mainstream human rights discourse wherein the exercise of civil and political rights vis-à-vis the state is presumed to be more important – and inherently more achievable and defensible – than the exercise of supposedly amorphous social, economic and cultural rights vis-à-vis 'society'. Further, building on the precedent set by ICERD, the Women's Convention recognizes that both state and non-state actors can play a role in violating rights and sustaining patterns of discrimination against women in everyday life (Article 2 (e)). Similarly, in proscribing actions with a discriminatory purpose or effect, CEDAW expressly encompasses direct and indirect forms of discrimination. The convention is also notable in underlining the positive duty of states to eliminate discrimination against women and promote equality across all spheres of life through the law and other measures (Article 2 and Article 3). This includes a call on states to 'modify social and cultural patterns of conduct' towards the elimination of gender-based prejudices and harmful customary practices (Article 5). In particular, CEDAW affirms and clarifies gender-specific understanding of the concept of 'special temporary measures' whereby neither programmes to redress the effects of sex-based discrimination nor 'permanent' maternity-based protections, for example, can be considered discriminatory (Article 4). While ICERD stands out among international human rights treaties as the first to bring together in one legally binding convention economic, social, cultural, civil and political rights, CEDAW takes this approach further. It moves beyond a simple enumeration of these rights and elaborates their content from the perspective of women. This includes detailed articles in areas of long-standing concern to the CSW addressing equality before the law (Article 15) and in public and political life (Article 7 and Article 8), recognition of nationality (Article 9), education (Article 10), employment (Article 11) and marriage and family life (Article 16). Additional substantive articles address relatively newer areas, brought to the fore in the context of the UNDW and a wider focus on development. These include the situation of rural women (Article 11) and access to healthcare and family planning (Article 12) and financial services (Article 13).

The implementation of the convention is monitored by a regionally balanced Committee on the Elimination of Discrimination against Women.

This consists of twenty-three 'members of high moral standing and competence in the fields covered by the Convention' (Article 17) who serve in a personal capacity for four-year terms. Its work primarily revolves around reviews of national reports, which each State Party must submit every four years. In this context, the committee also receives information from and engages in dialogue with NGOs that prepare alternative or 'shadow' reports to draw attention to gaps in implementation or flagrant abuses of rights by states. On the basis of each review, the committee issues 'concluding comments' that suggest areas for remedial action to be taken by the reporting state before its next review. The CEDAW committee has a particularly strong relationship with NGOs. Notably, IWRAW and more recently its Malaysia-based sister organization, IWRAW Asia Pacific, have played key roles supporting the work of the committee and have organized innumerable training and information sessions with NGOs and state actors to promote the application of CEDAW at national level.

The transformation of CEDAW: from legal blueprint to emancipatory tool?

Rhonda Copelon notes that 'in 1990 women's human rights issues were barely on the margin of the international human rights agenda' and that 'the Convention on the Elimination of All Forms of Discrimination Against Women was consigned to little more than window dressing' (Copelon 2003, 866). While CEDAW was recognized – mainly by feminist legal advocates – as a comprehensive charter on women's equality and human rights, it was also recognized as especially ineffectual among international human rights treaties. In particular, it had no complaints or investigative procedures that would allow women to challenge formally states that fail to implement the treaty's provisions or to allow the treaty-monitoring committee to undertake its own investigations into suspected violations.

Unlike the treaties on civil and political rights or torture, therefore, the CEDAW committee's concluding comments and general recommendations were the only form of censure available when states violated the rights set out in CEDAW. Further, after ten years in force, the committee was profoundly under-resourced. It met just once a year in New York – away from the centre of activity of the 'real' human rights world in Geneva – and had a major backlog of governmental reports to review. In addition, as noted earlier, the convention was (and continues to be) hampered by copious reservations and to have the dubious distinction of being the most reserved treaty. While Article 28 does not permit states to enter reservations 'incompatible with the object and purpose' of the convention, there are no mechanisms to enforce this restriction and, in reality, many of the reservations currently in place are directly at odds with the purpose of the convention.

During the 1990s, however, CEDAW and its committee underwent a significant revival. In 1991, as plans at the UN were underway to hold a second world conference on human rights in Vienna in 1993, the new Global Campaign for Women's Human Rights had begun to emerge. This multi-pronged initiative included renewed attention to CEDAW. As a result, a number of important concrete measures emerged that strengthened the convention and narrowed the gap between 'legal' and 'non-legal' strands of feminist advocacy, and, in doing so, laid the foundations for the reinvigoration of CEDAW as an emancipatory tool. In terms of its technical procedures, for example, the CEDAW committee was successful in securing changes that allowed it to meet more frequently and for longer periods. Since 1997, the committee has met at least twice a year for three weeks (where previously it met just once a year for two weeks). Aside from undertaking reviews of governmental compliance with CEDAW, the committee is also empowered to formulate 'general recommendations' directed at states in areas where it believes more action is needed to achieve full implementation of the convention.

As of 2006, the committee had made twenty-five such recommendations. Throughout the 1980s, however, these were generally brief and focused on technical issues. In 1991 the committee made a deliberate decision, reflecting the influence of the Global Campaign for Women's Human Rights, to use this function to develop more detailed analyses and guidelines around the meaning of specific articles and/or the application of the treaty to specific issues. From this new perspective, the committee produced detailed general recommendations on VAW as a form of discrimination (1992), equality within marriage and family relations (1994), women's right to health (1999) and the meaning and use of temporary special measures (2004).

Perhaps most importantly, during this time the convention was greatly strengthened by the introduction of new complaints and inquiry procedures. This hard-won gain began when WHR advocates successfully lobbied the Vienna conference to include among its main recommendations a call to 'quickly examine the possibility of introducing . . . an optional protocol' to CEDAW.[12] In 1995, an ECOSOC resolution called on the CSW to convene a working group to develop an optional protocol. Further encouraged by the Fourth World Conference on Women (Beijing, 1995)

(FWCW) and the resulting Beijing Platform for Action (1995), the working group was convened and commenced work early in 1996. Building on key inputs from the CEDAW committee and interested NGOs[13] and States Parties, the working group produced a draft optional protocol by 1997. The draft was the subject of intense debate at subsequent meetings in 1998 and 1999. While there was broad agreement that the protocol should include an individual complaints procedure, the process was almost halted by disagreements over whether third parties (especially NGOs) should be allowed to make complaints on behalf of individuals and, if NGOs were allowed to do so, whether or not the explicit consent of the individuals involved should be required (Gómez Isa 2003, 310).

This debate goes to the heart of the competing visions of the nature and role of human rights law. On the one hand, there are those who view NGO and civil-society engagement as key components in the process of bringing international human rights law to life, especially in the context of emancipatory projects. On the other hand are those who resist a wider role for civil-society actors in seeking implementation of human rights standards, reassert the primacy of state sovereignty and reaffirm a legalistic view of human rights wherein alleged victims defend their rights as individuals in the public sphere. Human rights groups like Amnesty International (AI) – influenced especially by the Global Campaign for Women's Human Rights – insisted that an overly narrow, legalistic procedure would render it useless to the most marginalized victims and those 'least able to come forward and speak of their suffering' (Gómez Isa 2003, 310). In the end a compromise was agreed allowing complaints to be submitted '*by or on behalf of* individuals or groups of individuals' (my emphasis) with the consent of the person or group involved 'unless the author [of the complaint] can justify acting on their behalf without such consent' (Optional Protocol, Article 2).[14]

In addition to receiving individual and group complaints, the Optional Protocol also gives the CEDAW committee the power to initiate inquiries into suspected 'grave or systematic violations . . . of rights set forth in the Convention' (Optional Protocol, Article 8). While the inquiry procedure can be initiated on the basis of 'reliable information' received, for example, from NGOs and other independent sources, the committee must also have the cooperation of the relevant State Party in order to proceed. The procedure clearly opens the door to developing further the advocacy and monitoring role of civil-society actors in making human rights a local reality. Unsurprisingly, this feature of the Optional Protocol was also strongly opposed by a minority of states that were particularly resistant to

an increase in international and NGO scrutiny.[15] Reflecting the conten-
tiousness of the debate, the working group agreed to include an opt-out
clause in the Optional Protocol (Article 10) that allowed states to ratify the
treaty without being bound by its inquiry procedure element. Hence, after
three years of intense debate, the text of the Optional Protocol was finally
agreed and adopted by the General Assembly in 1999, just in time to mark
the twentieth anniversary of the Women's Convention.

The reviews by the CEDAW Committee of complaints received under
the Optional Protocol since 2003 illustrate the ongoing development and
impact of this important mechanism. Of ten complaints considered through
2006, three were deemed inadmissible because domestic judicial remedies
had not been exhausted or the events occurred before the protocol was in
force. Of the remaining seven: one was a case of direct discrimination by
the Spanish state where an eldest daughter was denied the right to succeed
to her father's title, which a firstborn male would enjoy; another case
alleged indirect discrimination against older women with children in the
material consequences of German divorce law; three concerned physical
violence against women perpetrated by a spouse or estranged partner in
Hungary and Austria, which caused the death of the two women at the
centre of the complaints against the Austrian state; and, finally, two cases
addressed violations of women's social and/or economic rights, one relat-
ing to an incident of forced sterilization in Hungary and another concerning
the Netherlands' alleged discriminatory maternity benefit policy that disadvantaged self-employed women. With the exception of the maternity
benefit complaint, in each of these cases the committee concluded that the
state had violated or failed in its duty to protect specific rights set out in the
Women's Convention and states were requested to follow particular recommendations to remedy the situation. These developments are
noteworthy on a number of levels.[16]

The range of complaints appraised (spanning civil and political as well as
economic, social and cultural rights) and the nuanced analyses offered in
each case illustrate the committee's mandate in action to foreground the
indivisibility of WHR. In addition, NGOs played a key role in supporting
complainants through the process, thereby underlining its potential not
only as a redress route for particular individuals but also as focus for wider
mobilization around needed legal and policy reforms.[17] Similar points
apply regarding the committee's first completed inquiry conducted under
the Optional Protocol into the role of the state in addressing the unsolved
murders of more than 200 women in Ciudad Juarez, Mexico, since the
1990s. Feride Acar, Chairperson of the CEDAW committee, notes that the

request to undertake the inquiry was initiated jointly by NGOs in Mexico and the USA (Acar 2004, 1). In addition, once again underlining the centrality of the indivisibility of rights to achieving women's equality, Acar asserts that the committee's findings regarding Ciudad Juarez are most important because:

> [T]hey do not only respond to the concrete violations, their victims and perpetrators, but address the sociocultural background in which the events have taken place. Our analysis and recommendations place the specific crimes of Juarez in the context of women's human rights and highlight their gender-based nature. Our recommendations address the root causes and support mechanisms that feed this structural violence against women as well as the killings themselves. (Acar 2004, 2)

Conclusion

Throughout this discussion, I have underlined the ways in which international human rights law (like all law) is socially constructed and a site of struggle and contestation. Although the creation of international human rights law is motivated by a universal norm – recognition of the equal worth of all human beings – actual human rights agreements are inevitably contingent on a variety of levels. However, even as human rights agreements reflect prevailing power relations, along lines of gender, geo-politics, culture and so on, they often also capture moments of resistance. These contest and unsettle dominant notions of what constitutes human rights and under what conditions individuals are entitled to protection and redress vis-à-vis abuses they have suffered. While the overall trajectory of international human rights discourse since the inception of the UN, therefore, has been deeply shaped by hegemonic Western, neo-liberal, male biases, the account of feminist intervention presented here demonstrates the potential to disrupt this trajectory and create spaces where usually marginalized actors can achieve meaningful shifts in the exercise of power. More specifically, I have highlighted such moments of feminist engagement with the UN over its first four decades.

Beginning with the efforts of a few dedicated advocates seeking to ensure that women were explicitly addressed in the UN Charter and Universal Declaration of Human Rights, I have flagged subsequent processes surrounding key feminist achievements. Importantly, I highlighted the pivotal contributions of women's rights advocates – from the South and former communist countries, as well as from the North – in creating a range of new legal standards that enshrined in international law principles of sex-based equality and non-discrimination. In doing so, I hope to dispel the widely held belief that these developments were entirely Western-driven. However, while radical in challenging states to apply fully emerging human rights standards to women's lives, these efforts were limited insofar as they reinforced a traditional, top-down, approach to the law. Many of the leading feminist advocates noted in this chapter were also trained as lawyers and, arguably, accepted too uncritically the privileged positioning of the law (and its expert interpreters) in shaping societies and administering justice.

Ultimately, the expert-driven and law-centric focus of the early decades of UN-oriented feminist advocacy significantly undermined prospects for implementing the standards and principles that had been achieved. The radical potential of the gains made was limited in a changed UN climate in the 1960s and 1970s, which favoured programmatic initiatives as an alternative to legal standards in efforts to achieve ever more ambitious UN goals. Further, the dichotomy between 'law' and 'non-law' approaches, which was mapped onto an 'elite' versus 'grassroots' split in many people's minds, undoubtedly contributed to the unenthusiastic reception of CEDAW by the emerging, grassroots-oriented global women's movement of the UNDW (1976–85). These tensions further mirror ideological divides within feminism, which tend to suppose a dichotomy between 'top-down' liberal feminism and its emphasis on the law and individual rights and 'bottom-up' Third World, socialist and radical feminisms, which challenge structural inequalities, colonialism and racism, the sexual division of labour and the oppressive gender politics of family and personal relationships.

In fact, the UNDW laid the foundations for a more constructive dialectic between the 'legal' and the 'programmatic' streams of feminist activism. By making the UN more accessible as a site of deliberation and policy-making for growing numbers of women's NGOs, and by creating concrete opportunities for critical feminist engagement with gender-specific UN forums, the Decade opened up the possibility of similar and more targeted engagement with other arenas within the UN – including different areas of international law. This is evidenced in the reinvigoration of CEDAW through the adoption of an optional protocol in 1997. Other examples discussed in detail in subsequent chapters include successful campaigns to achieve recognition of violence against women as a violation of human rights, define sexual violence as a war crime and a crime against humanity in the statute of the International Criminal Court, and bring about the adoption of Security Council Resolution 1325 calling for the protection of women in conflict situations and their full inclusion in peace-building and post-conflict reconstruction. In the following chapter, I turn to a detailed analysis of the 1990s Global Campaign for Women's Human Rights and the 'feminist transformation of human rights' that it sought to effect.

4

Violence and Reproductive Health as Human Rights Issues

Introduction

Recognizing the importance of Amnesty International (AI) as a high-profile, human rights non-governmental organization (NGO) with an extensive grassroots base, long-time US women's rights activist Fran Hosken approached the organization to discuss the possibilities of AI working collaboratively with her project, Women's International Network (WIN) News. WIN gathered and disseminated information and editorials on women's rights concerns around the world (Hosken 1981). AI responded by saying that it could only concern itself with 'women as political prisoners'. This prompted Hosken to ask how it is that 'sexual assault, wife-beating, genital mutilation [and] depriving women of food, clothes, shelter, or gainful employment' are outside the 'self-ascribed domains or action fields of all so-called human rights groups?' (p. 8).

This early encounter between the then quite separate worlds of 'women's rights' and 'human rights' highlighted the absence of a broad-based movement dedicated to the realization of human rights in the lives of women on a par with AI. It also anticipated the central role that violations of bodily integrity, and gender-based violence in particular, would play in exposing the gendered limitations of the established human rights paradigm and shaping the new women's human rights (WHR) agenda. In the early 1990s, the Global Campaign for Women's Human Rights[1] became a central locus of this movement. While not without its faults and critics, it is fair to say that the Global Campaign was more broad-based and more global than all previous initiatives to advance women's rights within a human rights framework. In doing so, it moved beyond the narrowly legal focus of traditional liberal feminism and promoted instead a transformative vision of international law and standards, linked to bottom-up participation by women's movements in every region. Moreover, the success of the Global Campaign in framing violence against women

(VAW) as a human rights issue signalled the incorporation of radical feminist analysis into an important mainstream international policy arena.

The term 'radical feminism' is generally used to describe the strand of feminism at the critical edges of 1970s Euro-American 'second-wave' women's movements that highlighted personal relationships and women's bodies and sexuality as primary sites of oppression and political struggle. Popularizing the slogan 'the personal is political', radical feminism named and problematized patriarchal control over women's bodies and reproductive and sexual lives and the related repression of homosexuality. In this context, a focus on issues of sexual exploitation, rape, VAW and access to contraception and abortion has become synonymous with Euro-American 1970s feminism. The issue of VAW, in particular, remained a central preoccupation of established women's movements in the global North in the 1980s and also emerged as a primary issue for women's movements in the global South. Hence, when women's movements began to re-think the relevance of human rights ideas and practice to addressing women's and gender concerns in emerging 1990s global policy agendas, the human rights principle of respect for bodily integrity resonated strongly with established feminist agendas in every region.

In mainstream human rights discourse, bodily integrity has generally been seen as an aspect of 'civil and political' rights, grounded in the 'right to life' (ICCPR, Article 6), the right to 'liberty and security of person' (ICCPR, Article 9) and the right not to be subjected to 'torture or cruel, inhuman or degrading treatment' (ICCPR, Article 7).[2] In the context of evolving feminist critiques of human rights, however, the term 'bodily integrity' was used increasingly in naming particular forms of invasive physical violation as human rights abuses, usually centring on sexual violence and humiliation and interventions to control women's sexuality and reproductive lives (Wilets 1997). This change in how the term 'bodily integrity' was used is an important example of the impact of the Global Campaign on traditional human rights thinking. It unsettles the public–private divide and exposes the ways in which wider social and cultural mores and power dynamics are implicated in facilitating and concealing such abuses. From this perspective, I now turn to consider more closely the unique contribution of the 1990s Global Campaign, its strategies, gains and limitations.

The Global Campaign for Women's Human Rights: setting the context

Prior to the emergence of the Global Campaign for Women's Human Rights there had been no concerted effort to contest the gender bias of mainstream human rights practice, which was largely ignored by women's movements. From 1985, the Nairobi Forward-Looking Strategies for the Advancement of Women (FLS) reflected the global consensus on the 'advancement of women' under the rubric of 'Equality, Development and Peace'. Less concerned with women's legal status and more in tune with the emerging global women's movement of the UN Decade for Women (UNDW), the FLS placed greater emphasis on the structural, institutional and sociocultural changes that need to occur in societies everywhere if women are to be full and equal participants in public and private life (Bunch 1987, 322). Significantly, however, references to human rights standards and the role of human rights institutions in realizing the FLS vision were virtually absent. Furthermore, while VAW had begun to surface as a major concern of women's movements during the UNDW, it still occupied a marginal position on the FLS agenda. All of this, however, was set to change.

In the mid 1980s, in an early indication of a bottom-up, global WHR movement, GABRIELA (a network of women's organizations in the Philippines) began using the slogan 'women's rights are human rights'. Such a use of human rights language in this context rebuked the routine dismissal of women's rights advocacy as a Western or middle-class idea, secondary to national liberation and labour movements, and certainly not a matter of global politics. At the same time, the issue of VAW was increasingly being highlighted by grassroots women's movements as among their most pressing concerns. The Feminist Encuentro for Latin America, and the Caribbean, held in Bogotá, Colombia, in 1981, for example, declared 25 November as 'International Day against Violence against Women'. Efforts to counter domestic violence in Europe and North America through the establishment of women's refuges and shelters were also a principal focus of women's movement activity in the region. By the early 1990s, regional women's networks with broad-based constituencies – such as Women in Law and Development in Africa (WiLDAF), the Asia Pacific Forum on Women, Law and Development (APWLD), the Caribbean Association for Feminist Research and Action (CAFRA) and Women Living under Muslim Laws (WLUML) – had also developed programmes and strategies focusing on gender-based violence (Bunch and Reilly 1994).

Encouraged by the UNDW, the Nairobi conference and the vibrancy of transnational women's networking and advocacy, some scholars began to re-evaluate the relevance of international human rights standards and processes in pursuing gender justice (Cook 1994c, Schuler 1995, Peters and Wolper 1995, *American University Law Review* 1995). They explored issues such as state accountability for gender-specific abuses by private actors (Cook 1994a, 228), the prospects for tackling gender-specific economic inequalities as human rights concerns (Butegwa 1994, 495) and the value of human rights as a framework for feminist advocacy at different levels (Abeysekera 1995; Matus Madrid 1995; Bunch and Reilly 1995). Other scholars began to develop new feminist interpretations of human rights legal processes and procedures in order to seek the inclusion of other, previously ignored gender-specific violations in human rights agendas. This included, for example, arguing for recognition of the fear of female genital mutilation (P. Goldberg 1993) or lesbian persecution (S. Goldberg 1993) as grounds for political asylum. Further, voices from the South questioned the toleration in the established human rights community of cultural practices that are harmful to women and girls in the name of respecting religious or cultural identity (Afkhami 1995, Hom 1992, Shaheed 1995).

At the same time, new empirical research confirming the claims of women's movements that VAW was both pervasive and life-threatening provided additional impetus to the emerging movement for WHR (Heise 1989, Heise et al. 1994, Carrillo 1991). Notably, a study by Amartya Sen of recent demographic patterns in Asia indicated that as many as 100 million women were 'missing' in the region as a result of the discriminatory allocation of basic resources, as well as life-threatening cultural norms, such as son-preference (Sen 1990). Sen argued that these factors produced gender-specific abuses such as female infanticide, the systematic malnourishment of girl-children, and dowry-related deaths. Documenting the scale and seriousness of VAW in this way underlined the imperative of tackling both direct and indirect (structurally mediated) violence against women if the realization of WHR is to be taken seriously.

In terms of human rights practice, the CEDAW Committee – buoyed by the burgeoning Global Campaign and growing interest in the issue – formulated its second general recommendation (No. 19) on VAW in 1992. The recommendation defined gender-based violence for the first time as a form of discrimination, set out the ways in which it relates to interpreting the different articles of the Women's Convention and laid the foundation for the 1993 UN Declaration on the Elimination of Violence against

Women (Merry 2006, 76). During this time, women's networks and NGOs with a primary mission to highlight the UN's responsibility to women – such as the International Women's Rights Action Watch (IWRAW) and the International Women's Tribune Center (IWTC) – also turned their attention to the issue of VAW. In addition, influential funding bodies such as the United Nations Development Fund for Women (UNIFEM) made the issue a major programmatic area.

Major human rights NGOs also made significant advances towards greater recognition of WHR in the traditional human rights community. For example, AI conducted studies and issued reports on rape in detention as a form of torture and other gender-based forms of persecution on the part of state actors (Amnesty International 1991). Human Rights Watch, which has a somewhat broader mandate than Amnesty's focus on state-sponsored abuse, carried out numerous investigations into different forms of VAW including, for example, the use of virginity tests in Turkey (Human Rights Watch 1994) and trafficking of Burmese women and girls in Thailand (Human Rights Watch 1993).

The Global Campaign gathers momentum

When the UN resolved in 1991 to convene a World Conference on Human Rights as part of a series of conferences designed to shape positively post-Cold War global politics,[3] women and gender-specific aspects of human rights were completely absent from the proposed agenda. Yet, between 1991 and the time the World Conference ended in Vienna (June 1993), WHR became one of the most discussed topics in the international human rights community. The Vienna Declaration, the final statement issued by the 171 participating governments at the conference, devotes several pages to the 'equal status and human rights of women' as a priority for governments and the United Nations. Moreover, it makes a historic call for the elimination of 'violence against women in public and private life' as a human rights obligation. This progress on WHR did not happen suddenly or by accident. It was the result of well-organized, broad-based, transnational collaboration among diverse women's rights advocates and NGOs – wherein the activities of the Global Campaign for Women's Human Rights played a major part.

This Global Campaign was a multilevel initiative encompassing 'high-level' lobbying of national, regional and global bodies alongside broad-based popular education and mobilization strategies (CWGL 1993). In 1991, international, regional and local women's groups began to hold regular meetings to strategize on how to make WHR perspectives more visible at the Vienna Conference. In this way, the conference preparatory processes, as well as the actual conference and its 'parallel' NGO Forum, emerged as concrete sites of cosmopolitan feminism – that is, spaces where trans-formative visions of human rights were discussed, refined and championed effectively by women's rights advocates from different backgrounds and regions.

At official regional preparatory meetings for the Vienna Conference held in Tunis, San José in Costa Rica and Bangkok, representatives of women's NGOs challenged prevailing limited interpretations of human rights and insisted that WHR be discussed. For example, groups in Latin America organized a WHR conference called 'La Nuestra' (Ours) prior to the regional meeting in San José and prepared a nineteen-point agenda to take there.[4] WiLDAF held a series of subregional women's meetings to define WHR concerns, from which a regional African women's paper was written and presented at the final international preparatory meeting before the World Conference (Butegwa 1993). Similarly, women's organizations at the Asian regional meeting built on the work that had been done in the other regions and successfully integrated their perspectives into the final Asian NGO statement, despite opposition from their governments. The US-based Center for Women's Global Leadership (CWGL)[5] played a valu-able role in convening a global 'strategic planning meeting' where participants from different regions met to formulate common recommen-dations to advance at the international preparatory meeting and to develop plans for other activities of the Global Campaign (CWGL 1993). As a result, the final meeting of the International Preparatory Committee (IPC) in April 1993, which was charged with creating the draft Vienna Conference document, was a site of unprecedented coalitions across old divisions, not only along North–South lines but also across women's NGOs and women working in human rights NGOs and in government and UN agencies (Bunch and Reilly 1994).

This notable example of collaborative, transnational, feminist engage-ment with mainstream human rights agenda-setting processes succeeded in two important ways. First, it effectively pressured for the inclusion of text on women in the draft intergovernmental document, which was accepted by governments at the IPC meeting, thereby assuring its passage later in Vienna. Second, it formed the basis for women's advocates to con-tinue working together across their many differences in Vienna and beyond, especially around the world conferences on social development (Copenhagen, 1995) and population and development (Cairo, 1994) and in preparation for the Fourth World Conference on Women in Beijing in 1995.

In tandem with document drafting and lobbying activities, the Global Campaign created opportunities to foster bottom-up links to the Vienna Conference processes, as well as local ownership of the Global Campaign more generally. Most notably, this included three elements: (1) the 16 Days of Action against Gender Violence, a campaign of activities and events taking place around the world; (2) a four-year worldwide petition campaign (1991–5) initially launched to support the inclusion of women's concerns in the agenda of the Vienna Conference; and (3) the promotion of 'best practice' popular tribunals and hearings on WHR (Reilly and Posluszny 2006). The 16 Days, first launched in 1991, proved to be a pivotal strategy in broadening grassroots women's involvement in the Global Campaign and the movement for WHR beyond Vienna.[6] The 16 Days campaign links women's groups and networks in dozens of countries in every region of the world that organize events and actions each year to build public awareness of VAW as a human rights concern. During the first 16 Days in 1991, a worldwide petition drive was initiated in English, Spanish and French, calling upon the United Nations Human Rights Conference 'to comprehensively address women's human rights at every level of its proceedings' and to recognize 'gender violence, a universal phenomenon which takes many forms across culture, race, and class . . . as a violation of human rights requiring immediate action'. The petition was subsequently translated into more than twenty other languages and distributed by non-governmental sponsors at community, national and regional levels worldwide. By the time the Vienna Conference arrived, 1,000 sponsoring groups across every region of the world had gathered almost a half-million signatures in 124 countries.[7]

Adding to the momentum, a strategy of convening popular tribunals and hearings was launched as part of the second 16 Days campaign in 1992. These aimed to demonstrate more precisely the spectrum of issues behind the worldwide petition drive for recognition of WHR. During 1992–3, substantial hearings were convened by NGOs in Argentina, Costa Rica, India, Nepal and the United States, with dozens of smaller speak-outs in other locations where women voiced their concerns about denials of WHR. Building on this, organizers of the Global Campaign decided to convene the Global Tribunal on Violations of Women's Human Rights, which 'concretized in a dramatic way . . . the pervasive problem of violence against women . . . and [more generally] was instrumental in publicising and recording in the official Vienna Declaration' that women's rights were an integral and indivisible part of universal human rights (Romany 1995, 547). The 16 Days, petition drive and popular hearings all played a part in strengthening the claims of the Global Campaign for Women's Human Rights. They facilitated the mobilization and expression of bottom-up support for the campaign, promoted gender-conscious human rights education from the local to the global level, and bolstered 'high-level' lobbying efforts by women in relation to specific legislation and/or national policy debates, as well as UN or regional human rights implementation.

There have been criticisms of the Global Campaign for Women's Human Rights (Romany 1995, Grewal 1999). In particular, Celina Romany has raised concerns about the dominance of Northern activists and NGOs in the campaign, especially at the Vienna Conference itself.[8] Romany correctly notes that the structure of UN conference proceedings presents 'complex conceptual, strategic and organizational barriers' to women's organizations seeking to advance human rights (p. 546). Under such conditions, inexperienced entrants to a UN process that is already underway will often find themselves disempowered by the complexity of the rules and procedures, the regional politics, as well as the advanced stage of proceedings. To some degree, this was the case for some women who came to Vienna. From Romany's perspective, this meant that the greater 'financial and informational resources of the Northern NGOs determined their leadership role in feminist reconceptualisation of human rights' (p. 547). Regarding lobbying activities targeting the official intergovernmental document, she observed 'only a core of women at Vienna privy to strategy agendas' and noted how newly arrived participants in women's NGO caucuses heard 'with disbelief how a well-travelled working document, which had been discussed at regional preparatory meetings, failed to address the intersection of gender, class and ethnic subordination in its definition of discrimination' (p. 547). Romany highlights real difficulties and exclusions that arose at the Vienna Conference and its NGO Forum, especially around the frustrated expectations of women who joined the process at a point when most of the content of the Vienna Declaration and Programme of Action were effectively already agreed. However, these difficulties affected women from the North and the South; Romany's conclusion that they reflected the unilateral dominance of Northern feminists and the exclusion of 'Southern women in the re-conceptualization of a human rights dialogue' is not borne out by the full record of the Global Campaign, the diversity of its leadership from the start, and the unprecedented cross-regional grassroots support it attracted in the two years running up to Vienna and on through the Fourth World Conference on Women (FWCW).

The Global Tribunal on Violations of Women's Human Rights

The Global Tribunal on Violations of Women's Human Rights took place at the UN World Conference on Human Rights in Vienna (June 1993). It is an event widely recognized as a pivotal moment in the Global Campaign's struggle to seek recognition of women's rights as human rights (Friedman 1995, Copelon 2003).[9] In this context, the Vienna Tribunal offers a unique snapshot of the issues, analyses and strategies of the Global Campaign for Women's Human Rights at a formative moment.[10] As a strategy, the campaign built on a strong tradition in human rights and women's movements of using popular tribunals and hearings to raise public awareness and seek action to stop egregious violations (Reilly and Posluszny 2006). By documenting the 'facts' and recounting the consequences of particular violations, the tribunal sought to draw parallels between different forms of gender-based abuse and established categories of human rights violation such as 'torture', 'cruel and unusual punishment', 'persecution', 'slavery' and so on. The issues and analyses brought to life by the tribunal testifiers are as salient today as they were in 1993 – if not more so. Despite the very significant UN and governmental commitments to WHR that were achieved as a result of the Global Campaign, the implementation gaps remain wide and numerous. In this sense, the Vienna Tribunal serves as a benchmark from which to gauge progress on what has been achieved to date and to identify continuing points of resistance and contention in the struggle to realize WHR.

Thirty-three women from twenty-five countries presented testimonies in five topic areas: human rights abuse in the family, war crimes against women in situations of conflict,[11] violations of bodily integrity, violations of women's socio-economic human rights, and political persecution and discrimination (Bunch and Reilly 1994). Each cluster of testimonies aimed to expose the failure of traditional approaches to human rights to comprehend and respond to gender-specific violations of human rights in that particular category. The categories themselves were carefully formulated to build on the authority of traditional legal and human rights discourse while also deconstructing it and unsettling the expectations of tribunal 'witnesses' about the nature, scope and locations of human rights violations and perpetrators. In particular, the accounts of abuse in the family and of violations of bodily integrity drew attention to 'private' sites of violation – the home, family and hospitals – which are not normally linked to denials of human rights. These testimonies presented the realities of different forms of violence against women and girls in ways that underlined the magnitude of the abuses involved and made it difficult to trivialize such acts or to argue that they do not constitute human rights issues.

Further, the tribunal testimonies repeatedly showed how the subordinate position of women in social, economic and cultural terms, even where formal political and civil rights are in place, leaves women vulnerable to violence, harassment, intimidation and economic dependence in their daily lives. It is now well documented, for instance, that a major reason why women remain in abusive relationships is the fact that they are economically dependent on their abuser and/or have dependent children who they could not provide for alone. One testifier, Perveen Martha, who lived in extreme poverty in Bangladesh, described numerous incidents of beatings, burnings and death threats at the hands of her husband and other members of his family. Unable to read or write, and totally dependent on her husband, she was able to escape to her parents' home. She said 'they would take me back to my husband's house and plead with my in-laws to let me stay' (Bunch and Reilly 1994, 27). Her testimony demonstrates how the low status of women – economically, socially, culturally and politically – both constitutes and enables the further denial of human rights in gender-specific ways, often at the hands of family members, male and female.

Other testimonies highlighted how – notwithstanding the emphasis in the prevailing human rights regime on achieving formal legal rights – there persists a widespread failure on the part of legal and judicial systems around the world to ensure that cases of family violence are prosecuted and justly sentenced, and that women are protected from violence throughout these processes (Kelleher and O'Connor 1999). Margaret Dravu from Uganda, for example, recounted how she had been subject to frequent attacks from her partner. On one occasion, he beat and kicked her, after which he threw her 'onto the lit lamp . . . causing burns all over her body' (Bunch and Reilly 1994, 28). Yet, some years later, the perpetrator had not yet been located or arrested. This lack of national-level redress with respect to violence against women reflects a failure to implement women's civil and political human rights and is indicative of a prevalent gender bias in legal and judicial systems in every region.

While the tribunal testimonies exposed the limitations of the mainstream human rights regime's state-centric focus on civil and political rights, the intention, however, was not to discount the importance of civil and political rights or the need to limit state power. Rather, it was to assert the genuine interdependence – and the need to ensure the gender-aware definition and implementation – of all rights. This necessitates an understanding of the interconnection between abuses of civil and political rights on the one hand, and of economic and social rights on the other. Maria Lourdes de Jesus, who had migrated from Cape Verde to Italy, for example, testified to the human rights violations she and others in similar situations had experienced as migrant African women employed as domestic workers in Europe. She told of women who 'suffer sexual assault in silence in order to avoid being fired' and highlighted the fact that 'it is difficult to document the violations for various reasons, including the fact that many of the violations occur within private homes where migrant women fear losing jobs, or are ashamed and embarrassed to talk about experiences they would prefer to forget' (p. 65).

Finally, women's testimonies in Vienna challenged the idea that human rights violations only happen in the South. Rosa Logar, then Coordinator of the Austrian Women's Shelter Network, for example, reported that in all of Europe (excluding the former Soviet Union) more than 12 million women and girls are subject to violence annually (p. 222). In highlighting violence against women as a violation of human rights that is pervasive in countries of the North as well as the South, the Tribunal underlined the idea that human rights are a matter of domestic policy and not simply vehicles used selectively by Northern governments to criticize and condemn other, usually less powerful, countries.

Outcomes of the Vienna World Conference on Human Rights

The Vienna Declaration and Programme of Action (VDPA) were adopted by consensus by 171 Member States at the close of the Vienna World Conference on Human Rights in 1993. These documents remain the most authoritative statement of the international community's commitment to human rights as a framework for global politics and the realization of human rights in the twenty-first century (Boyle 1995). As such, it is important to highlight their most salient provisions here, especially in relation to WHR. A major theme of the declaration is its reaffirmation of the universality of all human rights, regardless of differences in political, economic and cultural systems. This is especially welcome in countering the eclipse of WHR in the name of protecting culture. Importantly, the declaration reiterates that all human rights are 'indivisible, . . . interdependent and interrelated', whereby formal legal, civil and political rights are understood to be only part of a comprehensive human rights agenda. Moreover, it recognizes that 'the human rights of women and of the girl-child are an inalienable, integral and indivisible part of universal human rights'.

The impact of the Global Campaign for Women's Human Rights is most evident in the section of the Vienna Declaration on the 'equal status and human rights of women'. In it, governments recognize the need to work towards the 'elimination of violence against women in public and private life' as well as 'the elimination of all forms of sexual harassment, exploitation and trafficking in women'. Regarding conflict situations, the declaration affirms that violations of WHR, including 'murder, systematic rape, sexual slavery, and forced pregnancy', are 'violations of the fundamental principles of international human rights and humanitarian law' (Paragraph 38). Concerning health and reproductive rights, women ought to enjoy the 'highest standard of physical and mental health throughout their life span' and have access to 'adequate health care and the widest range of family planning services' (Paragraph 41). This section also 'underlines the importance of the integration and full participation of women as both agents and beneficiaries in the development process' (Paragraph 36). It further asserts that the 'human rights of women should be integrated into the mainstream of United Nations system-wide activity' (Paragraph 37). The range of commitments to WHR, appearing together for the first time in an international human rights programme of action, offered a blueprint of the new WHR agenda and signalled the direction that subsequent campaigns and initiatives would pursue.

Consolidating global norms against violence against women

Encouraged by the Vienna Conference, in December 1993, the UN General Assembly adopted the Declaration on the Elimination of Violence against Women (DEVAW) which, for the first time, provides a definition of VAW that all of the Member States of the United Nations have agreed to work towards eliminating. The declaration states that VAW is: 'Any act of gender-based violence that results in, or is likely to result in, physical, sexual or psychological harm or suffering to women, including threats of such acts, coercion or arbitrary deprivations of liberty, whether occurring in public or private life' (Article 1). The definition names violence in the family, including battery, sexual abuse of female children, marital rape, dowry-related violence and female genital mutilation. It also specifies violence in the community, including rape, sexual abuse and sexual harassment at places of work, in educational institutions and elsewhere. Finally, the definition includes violence *perpetrated or condoned by the state, wherever it occurs*. Importantly, DEVAW stipulates the responsibilities of states to eliminate such violence at the national level as a matter of human rights policy by ensuring that women who are subjected to violence have 'access to the mechanisms of justice and . . . to just and effective remedies for the harm that they have suffered; states should also inform women of their rights in seeking redress through such remedies' (Article 4 (d)). It calls on states to develop 'preventative approaches [to gender-based violence] . . . and ensure that the re-victimisation of women does not occur because of laws insensitive to gender considerations' (Article 4 (f)). Governments are also called upon, unconditionally, to provide 'adequate resources for their activities related to the elimination of violence against women' (Article 4 (h)). Importantly, states are requested to 'facilitate and enhance the work of the women's movement . . . in raising awareness and alleviating the problem of violence against women' (Article 4 (o)). At the international level, states are asked to ratify the Women's Convention (CEDAW) and withdraw any reservations they hold to the convention (Article 4 (a)). Also, in the course of 'submitting reports as required under relevant human rights instruments of the United Nations, information pertaining to violence against women and measures taken to implement the present Declaration' should be included (Article 4 (m)).

In March 1994, the then UN Commission on Human Rights adopted a resolution on Integrating the Rights of Women into the Human Rights Mechanisms of the United Nations in which it decided to appoint a 'special rapporteur on violence against women (SRVAW), including its causes and consequences, who will report to the Commission on an annual basis' beginning in 1995 (Paragraph 6). The mandate of the SRVAW falls 'within the framework of the Universal Declaration of Human Rights and all international human rights instruments'; it entails a responsibility to 'seek and receive information on violence against women' and its 'causes and consequences' and to 'respond effectively' to that information. The SRVAW is required to cooperate with all aspects of the UN human rights machinery, but equally, all treaty-monitoring bodies are obligated to 'regularly and systematically include in their reports available information on human rights violations affecting women'. Radhika Coomaraswamy (Sri Lanka) held the position of SRVAW for almost a decade (1994–2003).

In 2003, the SRVAW mandate was renewed and Yakin Ertürk (Turkey) was appointed to the role. Since 1994, the SRVAW has carried out exhaustive investigations into policy and practice in relation to VAW in dozens of countries, from Afghanistan and Cuba to Russia and the United States.

Other reports have examined the interaction between VAW and critical thematic areas such as trafficking (2000), racism (2001), cultural practices (2002) and HIV / AIDS (2005). The SRVAW has played a vital role in keeping VAW on UN human rights agendas and continuing to deepen and expand understanding of gender violence and what is needed to eradicate it. In her final report, however, Coomaraswamy (2003) notes that despite 'great advances in standard setting' at the UN and regional levels and the 'development of jurisprudence and prosecution of perpetrators of VAW through international, regional, and national courts': 'Very little has changed in the lives of most women . . . Statistics continue to show high rates of violence and abuse [and] most cases of VAW result in impunity for the perpetrators . . . If the first decade [of the SRVAW] emphasized standard-setting and awareness-raising, the second decade must focus on effective implementation' (Coomaraswamy 2003, 20). Hence, Coomaraswamy underlines the imperative of taking an indivisible approach to WHR which addresses the 'root causes of violence, including women's poor economic, social and political status', ensures 'equal access to the criminal justice system', and stops 'impunity for gender-based violence' (p. 24). Building on Coomaraswamy's expansive body of work, Ertürk has continued to generate new analyses to meet the challenges of implementation in the current political climate. In particular, she has emphasized the need to strengthen the 'capacity of states to comply effectively with their obligations under international law' – especially in a context where 'conservative political trends and the response to global terror' threaten to undermine 'the universality of basic human rights for women and men' and where a 'global economic order' prevails in which non-state actors wield enormous power (Ertürk 2005, 22). More specifically, a recent report by the SRVAW has further elaborated the principle of 'due diligence' on the part of states in order to define more clearly the positive obligation on the part of states to 'prevent and compensate' and to hold non-state actors to account when they commit acts of violence against women (Ertürk 2007, 2).

Reflecting continuing pressure to address VAW as a priority global policy issue, UN Secretary General Kofi Annan commissioned a comprehensive report on the subject, 'Ending Violence against Women: From Words to Action' (2006). Given the backlash against WHR agendas in so many UN forums since the FWCW, the Secretary General's report gives a valuable political boost to transnational feminist advocacy (TFA) to combat VAW. It rearticulates the factors that render VAW such an intractable problem worldwide, especially deeply unequal gender power relations in public and private life, evident in every region. The report also reaffirms the UN's broad and multifaceted definition of VAW and provides useful examples of best practice in combating VAW. It is most useful in setting out the actions that are needed on different levels to ensure that global norms against VAW are translated into real change in women's lives. It calls on the UN to increase resources and to play a stronger role in the global effort to eliminate VAW. However, the report places the bulk of responsibility with states in a series of recommendations that call on them to:

- introduce immediate measures to secure gender equality and protect WHR;
- exercise political and social leadership at every level to end VAW;
- close gaps between international standards and national laws;
- build and sustain strong multi-sectoral strategies, locally and nationally;
- allocate adequate resources and funding to programmes to address and redress VAW;
- strengthen the knowledge base on all forms of VAW to inform policy development.

Seeking recognition of reproductive and sexual rights as human rights

Following the World Conference on Human Rights, WHR advocates turned their attention to ensuring that the gains secured at Vienna would be progressed further in the agendas and outcomes of other upcoming UN conferences. This strategy was most effective in relation to the International Conference on Population and Development (ICPD) held in Cairo in 1994 and the FWCW in Beijing in 1995. In tandem with the Vienna-focused activities of the Global Campaign, another critical mass of TFA gathered momentum around preparations for the ICPD. As a result, the Cairo Conference proved to be a major breakthrough along the way to recognition of reproductive health as a human right. Helped by the formal recognition of WHR in Vienna, the gains made at Cairo grew out of more than a decade of collaboration among women advocates across the global South and North, initially in the form of the Women's Global Network for Reproductive Rights (WGNRR).

The WGNRR was formed 'under pressure from Southern activists' (Corrêa 1994, 61) before the UN International Conference on Population in Mexico City in 1984. Participants from the South wanted to use the term 'reproductive rights' in the network's new title because it better conveyed their health agendas than its antecedent, the more Eurocentric International

Campaign on Abortion, Sterilisation and Contraception (ICASC) (p. 61). The basic principle underpinning the re-launched network was that 'women should be seen as subjects and not objects of population polices' (p. 62). While rights language had long been used by women's movements in struggles for access to contraception and abortion around the world, the term 'reproductive rights' was used to suggest an expansion beyond the right of individual choice to a more comprehensive understanding of the complex of rights that underpin reproductive well-being as an aspect of human development (p. 64). In doing so, WGNRR participants highlighted the macro conditions and global forces that obstruct the attainment of women's reproductive health and well-being in different contexts. This globalization of the reproductive health and rights movement reflected a significant turning point in deepening the links between 'reproductive health and rights' and 'gender and development' feminist advocacy.

The WGNRR challenged two major forces that had previously domi-nated international population debates. First, it contested neo-Malthusian orthodoxy, which treats women's fertility as a cause of poverty and an obstacle to development that must be controlled through the top-down implementation of biomedical and reproductive technologies. Second, at the other end of the spectrum, the WGNRR conflicted with currents of religious fundamentalism dominant in the international development community (especially Catholic), which generally oppose the idea that access to sex education, contraception and abortion are integral aspects of development. By the end of the 1980s, the network had made inroads into mainstream population discourse and major funding agencies, and the Population Council and World Bank had integrated the idea of reproduc-tive health into their population programming (p. 62).

By the early 1990s, in addition to the WGNRR, several established women's networks were also playing leading roles in what had become a global reproductive health and rights movement. Most notably, this included DAWN, IWHC and WEDO. While DAWN is a Southern-based and Southern-led network, the others have active regional offices around the world and/or – like the Center for Women's Global Leadership – routinely convene South–North meetings and consultations in setting and implementing agendas, as a matter of principle. Indeed, according to reproductive rights academic and transnational activist Ros Petchesky, from 1984 onwards 'women from the South were a leading and majority presence' in the global women's reproductive health movement (2003, 5).[12] Furthermore, Petchesky persuasively argues that 'despite political differences and disparities in access to power and resources . . . within and among countries and regions . . . activists and thinkers from the South assumed intellectual and political leadership in shaping a more holistic and integrative direction for the transnational women's health movement in the 1990s' (p. 5).

From the inception of the Global Campaign for Women's Human Rights in 1991, there were strong links between its leading advocates and participating organizations and those involved in the global reproductive health and rights movement.[13] The influence of the reproductive health and rights movement, for example, is evident in the inclusion of testimonies in the Vienna Tribunal on female genital mutilation in Sudan and botched obstetric care in Nicaragua, and the subsequent coordination of a Cairo Hearing on Reproductive Health and Human Rights as part of the Global Campaign's post-Vienna activities (CWGL 1995). More generally, the ICPD – which took place after the Vienna Conference and before the FWCW – proved to be a particularly significant moment of synergy between WHR, reproductive health and gender and development (GAD) advocacy campaigns. Like Vienna, the Cairo Conference and its preparatory processes afforded concrete opportunities for the confluence of UN policy lobbying, broad-based mobilization and new feminist thinking and scholarship[14] on reproductive and sexual rights.

Evolving activist thinking on reproductive and sexual rights as human rights is illustrated by the declaration of the NGO International Women's Health Conference in Cairo, held in January 1994 (Corrêa 1994, 65). The document clearly contextualizes women's reproductive health concerns in relation to the persistent subordination of women in most societies, as well as the gendered impacts of neo-liberal globalization, rising fundamentalisms and conflict. From this perspective, it articulates a feminist, human rights vision of reproductive health wherein: 'Reproductive rights are human rights which are inalienable and inseparable from basic rights such as the right to food, shelter, health, security, livelihood, education and political empowerment' (p. 66). Elaborating this indivisible human rights approach, the NGO declaration calls for reproductive health services to include 'not only safe contraception but also safe abortion and prevention and early diagnosis and treatment of sexually transmitted diseases, including HIV / AIDS' (p. 65). Further, blending a critical approach to traditional human rights discourse with a radical feminist perspective, it asserts that: 'Women are entitled to bodily integrity . . . [where] violence against women and harmful practices like female genital mutilation must be recognized as a major reproductive rights and health issue . . . [and] governments held accountable for taking measures to combat such practices' (p. 65). Finally, the declaration insists that, in addition to better health services, 'sexuality and gender power relations must be addressed as a central aspect of reproductive rights' (p. 65).

While the official Cairo Programme of Action (POA) falls short of the more radical aspirations of the global reproductive health and rights movement, it nonetheless reflects a major leap forward in global policy discourse.[15] In particular, it signalled a paradigmatic shift away from top-down 'population control' to one of respect for 'reproductive health' and 'reproductive rights'. It provided a comprehensive definition of reproductive health, including sexual health (Paragraph 7.2). Importantly, for the first time it clearly defined reproductive health as a human right, grounded in established international human rights commitments:

> Reproductive rights embrace certain human rights that are already recognized in national laws, international human rights documents and other consensus documents. These rights rest on the recognition of the basic right of all couples and individuals to decide freely and responsibly the number, spacing and timing of their children and to have the information and means to do so, and the right to attain the highest standard of sexual and reproductive health. It also includes their right to make decisions concerning reproduction free of discrimination, coercion and violence, as expressed in human rights documents. (ICPD POA Paragraph 7.3)

Other notable achievements of the Cairo POA include recognition that VAW is a reproductive health concern, an acknowledgement of diverse family formations, and the inclusion of antenatal, obstetric and postnatal care, as well as sexual health and reproductive cancer care, in a very broad definition of reproductive health (Petchesky 2003, 44–5). Most disappointingly from a feminist perspective, the Cairo POA did not include access to safe and legal abortion as part of reproductive health and rights and it failed to affirm sexual rights, including freedom of sexual expression and orientation (pp. 44–5).

Since 1994, a powerful backlash against WHR agendas in global policy forums has worked to reverse or prevent progress on the advancement of reproductive and sexual rights. The official UN five-year review of implementation of the ICPD POA took place in New York City in 1999. The network Health, Empowerment, Rights, and Accountability (HERA) coordinated a major NGO initiative – the Women's Coalition for the International Conference on Population and Development – which included more than 100 groups from the South and North. Petchesky reports that the coalition was hampered on two main fronts. First, the Vatican and other fundamentalist allies operated in a highly coordinated manner with a focus on a few key issues, and, second, a decision by the G-77 countries to act as a bloc slowed down proceedings and made agreement on substantive issues virtually impossible (Petchesky 2000, 26). In addition, Petchesky notes that many of the governmental delegates were inexperienced and unfamiliar with the ICPD and its POA, rendering the work of the NGOs all the more difficult. Notwithstanding these obstacles, the active presence of the coalition ensured that the POA was reaffirmed and some small gains were made, most notably in the adoption of a new provision calling for the training of health service providers to ensure that abortion is 'safe and accessible' in situations where it is legal (p. 26).

The ten-year review of the Cairo POA in 2004, which took place during the 37th Session of the UN Commission on Population and Development (CPD), was similarly held hostage to conservative political forces. This time the United States led the backlash and opposed implementation of the POA throughout the preparatory process and attempted, unsuccessfully, to introduce a provision condemning abortion. Once more, dozens of major international reproductive rights organizations worked in concert as the International Sexual and Reproductive Rights Coalition (ISRRC) to counter the US-led backlash. The coalition lobbied to ensure that in the end, a final resolution by governments reaffirmed the 1994 POA and underlined the centrality of the Cairo commitment to women's empowerment and gender equality in achieving the Millennium Development Goals. Nonetheless, at the close of the Cairo ten-year review, an NGO statement issued by the ISRRC once more highlighted the imperative of continuing to seek UN recognition of 'the right of women to legal abortion services and the ability to express one's sexual orientation without violence or discrimination' (ISRRC 2004).

On the positive side, while the backlash against reproductive and sexual rights has predominated global policy deliberations over the past decade, many governments have made progress in implementing their ICPD commitments. Mariane Haslegrave notes that Mexico, Ghana, South Africa and Thailand, in particular, have 'shown considerable success in integrating sexual and reproductive health care into primary health care' (Haslegrave 2004). In addition, a great deal of work has been done to develop international human rights legal thinking and practice around defining and monitoring the reproductive rights (Cook et al. 2003). Linked to this, much progress has been made within the UN human rights machinery to elaborate and strengthen the right to 'the highest attainable standard of physical and mental health'. In particular, the treaty-monitoring bodies that oversee implementation of the International Covenant on Economic, Social and Cultural Rights, the Women's Convention, and the Children's Rights Convention have all produced general comments or recommendations on the right to health, including sexual and reproductive health. In addition, the UN Commission on Human Rights passed a resolution on the right to health (2003) and appointed Paul Hunt as Special Rapporteur on the Right to Health (2002–8), whose work addresses reproductive and sexual rights in some detail.

Beijing World Conference on Women

The FWCW produced the Beijing Declaration and Platform for Action (BPA) – the most comprehensive global governmental agreement to date on the status of women and what is needed to achieve substantive gender equality and WHR. It sets out detailed analyses and recommended actions across twelve 'critical areas of concern': poverty, education, health, VAW, armed conflict, the economy, decision-making, institutional mechanisms, human rights, media, the environment and the girl-child (UN 1995).

Governmental negotiations to draft the BPA, however, were contentious and WHR advocates were not successful in their efforts to maintain a cross-cutting human rights perspective throughout the Platform. As a result, 'human rights' appears as one of twelve critical areas of concern and is not used explicitly as the organizing framework for the entire document. This partly reflected 'concerted efforts by religious fundamentalists and secular conservatives to narrow the reach of human rights' (Bunch and Fried 1996). Signalling the shape of the emerging backlash against WHR, which had dominated international forums where women and gender issues were being discussed since Beijing, these debates centred on objections to the inclusion of terms such as 'gender', 'sexual rights' and 'sexual orientation' because they threatened traditional concepts of the family and gender roles (p. 202). Significantly, the term 'universal' was also resisted in relation to WHR by the Vatican and some Islamist governments on the grounds that it implied 'disrespect for religion and culture and overzealous individualism' (p. 203). Notwithstanding an increasing hostility to WHR discourse, however, the BPA contained a whole section on the issue of VAW, which recognized that its eradication is integral to the realization of equality, development and peace. Further, despite the failure to include the terms 'reproductive rights' or 'sexual rights' in the Platform, WHR advocates secured recognition that 'the human rights of women include their right to have control over and decide freely and responsibly on matters related to their sexuality, including sexual and reproductive health, free of coercion, discrimination and violence' (Paragraph 96).

Since 1995, formal monitoring of governmental implementation of the Beijing Platform has taken place primarily in the context of annual meetings of the Commission on the Status of Women and one Special Session of the UN General Assembly (UNGASS) in 2000. During the UNGASS or 'Beijing plus Five' review in 2000, opposition to the BPA from traditionalist and conservative governments and NGOs intensified. Consequently, pro-BPA advocates were forced to focus on protecting the Platform provisions rather than advancing its implementation (CWGL and WEDO 2000). Combined with the structural limitations of UNGASS meetings (in contrast to world conferences) and related severe restrictions on NGO participation, this created an extremely frustrating environment for the 'record numbers' of women and men who came to affirm and support the BPA. Despite these difficulties, however, there were some noteworthy steps forward at the 'Beijing plus Five' meeting in relation to recognition of different forms of VAW. Specifically, 'honour' crimes were put on the agenda, language to combat dowry-related deaths and violence was strengthened, governments were called on to introduce legislation on marital rape, and racially motivated crimes and acid attacks were named as forms of VAW (Obando 2004).

There were, however, further setbacks in 2003 at a meeting of the Commission on the Status of Women to review governmental implementation of commitments in a number of BPA critical areas of concern including 'violence against women'. Once more alliances among conservative forces in the North and South threatened to reverse principles established by the BPA. In particular, the delegate from Iran, with support from Egypt, objected to the inclusion of a paragraph that called on governments to 'condemn violence against women and refrain from invoking any custom, tradition, or religious consideration to avoid their obligations with respect to its elimination as set out in the Declaration on the Elimination of Violence against Women'. Later in 2005, at the 'Beijing plus Ten' review under the auspices of the CSW, the US government played a leading role in obstructing the adoption of a straightforward declaration reaffirming the BPA. In the end, the USA failed to break the international consensus in favour of the declaration and withdrew its controversial proposed amendment, which stated that the BPA and the outcome document of the 'Beijing plus Five' review in 2000 'do not create new international human rights and do not include the right to abortion'. After this qualified success, underlining the low expectations that prevail within the WHR movement in comparison to the early 1990s, leading advocates noted that the 'US decision to withdraw its anti-human rights amendment marked a significant victory in support of women's human rights worldwide' (CWGL 2005).

Conclusion

This chapter has focused on transnational advocacy for WHR in the 1990s and beyond, especially the 1990s Global Campaign for Women's Human Rights and the linked movement for reproductive and sexual health and rights. These efforts were marked by two notable features. First, earlier WHR initiatives worked largely within traditional liberal discourse and its pursuit of laws and norms as end goals. In contrast, the WHR advocacy considered here demonstrates an emancipatory cosmopolitan engagement with mainstream human rights discourse wherein feminist NGOs and advocates and transnational collaboration are understood to play a pivotal role in shaping and realizing the radical promise of human rights.

Second, while the activities of the Global Campaign regularly highlighted the entire range of human rights concerns affecting women, ultimately issues of bodily integrity – especially VAW and reproductive and sexual health – dominated the advocacy agenda, with different degrees of success. In doing so, WHR advocates exposed the prevalence and multiplicity of different forms of VAW, including denials of reproductive and sexual health, across all regions, North and South. Importantly, however, they repeatedly underlined the interdependence of all human rights in women's lives whereby economic, social and cultural marginalization fosters vulnerability to violations of the 'civil right' to bodily integrity – whether in the form of battery, rape, trafficking or denials of reproductive and sexual health.

Advancing a distinctly feminist understanding of bodily integrity, WHR advocacy in the 1990s unsettled the public–private divide and narrow understandings of state accountability in mainstream human rights discourse. It highlighted how implementation of WHR calls for scrutiny of violations whether they are perpetrated in public or private contexts, by state or private actors, through acts of commission or of omission. In this regard, WHR advocacy is integral to a wider, ongoing shift in established human rights thinking – away from a state-centred, 'negative rights' paradigm, towards a gender-conscious, positive notion of human rights that takes account of the root causes of violations and the ways in which power operates in economic, social and cultural processes and structures.

Overall, however, the 1990s movement for WHR is known for achieving international recognition that VAW is a violation of human rights, and for securing a raft of new global standards and mechanisms aimed at its elimination. The period 1991–5, however, proved to be a high point of achievement. Almost immediately following Vienna, a backlash against the new commitments to WHR began to take shape. The backlash has centred primarily on blocking advancement of reproductive and sexual rights, but has also entailed resistance to addressing harmful traditional practices as forms of VAW. This raises critical questions about how far the boundaries of human rights discourse can be pushed, what its limits are, and who gets to decide those limits.

While acceptance of the claim that VAW is a violation of human rights signals a major departure in human rights thinking, important caveats should be noted. First, the gaps between global commitments and practice on the ground are still enormous, and efforts against VAW must remain a priority for governments and women's movements everywhere in order to ensure that real progress is made. Second, the successful inclusion of 'violence against women' on the international agenda, while reflecting the impact of WHR advocacy, also indicates a degree of receptiveness to the issue within the mainstream human rights regime that does not apply to a more comprehensive WHR agenda. In particular, it builds on well-established 'civil rights' norms and prohibitions against egregious acts of physical violence (outside of conflict situations). In this regard, securing recognition of reproductive and sexual health as human rights demands an even bigger leap. On the one hand, it introduces ideas of self-determination and bodily integrity into an arena in which women have long been subject to powerful patriarchal forces – whether through conservative familial, cultural and religious mores or top-down medical and social policy practices. On the other hand, it demands a proactive understanding of the 'right to health', an evolving socio-economic right that has never been treated with the same urgency as the 'civil right' to bodily integrity.

Third, and related to the preceding point, there are concerns that the movement for WHR has been too narrowly focused on VAW and has failed to gather momentum around a more comprehensive and indivisible account of human rights. Indeed, the relative openness to recognizing VAW as a human rights issue partly stems from the degree to which it can be understood as a violation of the individual, rather than a manifestation of profoundly unequal, structural power relations that foster and conceal denials of human rights. Furthermore, as the hegemony of neo-liberal models of globalization and free-market ideology has deepened, so has the antipathy of states to committing the resources necessary to implementing more expansive visions of human rights. The challenge of implementing women's universal and indivisible human rights effectively, therefore, is a complex and difficult one that requires continual vigilance and political mobilization on the part of all progressive movements for human rights. I return to this question again in chapter 6 when I consider why, in comparison to issues of VAW, relatively little progress has been made in contesting women's economic, social and cultural marginalization per se as human rights violations, especially in a context of deepening global inequalities.

Nonetheless, it is important to recognize the successes of the 1990s and to acknowledge the many new commitments to WHR that were secured at world conferences, especially in Vienna, Cairo and Beijing. Each of the next three chapters explores a particular avenue of transnational WHR advocacy that is critical to the implementation of the gains secured during the 1990s. This includes, in the next chapter, campaigns to gender-proof international criminal tribunals and peace-building and post-conflict reconstruction processes. It also encompasses more tenuous initiatives to formulate and implement gender-sensitive understandings of the indivisibility of human rights in a context of globalization (chapter 6). Last, but not least, chapter 7 looks more closely at the rise of fundamentalist and traditionalist projects intent on preventing or reversing recognition of WHR, and the role of women's movements and cosmopolitan feminist practice in countering them.

5

Women's Human Rights in Conflict and Post-Conflict Transformation

Introduction

Contrary to popular representations of war as something that is waged between armies, most violent conflicts, past and current, have been fought significantly amidst civilian populations. Between 1990 and 2000, for example, an estimated 118 conflicts around the world resulted in approximately 6 million deaths, three-quarters of which were civilian (Abeysekera 2006, 3). Recognition of this reality makes it increasingly difficult to ignore women's experiences and gender concerns in analysing conflicts and in formulating effective preventive and remedial actions. Women are now at the centre of conflicts in unprecedented ways: as combatants, as grassroots peace advocates, as targets of physical and sexual violence, as the bearers of contested communal identities, and as the group in society that is expected to sustain everyday life, even under catastrophic conditions. Hence, women clearly have a major stake in how justice and human rights are conceptualized and enacted in relation to conflicts, and how a society reinvents itself in the move away from violent conflict.

Reflecting this, there is now a considerable body of feminist scholarship that explores women's experiences of conflict and the gendered nature of mainstream war and security paradigms (Cohn 1987, Yuval-Davis 1997, Enloe 1990, Cockburn 2007). There is also a sizeable literature in comparative politics which focuses on the role of women and gender relations in transitions from repressive to democratic regimes (Alvarez 1990, Waylen 2000). More recently, a body of law-oriented work has begun to emerge that interrogates women's experiences in transitions from conflict (Chinkin and Paradine 2001, Coomaraswamy and Fonseka 2004, Rubio-Marin 2006). This work seeks to deepen the 'women and conflict' agenda beyond questions of wartime sexual violence to explore women's wider experiences of conflict, their extensive contributions to peace initiatives and the significance of pervasive gender inequalities and biases in limiting women's inclusion and meaningful participation at every level and stage of post-conflict transition.

On the advocacy side, the Global Campaign for Women's Human Rights laid the groundwork for further transnational advocacy around the gender dimensions of conflict and post-conflict transitions. The 1990s war in the Former Yugoslavia, in particular, stimulated a surge in research and advocacy on issues of wartime sexual violence in conflicts and the pursuit of post-conflict 'justice' for women. This chapter reflects upon these developments in light of the growing feminist literature on women in conflict and transitions from conflict noted above. In particular, I highlight the role of transnational feminist engagement with public international law as a mode of transformative practice. A central theme running throughout this chapter, therefore, concerns the potential use of international commitments to women's human rights (WHR) and gender mainstreaming in defining and advancing a comprehensive vision of gender justice in post-conflict transitional contexts. From this point of departure, I focus on two recent areas of feminist engagement with international law. Both of these areas have roots in the Global Campaign for Women's Human Rights and are particularly salient to the project of seeking gender justice in post-conflict transitions. They are campaigns to: (1) ensure the inclusion of gender-sensitive definitions and provisions in the statute and procedures of the International Criminal Court (ICC), and (2) secure the adoption and implementation of Security Council Resolution 1325 on women, peace and security.

Ultimately, I argue that these examples of transnational feminist advocacy (TFA) signal a broader, deeper, bottom-up vision of 'justice' and the 'rule of law' than is found in mainstream understandings of post-conflict transitional justice. Such feminist accounts are grounded in critically interpreted global WHR norms, which contest and seek to transform male-centric definitions and practice in transitions from conflict. As such, they resonate with critiques in feminist legal scholarship that expose the gender biases and exclusions that are (re)produced by traditional models of 'ordinary' (punitive), 'liberalising' and 'restorative' transitional justice (Bell and O'Rourke 2007). Moreover, they demonstrate the inescapable links between achieving gender justice in transitions and extending the scope of transitional justice to encompass consideration of social, economic and cultural inequalities (Chinkin and Charlesworth 2006).

The chapter is divided into three main parts. The first provides an overview of the theoretical and analytical framework that broadly informs the discussion. It flags pervasive discursive obstacles facing efforts to achieving gender justice in transitions, both within mainstream transitional justice discourse and related discourses, such as security and nationalism. The second part reviews successful feminist interventions to remedy the previous exclusion of gender-based crimes from international humanitarian and criminal law with a focus on international criminal tribunals. These efforts offer important insights into balancing two fundamental concerns of WHR advocates: first, to minimize the risk of re-victimizing women within adversarial legal proceedings; and second, to retain a critical commitment to 'objective' values of fairness, transparency and accountability towards the advancement of gender equality and human rights for women.

The third part of this chapter examines UN Security Council Resolution (SCR) 1325 as a potential vehicle to achieve a more comprehensive account of gender justice in transitions. By purposively shifting the focus from 'women as victims' of conflict to women as agents of transition, SCR 1325 signals an important contribution to expanding the definition of transitional justice beyond (quasi-)legal responses to past harms. In this sense, it sits within an emerging consensus among feminist legal scholars and advocates that transitional justice must be framed within a wider process of forward-looking social transformation (Chinkin and Charlesworth 2006, Abeysekera 2006). I consider the potential role of SCR 1325 in contributing to such a transformative approach and ask what more is needed to underpin the necessary paradigmatic shift from the perspective of women. Finally, I conclude that the prospects for realization of a comprehensive, gender-sensitive vision of justice in transitions are integrally tied to the wider, bottom-up drive for implementation of international commitments to WHR.

Dominant theoretical frameworks and discourses

The terrain of transitional justice has evolved a great deal since the post-World War II period, when the prosecution and punishment of war criminals (who were mostly individual state / military actors on the defeated side) were established as the principal mode of pursuing post-war justice. As will be discussed below, even within this narrow purview, gender bias has ensured that war crimes against women did not enter the equation until very recently. At the same time, the presumption that all wars follow the pattern of World War I and World War II has been called into question. The majority of conflicts are internal rather than interstate, involve non-state as well as state parties and are fought amidst civilians. In such divided societies, criminal prosecutions of individuals on one side or another may not be the best way to underpin the transition to 'peace'. Instead, 'justice operates pragmatically . . . when it functions to facilitate the workings of the political sphere by absolving the need for absolute accountability' (Ní Aoláin and Turner 2007, 231). The core problematic for those most engaged in the field of transitional justice, therefore, has become one of balancing the normative imperatives of justice against the pragmatic requirements of peace and reconciliation (Bell et al. 2004).

This balancing act usually entails a shift away from formal retributive to informal restorative models of justice. The latter are generally oriented towards 'resolving the original conflict, integrating all affected parties, healing the pain of victims through apologies and restitution, and preventing wrongdoing through community-building measures' (Anderlini et al. n.d.). While there is now a well-developed feminist critique of traditional retributive approaches to post-conflict criminal justice (Askin 1997, Ní Aoláin 1997), only recently has attention been paid to the gendered impact of restorative transitional justice processes and mechanisms. On the surface, because they appear to be non-adversarial, holistic and inclusive, such approaches to transitional justice might seem more amenable to recognizing women's experiences and needs in conflict and transitional contexts. Recent research, however, indicates that this is not the case (Ní Aoláin and Turner 2007, ICTJ 2007, Ross 2003).

Examining the construction and operation of truth commissions in Chile and Guatemala, for example, Ní Aoláin and Turner highlighted how gendered logic has operated in these contexts to exclude female subject positions and experiences (Ní Aoláin and Turner 2007). In explaining such patterns, Ní Aoláin and Turner underline the gendered exclusions produced by the uncritical incorporation of traditional international human rights hierarchies into transitional justice practices. Hence, despite the fact that both the Chilean and Guatemalan commissions had broad mandates to effect social reconciliation and restitution, in practice they took a very narrow 'civil and political rights' view of the harms that needed to be addressed. In doing so, both processes closed off consideration of the forms and locations of conflict-related harm to women, including, for example, domestic violence or conflict-induced impoverishment. Other scholars note similar outcomes in a variety of contexts from Afghanistan and Timor-Leste to Rwanda and South Africa, despite considerable efforts by women's non-governmental organizations (NGOs) to ensure the comprehensive inclusion of women and gender perspectives in transitional mechanisms and policies (Ross 2003, Grenfell 2004, Rubio-Marin 2006).

While the gendered exclusions of different approaches to dealing with the past are important concerns, it is also vital from a gender perspective that the scope of transitional justice should not be confined to consideration of legal, institutional and procedural aspects of dealing with past abuses only. Doing so limits exploration of the potentially transformative role of the law during a highly formative moment of renewal in transitional societies, including the role of international human rights standards and related transnational solidarity links. Under such conditions, there are opportunities to revisit inequalities, not only in relation to the dominant fissures around which the conflict has ostensibly revolved, but also in relation to other patterns of discrimination and marginalization, especially along lines of gender that are often rendered invisible in the wider conflict meta-narrative (Bell et al. 2004, 320). Recognizing this transformative potential of transitions, the present chapter focuses on the role of bottom-up, feminist engagement with international law in promoting such potential.

Understanding and contesting gender bias in mainstream theories of transitional justice builds on feminist critiques of other dominant narratives that shape our understanding of war, conflict and the objectives of transition. If 'transitional justice' is to include gender justice, the gender biases underpinning ideas of nationalism, war/peace/security, human rights, liberalism and so on must also be problematized in the process. A commitment to protecting women's rights in conflicts and ensuring gender justice in transitions, for example, calls for an understanding of how patriarchy, militarism and nationalism (including different forms of racism) interact to produce gendered identities and experiences that are inimical to women in conflicts and transitions. This process also demands critical scrutiny of top-down, minimalist, liberal models of the 'rule of law', democracy and human rights as the uncontested end-goals of transitions.

Feminist scholars have effectively demonstrated the ways in which war, conflict and the processes that surround them are deeply gendered and experienced differently by women and men (Enloe 1990, Cockburn and Zarkov 2002). Simplistic binaries, however, that cast women solely as pacifist victims of war and men as its belligerent perpetrators fail to capture the complex ways in which gender structures how we represent, understand and experience war, conflict and the human rights abuses that arise therein (Bos 2006, 999). While war and security discourses are dominated by men and the logic of masculinity, women's labour and bodies have always been integral to war-making in multifaceted ways – whether as combatants, 'army wives' and munitions factory workers (Enloe 2000) or as wartime 'booty' (Copelon 2000, 223). Exposing the many ways in which women are affected by and involved in conflicts is an important part of debunking the myth that war and security issues, including the orchestration of transitions 'from war to peace', are the 'natural' preserve of men.

Others have shown how nationalisms promote regressive visions of women's roles in the ongoing construction of national or ethnic identity and how this produces particular patterns of violence against women (VAW), especially in times of conflict (Yuval-Davis 1997, Lentin 1998, Nikolic-Ristanovic 1998). Feminist commentators have also called into question gender biases in the war–peace dichotomy per se and highlighted instead the continuities that prevail for women in transitions from 'conflict' to 'peace'. For example, women can experience increased and new forms of domestic violence as a result of the general normalization of violence during conflict situations (Kesic 2003). Equally, domestic violence can escalate following a conflict when soldiers rejoin civilian life and continue to be violent in the private sphere. Such analyses challenge male-defined notions of 'peace' as the cessation of certain forms of 'public' violence (Ní Aoláin 2006) and underline instead the interrelation of all forms of violence, that is, the 'continuum of violence running from bedroom, to boardroom, factory, stadium, classroom and battlefield' (Cohn and Ruddick 2004).

The foregoing analyses are also linked to well-honed feminist critiques of the liberal rule of law and the public–private divide (Smart 1989, Pateman 1988). Mainstream accounts of transitional justice generally accept top-down notions of the 'rule of law', formal equality and minimal representative democracy as the uncontested end-goals of transitions (Dyzenhaus 2003, 165). It is well known, however, that even under such conditions in established liberal democracies, women are marginalized in political life, and gender inequalities in social, economic and cultural spheres persist (Young 2000). In particular, the liberal public–private divide has meant that domestic abuse and sexual violence usually go unrecognized and unpunished. Further, gender equality in the liberal public sphere (i.e. equal access to political power) is directly impeded by gender inequalities in the private sphere (i.e. women's disproportionate responsibility for childcare).

Such deep-seated inequalities invariably reassert themselves in transitions. Even when women are integrally involved in conflicts and/or play key roles in peace initiatives, they are routinely cut out of political power after peace agreements are put in place (Bell et al. 2004, 320–1). In effect, therefore, models of transitional justice, which accept a traditional, territorially bounded, liberal public–private divide and male-dominated public sphere as the outcomes of transition, fail to operationalize transitional justice as if women's equality and human rights matter. In doing so, they dissipate a valuable opportunity to frame transition as a process of bottom-up transformation underpinned by critically interpreted human rights norms.

In the following sections, I turn to the achievements and wider implications of specific advocacy initiatives by women's movements to tackle the kinds of gender gaps and exclusions outlined here. These exemplify feminist engagement with international law as a site of contestation and potential transformation in the effort to foreground gender and women's experiences in post-conflict contexts. The first section focuses on efforts to remedy the previous exclusion of gender-based crimes from international humanitarian and criminal law while the second addresses obstacles to women's full and equal participation in transitions from conflict to peace. As such, these initiatives reflect significant practical contributions and offer valuable insights vis-à-vis the challenge of achieving gender justice in transitional contexts and the role of transnational, bottom-up approaches to international law therein.

Gender crimes in post-conflict tribunals

Wartime sexual violence

The increased vulnerability of women to rape and sexual violence has always been a feature of war (Chinkin 1994). There are well-documented accounts of many thousands of women being raped during conflicts by both enemy and 'friendly' forces, for example during World War II (Bos 2006), the 1971 Indo-Pakistani War (Menon and Bhasin 1998), wars in the Former Yugoslavia (Human Rights Watch and Helsinki Watch 1993, 163–5) and Rwanda (Human Rights Watch and Fédération Internationale des Ligues des Droits de l'Homme 1996) as well as in internal conflicts in Peru, Liberia and Timor-Leste (Chinkin 1994). The impact of such sexual violence in women's lives is profound. In addition to the immediate physical and emotional harm inflicted, the trauma produced can be prolonged and exacerbated if the violence also results in pregnancy or sexually transmitted disease.

Despite the prevalence and gravity of different forms of VAW in contexts of militarization, war and conflict, these issues did not begin to receive serious international attention until the 1990s. A variety of factors contribute to the impunity of perpetrators of sexual violence and the failure to date to achieve justice with respect to gender-based war crimes. These include deeply engrained perceptions that rape and other forms of sexual violence are unavoidable aspects of the breakdown in social order that accompanies war (Chinkin 1994), as well as women's own fears of social stigma and/or rejection by spouses, families and communities (Chinkin 1994, Rubio-Marin 2006). Even if these kinds of barriers can be surmounted, intimidation of women who report abuses, legislation preventing the prosecution of war crimes, or amnesties under peace agreements can all militate against the prosecution of wartime rapes and sexual violence.

Shortly, I look in more detail at feminist efforts to mainstream gender in the ICC as a way of countering some of the obstacles noted here and to address the persistent limitations of a criminal justice approach to achieving gender justice in post-conflict situations. To further contextualize that discussion, it is helpful to highlight entrenched gender biases in international humanitarian law vis-à-vis crimes against women, which the ICC women's initiative directly challenged.

Gender-based crimes in international law

Prior to the 1990s, the treatment of wartime rape and sexual violence in international humanitarian law was very ambiguous. Article 6 of the Nuremburg Charter (1945) establishes the core concepts used in the prosecution of war criminals after World War II.[1] It defines 'war crimes' as 'violations of the laws or customs of war', including 'but not limited to, murder, ill-treatment or deportation to slave labour'. Article 6 also defines the category of 'crimes against humanity', which is primarily concerned with violations against civilians within a wider context of conflict. It encompasses 'murder, extermination, enslavement, deportation, and other inhumane acts committed against any civilian population, before or during the war' and expressly outlaws 'persecutions on political, racial or religious grounds'. Notwithstanding the 'not limited to' caveat, the fact that rape and sexual violence were not explicitly listed as examples of 'violations of the laws or customs of war', or as forms of crimes against humanity, ensured that wartime rape and sexual violence did not feature in the Nuremburg trials (Copelon 2000, 227) and received very limited attention in the International Military Tribunal for the Far East.[2] Likewise, the failure to list gender-based persecution alongside political, racial and religious persecution both reflected and reinforced the invisibility of women and gender-specific experiences, not only in war and conflict situations and post-conflict justice processes but in society more generally.

The patriarchal mores of the Geneva Conventions are evident in Article 27 of the Fourth Geneva Convention on the protection of civilians in international conflict. It asserts that 'women shall be especially protected against any *attack on their honour*, in particular against rape, enforced prostitution, or any form of indecent assault' (my emphasis). Hence, sexual violence is recognized as a breach of social mores (i.e. damaging to a woman's reputation or her value from the perspective of men) but not as an expressly prohibited war crime that demands prosecution. In contrast, Article 3, common to all four Geneva Conventions, expressly prohibits other egregious acts against non-combatants in and of themselves, including murder of all kinds, violence to life and person, torture, the taking of hostages, and 'outrages upon personal dignity, in particular humiliating and degrading treatment'. Similarly, enforcement of the conventions relies on a requirement that states enact legislation and ensure punishment of 'grave breaches' of the conventions (Article 49). However, wartime rape and sexual violence are not explicitly enumerated in the list of grave breaches given in Article 50, which includes 'willful killing, torture or inhuman treatment, [and] . . . willfully causing great suffering or serious injury to body or health'.

Even though it is not difficult to see how rape and sexual violence could be interpreted as war crimes and/or crimes against humanity under the foregoing provisions, this did not begin to happen in a significant way until TFA mobilized around the issue in the 1990s. In the case of World War II, because the impact on women was not expressly included as part of the post-war justice agenda, violations against women were ignored. At the same time, gender bias permeated the processes established to prosecute World War II criminals. In particular, some have argued that the fact that wartime sexual violence was perpetrated with equal ferocity by all sides, and not by the German and Japanese forces only, created incentives to downplay the gravity and extent of VAW during the war (Chinkin 1994, Copelon 2000).

Mainstreaming gender in the International Criminal Court

In the early 1990s the Global Campaign for Women's Human Rights ensured the unequivocal recognition of women's rights as human rights at the World Conference on Human Rights (Vienna 1993). The confluence of these gains, together with a growing awareness of crimes against women in the conflict in the Former Yugoslavia, and a burgeoning campaign for justice for 'comfort women', energized a new transnational campaign to challenge past failures to ensure gender justice in international humanitarian and criminal law. At this juncture, WHR advocates were keenly aware that, if gender justice was to be effectively pursued in relation to ongoing and future conflict situations, women's movements needed to monitor closely and shape the statutes and procedures of the ad hoc International Criminal Tribunals for the Former Yugoslavia (ICTFY) and Rwanda (ICTR), but especially of the proposed permanent ICC.

Responding to this imperative, the ICC NGO Women's Caucus for Gender Justice was formed in 1997 to work in tandem with the wider NGO Coalition for the International Criminal Court. Significantly, members of the ICC Women's Caucus had participated in previous women's NGO caucuses at UN conferences, especially Vienna, Cairo and Beijing, and used this experience to influence the ICC process (Copelon 2000, 219).[3] Like the Global Campaign for Women's Human Rights and the transnational movement for reproductive health and rights, the ICC Women's Caucus coordinated a multifaceted strategy of highly technical drafting and lobbying efforts alongside North–South networking, training and mobilization initiatives.[4] Vahida Nainar, director of the ICC Women's Caucus through 2001, explains its bottom-up ethos and mode of operation: 'The Women's Caucus is . . . a network of individuals and groups committed to strengthening advocacy on women's human rights and helping to develop greater capacity among women in the use of international law, including the International Criminal Court, the Optional Protocol to CEDAW and other mechanisms that provide women avenues of and access to different systems of justice' (Nainar 1999).

Thanks to the efforts of the ICC Women's Caucus, the resulting Rome Statute of the International Criminal Court (1998) reflected a major leap forward in the effort to mainstream women and gender-specific concerns in international humanitarian and criminal law. By expressly defining a wide range of gender crimes as crimes against humanity and as war crimes, the statute eliminates much of the ambiguity that had closed off the possibility of prosecuting crimes against women in previous post-war accountability processes. Included in the statute's list of crimes against humanity are 'rape, sexual slavery, enforced prostitution, forced pregnancy, enforced sterilization, or any other form of sexual violence of comparable gravity' (Article 7). In addition, enumerated war crimes, in both international and internal conflicts, include 'committing rape, sexual slavery, enforced prostitution, forced pregnancy, . . . enforced sterilization, or any other form of sexual violence also constituting a grave breach of the Geneva Conventions' (Article 8).

Importantly, having closely observed the practices of the ad hoc tribunals, the ICC Women's Caucus was aware that, in addition to legal definitions, technical and procedural matters had the potential to close off consideration of gender-specific cases and discourage participation by women (Copelon 2000, 238). In an effort to minimize these obstacles in the operation of the ICC, the ICC Women's Caucus successfully pressed for the codification of a range of gender-sensitive provisions in the Statute and rules of procedure. Most notably, the Court is required to establish a Victims and Witnesses Unit to ensure the safety of victims and witnesses and to provide counselling and other necessary services, especially where sexual violence is involved. Furthermore, rules of evidence are also in place to prevent attacks on the credibility of victims or witnesses based on past sexual behaviour. The Statute also calls for the appointment of legal advisers with expertise on VAW, and for gender balance among judges and all ICC personnel. Finally, victims can participate directly in Court proceedings whether or not they are called as witnesses, thereby opening up potentially less stressful avenues for women's voices to be heard.

Feminist commentators have raised questions about the extent to which the international prosecution of wartime rapes can advance the interests of survivors (Mertus 2004, Ní Aoláin 1997). Analysing women's experiences vis-à-vis the Foča case[5] examined by the ICTFY, Julie Mertus concludes that court testimonies do not allow for the 'production of a narrative that reflects women's experiences, promotes agency, and addresses their need for closure and healing' (Mertus 2004, 110). Notwithstanding women's best efforts to resist dominant legal narratives, Mertus cautions against the inherent tendency of adversarial legal practices to promote gender and cultural essentialism and reinforce the notion of 'woman as victim'. Ultimately, she calls on WHR advocates to examine more critically the limits of international tribunals and explore complementary and alternative justice mechanisms.

These are very important and valid criticisms. In responding, it is important not to create artificial either/or options around the 'best' way to promote and safeguard the human rights and well-being of individual women. The failures of the adversarial legal system from a feminist perspective are well documented. Indeed, highlighting and transforming gender biases in traditional legal procedures (e.g. eliminating hostile questioning of rape victims about their past sexual activities), is a core tenet of feminist engagement with the law. Interventions like those of the ICC Women's Caucus, therefore, which challenge procedural as well as defini- tional aspects of the law and facilitate bottom-up participation in related processes, exemplify critical feminist human rights praxis at the interna- tional level.

At the same time, there is no doubt that protecting the interests of indi- vidual women in criminal trials is always going to be difficult and requires the ongoing participation and vigilance of WHR advocates. In the context of a body like the ICC, therefore, it is imperative that any woman who has been subject to abuses directly or indirectly, and is a potential witness or testifier, is made fully aware of the difficulties and limitations, as well as the wider benefits, associated with her participation in the trial and surround- ing processes. In addition, comprehensive steps must be in place to ensure the security and well-being of all victims and witnesses who choose to par- ticipate, especially in cases of sexual violence.

It is too soon to evaluate the impact of gender-sensitive provisions in the operation of the ICC and the extent to which they ameliorate the specific concerns raised by Mertus and others in relation to the ICTFY. Even under optimal conditions, however, it could be argued that women's participa- tion in international criminal tribunals is better understood primarily as a political act aimed at contesting the gendered exercise of power at a struc- tural level, rather than as a process for achieving justice on an individual level. In this regard, close attention must be paid by WHR advocates to the mechanisms through which women ultimately opt to participate in inter- national tribunals. In particular, efforts are needed to strengthen women's political agency throughout the entire process.[6] Ultimately, in the wider struggle to secure meaningful justice for women in transitions, formal criminal prosecutions of wartime sexual violence will only be part of the solution some of the time.

Regarding alternative transitional justice mechanisms, there is a growing awareness that quasi-legal, non-adversarial mechanisms, as noted earlier, such as truth commissions, are no less gender-biased in their operation than traditional court models (Ní Aoláin and Turner 2007). Feminist schol- ars and advocates, therefore, must problematize the operation of gender bias and gendered power relations in framing and operationalizing both formal retributive and informal restorative modes of justice (ICTJ 2007). This entails contesting the biased premises and parameters that privilege certain harms in certain contexts, thereby creating exclusions along lines of gender, race, class and so on. Equally importantly, it means continuing to pay close attention to the formulation of procedures and practical strategies in order to redress biases and monitor implementation of gender-sensitive measures on a continuous basis.

Another approach: feminist uses of popular tribunals

Notwithstanding the persistent difficulties around women's participation in formal legal processes, the radical import of feminist initiatives to establish gender-sensitive legal practices in the ICC (and earlier in ad hoc criminal tribunals) should not be understated. These actions constitute an important practical critique of the gendered exercise of power in male-dominated international legal and political structures. Further, by relying on broad-based participation and solidarity from other women's movements, they have undoubtedly helped to extend advocacy networks, raise awareness and enhance capacity among women's NGOs towards further transformative engagement with the law. Furthermore, they established important legal principles and precedents that can be used by women's movements to advance WHR in safer 'informal' contexts.

For example, the increasing use of popular tribunals by women's movements is indicative of evolving efforts to reconcile two fundamental concerns of WHR advocates. The first is to counter the potential threat of re-victimization of women survivors of gender crimes in the context of formal, top-down, legal proceedings. The second is to affirm nonetheless a commitment to 'objective' values of fairness, transparency and accountability and to appropriate the legitimacy and authority of the law towards the advancement of meaningful equality and human rights for women. Popular tribunals are generally framed in terms of international human rights and/or humanitarian law. They simulate to one degree or another formal legal procedures and practices and often enlist the expertise and support of established legal practitioners and judges. In addition to the Vienna (1993) and Beijing (1995) tribunals of the Global Campaign for Women's Human Rights (Bunch and Reilly 1994, Reilly 1996), recent examples include the Tokyo Tribunal (Chinkin 2001), a related public hearing on crimes against women in contemporary conflicts, and the International Initiative for Justice in Gujarat 2002 (Cockburn 2007).[7]

The Tokyo Tribunal is a particularly striking example of the political impact of the wider campaign for gender justice in criminal tribunals. It was the culmination of several years of advocacy on behalf of 75 former 'comfort women' who were kidnapped and held in sexual slavery by the

Japanese military during World War II (Chinkin 2001). Many of the advocates involved in the tribunal had also been part of the ICC campaign. The former 'comfort women' came from China, Timor-Leste, Indonesia, Malaysia, Korea (north and south), the Philippines and Taiwan, as well as Japan. They were among approximately 200,000 women who were raped up to forty times each day in what has been described as the 'unprecedented industrialization of sexual slavery' (Copelon 2000, 222). The Tribunal was notable in replicating a high degree of legal formality, which has served to enhance its legitimacy and impact in the international community. The final judgment found Emperor Hirohito and several high-ranking members of the Japanese military to be 'guilty' of crimes against humanity (Women's International 2001, Paragraph 817). It also found that the current Japanese government has a 'duty to provide reparation in various forms' (Paragraph 1085). More recently, a climate of backlash and revisionism has seen the Japanese government fall back from an earlier tentative acknowledgement of the harms suffered by the 'comfort women' (McNeill 2007).

Under these conditions, the Tokyo judgment is likely to be the final response these women receive, since most of them are eighty years old, or older. As such, the significance of the formality employed throughout the proceedings is heightened as the judgment of a popular tribunal becomes, de facto, an 'official' judgment. The example of the Tokyo Tribunal represents transformative, bottom-up, feminist engagement that innovatively negotiates the nexus between formal and informal uses of the law, within a framework of transnational solidarity, in the pursuit of justice for victims of wartime sexual violence. In this sense, it suggests a third approach to dealing with post-conflict justice that can inform gender analyses of formal and informal transitional justice mechanisms and the relation between the two.

This section has focused primarily on questions of dealing with abuses during wars and conflicts. Developing gender-sensitive formal and informal justice mechanisms to account for particular wartime crimes against women is a vital area of concern that requires sustained feminist analysis and advocacy. However, women's experiences of conflict and transition are complex and a comprehensive vision of gender justice in such contexts cannot be achieved if we stop there. Recognizing this, another major transnational, feminist campaign emerged in the late 1990s and shifted the focus from women as victims of war to women as agents of change in transitions. Specifically, using international law as a bottom-up tool, it sought the adoption and implementation of a Security Council resolution on women, peace and security. The following section explores the contribution of this initiative to the project of developing a more comprehensive account of gender justice in post-conflict transitions.

Women's participation and gender equality in transitions

Ostensibly, transitions offer extraordinary opportunities for recasting societies and transforming the pre-existing terms of power – social, economic, cultural and political – especially for the benefit of those previously denied human rights and access to decision-making processes. Importantly, they offer 'an opportunity to consolidate some of the more positive changes that occurred as a result of the conflict [including] . . . opening up new spaces of life and work for women' (Abeysekera 2006, 4). In practice, however, scholars and activists have highlighted the paradox of women's extensive engagement in peace-building activities (Bell et al. 2004, Goetz and Hassim 2003), and in national liberation/pro-democracy struggles (Alvarez 1990, Basu 1995, Waylen 2000), being followed by their subsequent marginalization from formal peace negotiations and newly formed governance institutions and processes (Abeysekera 2006, Chinkin and Paradine 2001, Porter 2003, Chinkin and Charlesworth 2006).

Achieving gender justice in transitions, therefore, demands close scrutiny of the causes and consequences of women's marginalization in high-level political decision-making. This is especially critical in the negotiation of peace settlements and drafting of constitutions, which represent particularly important windows of opportunity because they establish the legal and political framework for transition over the long term (Coomaraswamy and Fonseka 2004). At the same time, seeking gender justice in transitions calls for greater recognition of the vital role played by women through informal peace-building activities (Porter 2003, 256). This includes, for example, sustaining grassroots links across divided communities throughout conflicts (Abeysekera 2006, 15; Chinkin and Paradine 2001, 150).

More broadly, research on women involved in peace-building activities indicates that they embrace an expansive and multilayered understanding of what is involved in securing a sustainable transition from 'conflict to peace' (Porter 2003, 257). Contesting narrowly interpreted liberal norms, feminist peace-building practice reflects a vision of justice in transitions that incorporates traditional, legally framed justice into a more comprehensive account of social justice. This includes 'gender justice, demilitarization, the promotion of non-violence, reconciliation, the rebuilding of relationships, gender equality, WHR, the building of and participation in democratic institutions, and sustaining the environment' (p. 257). Implicitly, this account of justice rejects the public–private configuration at the heart of traditional accounts of law and democracy, which conceals a range of abuses in private contexts, especially VAW. Importantly too, for most women, their participation in peace-building work springs directly from their daily struggles to 'meet the urgency of ordinary daily needs' (p. 257). Viewed from this perspective, ensuring gender justice in transitions necessarily means treating socioeconomic inequalities and exclusions, which disproportionately affect women, as no less urgent than legal and political issues.

Feminist critiques underline the need for greater and more nuanced understandings of the ways in which prior gender inequalities shape women's experiences during conflicts and transitions. That is, pre-existing patterns of gender-stereotyping, sex-based discrimination, sexual exploitation, VAW, and female impoverishment and under-representation in decision-making inevitably shape women's experiences of war, conflict and post-conflict. Hence, in addition to the heightened risk of wartime sexual violence, women are adversely affected by conflicts in a range of everyday ways. For example, women's trauma at losing male family members is usually exacerbated by a loss of income or property and the need to assume sole financial responsibility for the care and survival of other family members (Turpin 1998, 7). Further, conflict-induced poverty means that women are often forced into prostitution or become victims of trafficking (p. 6). More generally, because of their traditional gender roles as carers, women usually bear the brunt of coping with the destruction of basic amenities as they struggle to procure food, water, accommodation and healthcare for their dependents.

Realizing gender justice in transitional contexts, therefore, demands an understanding of the specificity of the hardships that women encounter in violent conflicts, how these are linked to 'peacetime' gender inequalities and why women may be more interested in transformation than 'reconstruction' in moments of transition. Viewed from this perspective, achieving justice for women in transitions entails actively contesting these underlying and often invisible inequalities. To do so, the architects of transitions must work closely with local women's movements to underpin and institutionalize a broader shift towards gender equality and respect for WHR. As will be discussed below, however, at present the opposite is true.

Security Council Resolution 1325 on women, peace and security is an important example of the innovative use of international law in the effort to underpin women's participation and gender equality in transitional contexts. The following section looks at the campaign to adopt and implement SCR 1325 and considers the significance of the resolution and the movement that created it in the wider bid to achieve gender justice in post-conflict situations.

Security Council Resolution 1325

The story of SCR 1325 begins with the Beijing Platform for Action (BPA) (UN 1995), which included 'women and armed conflict' as one of twelve critical areas of concern. The UN Commission on the Status of Women (CSW) subsequently met in 1998 to review progress on implementing the BPA, with a particular focus on its commitments in relation to gender and conflict issues. In this context, the Women's International League for Peace and Freedom (WILPF) began to coordinate the Women and Armed Conflict Caucus and later the NGO Working Group on Women and International Peace and Security,[8] which continued to advocate for the implementation of the BPA provisions beyond the CSW session (Hill 2001).

Many months of sustained advocacy yielded positive results when Namibia agreed to host an open session on women, peace and security under its presidency of the Security Council in October 2000.[9] In addition to speakers from the NGO Working Group, women from Guatemala, Sierra Leone and Somalia made presentations to the Security Council on the gender-specific impact of conflict in their countries and the need to include women in finding and effecting solutions (Hill et al. 2003, 1259). Following the meeting, Resolution 1325 was adopted and greeted by women's movements as a major success; it contained much of the same language as the Draft Resolution produced by the NGO Working Group and circulated previously to Council members (p. 1260).

Historically, the Security Council has dealt with women only peripherally, as victims or as a vulnerable group (Cohn 2004). Resolution 1325, therefore, marks the first time that the Council focused its attention exclusively on women as subjects in their own right in situations of conflict and transition from conflict. The resolution is significant, therefore, not only for recognizing the disproportionate and gender-specific impact of conflict on women but also for highlighting the undervalued role of women in the prevention and resolution of conflicts and in peace-building and post-conflict reconstruction. Specifically, it calls for the 'increased representation of women at all decision-making levels . . . in the prevention, management, and resolution of conflict' (Article 1). Importantly, the resolution also requires all participants in the negotiation and implementation of peace agreements to 'adopt a gender perspective' (Article 8).

Notwithstanding the politicization and selective enforcement of Security Council resolutions, because SCR 1325 is legally binding – in contrast to the BPA, for example – it has more potential as a tool to bolster WHR claims in transitional contexts. Resolution 1325 is also exceptional in being the product and continued focus of an unprecedented level of women's mobilization and engagement with the Security Council (Cohn 2004). Since October 2000, participants in the NGO Working Group on Women and International Peace and Security have lobbied intensively at state and UN levels and organized numerous events aimed at progressing implementation of the resolution (Hill et al. 2003, 1261–5). In particular, the PeaceWomen project,[10] coordinated by WILPF, plays a vital role documenting and mobilizing initiatives to translate Resolution 1325 into action. Reflecting the impact of these efforts, the Security Council has since convened two follow-up sessions with NGOs (in 2001 and 2005) which have sustained the pressure for concrete actions to realize the resolution.

Resolution 1325 has begun to have some impact on the ground. For example, to assist its implementation, the United Nations Development Fund for Women (UNIFEM) has supported dozens of targeted activities including the following: establishing women's centres in areas for refugees and internally displaced people in Afghanistan in order to improve access to humanitarian assistance (UNIFEM 2004a, 15); building women's coalitions and capacity to influence peace negotiations in the Democratic Republic of Congo, Somalia and Burundi (pp. 19, 21); and running training courses with peacekeeping personnel on the interrelation of gender, human rights and HIV / AIDS in Sierra Leone (p. 17).

Despite these and other UN-led initiatives, however, there is a consensus among advocates that the struggle for concrete realization of Resolution 1325 is in its very early stages and faces myriad obstacles (WILPF 2007, 1). With regard to Iraq, for example, it has been noted that 'women's political participation in . . . the design of the new political order has regularly been sacrificed to pacify vocal religious groups' (Chinkin and Charlesworth 2006, 939). Moreover, despite the adoption of SCR 1325, subsequent 'peace negotiations in the Middle East, in Burundi and in Sudan either did not include women or did not ensure that women were represented at high levels' (Porter 2003, 254). Similarly, over a period of twenty years of inter-mittent peace negotiations in Sri Lanka, Sunila Abeysekera notes that 'in none of these were women a part of the process; nor was there any discus-sion of their absence or lack of participation' (Abeysekera 2006, 15). Responding to the exclusion of women from peace talks after the 2002 Sri Lanka – Liberation Tigers of Tamil Eelan (LTTE) Ceasefire Agreement, and encouraged by SCR 1325, autonomous women's groups throughout Sri Lanka mobilized around the issue and achieved the creation of a Sub-Committee on Gender Issues (p. 15).

The limits of SCR 1325

The difficulties in implementing SCR 1325 are similar to those facing any liberal feminist equality agenda. On one level, SCR 1325 reflects a radical departure in the male-dominated context of 'war and security' law and policy at the UN Security Council. Its radical potential is stymied, however, by an overly narrow focus on women's equal participation in public life. The full and equal participation of women in political decision-making and policy design and implementation – in transitions or otherwise – requires positive measures to counter gender inequality across the board: eco-nomic, social, cultural, legal and political. Speaking directly to the challenges of implementing SCR 1325 in Burundi, women's rights activist, Schola Harushiyakira[11] acknowledges unprecedented successes in the use of quotas to secure 30 per cent representation of women in national repre-sentative bodies. However, she also raises concerns about the absorption of these women into mainstream political parties that have little interest in gender equality; and the need for greater awareness of the issues affecting the majority of women on the ground among the elected female repre-sentatives. Perhaps most importantly, she named extreme poverty as the single biggest obstacle to broad-based civic and democratic participation by women.

These comments underline widespread doubts about whether women's sustained and equal political participation in decision-making and post-conflict transformation is possible without a radical re-conceptualization of the kinds of democratic institutions and processes that are needed to achieve justice for women in transitions. Equally, however, they highlight the interrelation of denials of human rights in women's lives and the imperative of addressing gender-based social and economic inequalities as major obstacles to the achievement of women's equal political participa-tion in the transformation of transitional societies. This is all the more urgent given that the majority of conflicts take place in the 'developing' world and that current patterns of globalization have a disproportionate, negative impact on women (Molyneux and Razavi 2006). From this perspective, the challenge of implementing SCR 1325 and achieving women's empowerment in transitions is integrally linked to challenging gendered inequalities fostered by neo-liberal globalization.

Towards an integrated approach to justice, equality and human rights for women in transitions

Recognizing the limitations of the remit of SCR 1325 and the failures to implement its provisions to date, sceptics will be tempted to discount the resolution as purely tokenistic. In contrast, I argue, the transformative potential of SCR 1325 relies upon it being understood as an interlocking piece in a growing body of international commitments to WHR, gender equality and gender mainstreaming. Reflecting this perspective, Chinkin and Charlesworth map the main elements of this international legal framework, which underpins claims for gender equality and WHR in transitions to peace (Chinkin and Charlesworth 2006). In addition to SCR 1325 and the gender-sensitive provisions of the ICC, they include in this framework *inter alia* the Vienna Declaration and Programme of Action (1993), the BPA (1995) and, the Convention on the Elimination of All Forms of Discrimination Against Women (CEDAW) (1979), as well as the international bill of rights and the conventions on children's rights and against racism.

The potential of international human rights standards to promote gender justice in transitional contexts is multifaceted. On one level, women's groups and others can lobby at the local level for the incorporation of international norms of non-discrimination and sex-based equality into emerging national legal systems, including customary and religious laws (2006, 944). This is particularly important in assisting women's movements, which in recent decades have been at the forefront of resisting resurgent traditionalism and new fundamentalisms (Shaheed 2001, Freedman 1996).

More broadly, however, there is much undeveloped potential for women's organizations to utilize the entire array of international human rights treaties in seeking gender justice in transitions. Given the traditional neglect of socio-economic rights in mainstream transitional justice and human rights paradigms, treaties like CEDAW and the International Covenant on Economic, Social and Cultural Rights (ICESCR) (which afford particular protection to the rights to health, decent conditions of work, social security, education and so on) have a particularly pivotal role to play in ensuring WHR in transitions (Chinkin and Charlesworth 2006, 946). Tapping this potential, however, will require sustained engagement by women's NGOs with the treaty-monitoring processes, in order to hold governments accountable for the local implementation of global gender equality and WHR standards. Beyond the possibilities of pursuing 'legal' strategies and bringing individual or group complaints under some treaties, all conventions require governments to participate in periodic reviews of their observance of the convention. These reviews create 'political' opportunities wherein women's organizations and individual activists can legitimate their local claims and secure benchmarks that can be repeatedly invoked and revisited. As such, reviews of a government's compliance with human rights standards are important civic/political processes in their own right. They afford women valuable opportunities for political engagement and negotiation with governments at the international level, which might not be available at state level. In addition, they foster transnational solidarity links with non-state and civil-society actors who share a commitment to advancing WHR.

Significantly, the Committee on the Elimination of Discrimination against Women is increasingly playing a lead role in monitoring implementation of SCR 1325. The committee now asks governments to report on the implementation of SCR 1325 as part of their overall compliance with CEDAW (UNIFEM 2004b). In 2007, thirteen out of thirty-six countries up for review before the committee were in conflict or post-conflict situations. In this context, women's organizations have very real opportunities to use their governments' obligations under CEDAW to reinforce implementation of SCR 1325. Moreover, the existence of well-organized transnational NGO networks that have grown up around both instruments[12] maximize the potential for local groups to use these international standards strategically in tandem to achieve substantive justice for women in post-conflict transitions.

Conclusion

This chapter has explored the prospects for achieving a comprehensive vision of gender justice in transitional contexts, with a focus on the potentially transformative role of international norms and TFA. In particular, I examined the significance of recent feminist initiatives targeting the ICC and the adoption of Security Council Resolution 1325. In the case of the former, I reviewed various levels of gender bias, especially in international humanitarian law, which have underpinned failures to account adequately for wartime crimes against women until the 1990s. Ultimately, I argue that efforts to date to engender war crimes prosecution are best understood as part of a wider 'political' process to contest and constitute global legal norms in ways that underpin principles of gender equality and WHR, and not *primarily* as avenues to seek justice for individual women. Further, I argue that the transformative value of such norms is especially evident when they are used in the context of bottom-up, quasi-legal initiatives such as the Tokyo Tribunal. More generally, women's movements and feminist critics must remain vigilant in exposing gender biases in determining what counts as conflict-related harms and in advancing ways and means to eliminate such biases in both formal and informal modes of dealing with past abuses.

Recognizing the imperative of extending the purview of justice in transitions beyond dealing with abuses during conflicts, I considered the potential of SCR 1325 as a tool of women's movements to capitalize on the transformative opportunities opened up by transitional moments. Despite the exceptional opportunities transitions offer to redefine and re-envision a society emerging from conflict, more often than not women find themselves sidelined in post-conflict politics and under pressure to return to traditional, subordinate roles. This tendency is exacerbated by the fact that male-centric models of representative democracy, together with the classic liberal public–private divide, are uncritically embraced as the final goal of transitions. The effect of these gender biases is to ignore structural social and economic inequalities, including global inequalities, which disproportionately disadvantage women in conflicts and transitions and impede their full and equal political participation. Further, the exclusion of women from the exercise of power is deepened by a widespread willingness – among progressives and conservatives alike – to discount calls for gender equality in the name of respecting collective 'cultural' claims.

UN Security Council Resolution 1325 is an important tool in promoting a more comprehensive vision of gender justice in transitions. However, in isolation, it cannot address the deep-seated gender inequalities which are produced by and reflected in legal, political, social, economic and cultural practices, institutions and identities. Rather, the transformative potential of SCR 1325 is enhanced if it is understood as one among an array of evolving international commitments to gender equality and WHR, within a framework of universal and indivisible human rights. The realization of justice for women in transitions is particularly tied to the bottom-up imple-mentation of CEDAW and the ICESCR, as well as the BPA, SCR 1325, the Protocol on the Rights of Women in Africa, and so on. Taking up this theme in more detail, the following chapter considers the modest gains and persistent obstacles surrounding the advancement of feminist visions of indivisible human rights.

6

Development, Globalization and Women's Human Rights

Introduction

Persistent advocacy by women's movements has ensured some positive steps towards gender equality in most regions of the world. Girls' participation in primary and secondary education, for example, has greatly increased (Molyneux and Razavi 2006, 4); fertility rates and the associated burden of care work carried by women have declined somewhat (p. 4); the proportion of women in elected assemblies has risen to a global average of 16 per cent (p. 7); and a larger proportion of women than ever before is in paid employment (p. 6), with many experiencing real gains in income and economic independence as a result. However, the global challenge of achieving full gender equality and human rights for women remains enormous. Given the very low baseline from which progress must be measured, and the unprecedented mobilization of efforts to improve the status of women, especially since the beginning of the UN Decade for Women (UNDW) (1976–85), the concrete improvements achieved to date are extremely modest.

The majority of societies worldwide remain highly patriarchal. Upper-echelon decision-making in political, economic and cultural life is still monopolized by men who, by and large, earn higher incomes and enjoy greater access to economic and social resources than women do. Further, most men continue to benefit hugely from women's unpaid work in the household economy and domestic life. Moreover, the hegemony of neo-liberal globalization, characterized by persistent privatization and deregulation pressures and new levels of deference to commercial logic, has eroded or thwarted the development of labour protection and social-security provisions. Importantly, these processes are not gender neutral; neo-liberal social and economic policies assiduously shift the burden of social care (that is, care for children, people with disabilities, the sick and elderly, etc.) from state agencies to private actors, the vast majority of whom are women.

These deeply rooted and widely normalized structural inequalities both reflect and reproduce patterns of discrimination and marginalization that make the majority of women and girls disproportionately susceptible to poverty, dispossession, economic exploitation and the many negative effects of globalization in both the global South and the North. Moreover, under such conditions, women are at greater risk of being subject to different forms of gender-based violence – including female infanticide, trafficking, sexual exploitation, wartime sexual violence, domestic abuse and rape. They are also disproportionately exposed to the harms caused by different forms of structural violence – from war and conflict to disease pandemics, 'natural' disasters or the massive upheaval of major infrastructural projects.

Viewed from the perspective of women and girls, therefore, the struggles to achieve human development, human security and human rights are inextricable. Arguably, you would expect human rights ideas, standards of protection, and avenues of redress to play a central role in promoting and protecting social and economic well-being, as well as inclusive, fair and sustainable models of development. Yet, this has not been the case. Instead, a persistent chasm divides dominant human rights and development paradigms and militates against framing economic and social development as human rights issues. From the beginning, UN development and human rights fields were constructed as two distinct areas of activity that address different types of problems. On the one hand, the principal goal of mainstream development is to narrow the gap in economic prosperity between 'developed' and 'developing' countries. On the other hand, a human rights regime has evolved that is largely concerned with promoting civil and political rights as checks against abuses of state power but fails to take seriously social and economic rights and global inequalities.

Contesting the second-class status of social and economic rights in dominant approaches to human rights is a major challenge. In meeting this challenge it is important to understand the arena of social and economic rights as a site of contestation where state actors, human rights 'experts', NGOs and transnational social movements engage in ongoing battles over malleable meaning and practice. Hence, the struggles to create, adopt and implement the International Covenant on Economic, Social and Cultural Rights (ICESCR) (1966), the Charter of Economic Rights and Duties of States (1974) or the Declaration on the Right to Development (1986) can all be seen as attempts to de-centre Western-biased and neo-liberal accounts of human rights in the international arena and to narrow the gap between human rights and development paradigms.

As noted in previous chapters, the early 1990s brought fresh attempts to reframe human rights discourse as a global ethical and legal template in the post-Cold War era. In this context, proponents of alternative approaches to human rights, including women's human rights (WHR) advocates, wished to transcend old tensions between those (mainly Western governments) who reduced 'human rights' to limited civil and political rights and those (mainly former socialist and Third World governments) who conceded only the value of certain forms of economic and social rights or the collective 'right to development'. Hence, along with the unprecedented recognition of WHR, the most significant outcome achieved at the World Conference on Human Rights (Vienna 1993) was a strong reaffirmation by governments that 'all human rights are universal, indivisible, interdependent and interrelated' (UN 1993). Building on this mini renaissance in human rights thinking, development scholars, NGOs and grassroots activists began to consider the transformative potential of framing development in human rights terms (Sen 2004, Rajagopal, 2003, Cornwall and Molyneux 2006, Elson and Gideon 2004).

Despite the openness to alternative approaches to human rights in the early 1990s, there have been many challenges to sustaining, expanding and building linkages between the 'gender' and 'indivisibility' critiques of human rights as articulated in Vienna. This chapter explores these challenges and the different factors that drive a wedge between the fields of human rights and development, with a particular focus on the gender dimensions involved. Building on recent discussions of the links between advocacy in the two fields (Cornwall and Molyneux 2006, Cornwall and Nyamu-Musembi 2004, Alston 2005), this chapter focuses especially on how these issues play out in interactions between 'women's human rights' and 'gender and development' (GAD) streams of advocacy, and in efforts to shape 'human rights' or 'rights-based approaches' to development (RBA) from feminist perspectives. Undoubtedly, points of contention exist between the two streams. For example, some GAD advocates have expressed concern that WHR approaches focus too narrowly on issues of violence against women (VAW) while women's experiences of marginalization and exploitation, especially within globalization and development processes, have not achieved the same level of recognition as human rights concerns. In response, I consider the factors behind the relatively limited impact to date of WHR advocacy on socio-economic rights and development issues, and I contextualize these gaps in terms of the wider constraints that permeate human rights and development discourses.

At the same time, there are grounds to be optimistic about the prospects for deepening the links between GAD and WHR analyses and strategies, especially in the context of evolving feminist accounts of rights-based development. Later in this chapter I highlight recent developments in human rights standard-setting and advocacy initiatives that strengthen women's claims to all human rights, but especially social, economic and development rights. In particular, I consider the gender dimensions of the UN Millennium Development Goals (MDG) initiative, which currently is the most important UN interface between human rights and development agendas. Arguably, if approached from a bottom-up, WHR perspective, the MDG initiative can foster the expansion of gender-sensitive, rights-based approaches to development and serve as a springboard for transformative action to eliminate gender inequalities that are impeding achievement of the Goals.

Before examining examples of positive synergy at the nexus of human rights and development, the next two sections highlight some of the main debates and issues that shape the political and conceptual terrain in which WHR and GAD advocacy operate. First, I discuss briefly the limitations of mainstream development paradigms and the emergence of alternative feminist and rights-based approaches to development. Second, I examine the uneasy relationship between human rights and development discourses, including conceptual and technical impediments to advancing social and economic rights agendas, and how this shapes the relationship between WHR and GAD advocacy. The remaining sections focus on specific concrete efforts to link development to human rights and their potential role in advancing WHR, especially vis-à-vis the MDG initiative.

Development and its critics

Embedded in a linear modernization narrative, dominant liberal and neo-liberal accounts frame 'development' as a process wherein 'backward' developing countries are assisted and 'incentivized' to catch up with mostly Western, economically 'advanced' economies. Viewing development in this way is problematic because it precludes consideration of how (global) capitalism fosters or relies upon inequalities both within and across countries and regions, including gender-specific inequalities. Ignoring such inequalities, mainstream approaches to development focus on how best to integrate poorer economies into the global economy on the basis of their 'competitive advantage' – often as a source of cheaper primary goods and labour. There have been some shifts in thinking within this dominant modernization paradigm since development first became a focus of the international community after World War II. In the 1950s and 1960s development was understood in narrow economic terms, in which rising national income was the principal indicator of success and the state and public sector was assumed to be a key catalyst of economic growth. During the 1970s, high inflation and stagnant growth in dominant Western economies encouraged a return to laissez-faire principles that emphasized small government, fiscal and monetary conservatism, and the role of free-market mechanisms in generating economic growth and development. This neo-liberal turn has affected women's lives in gender-specific ways. While gender critiques of the paternalism of the Keynesian welfare state are well documented, neo-liberalism, which seeks to limit the size and role of the state, presents other gender challenges in disproportionately exacerbating the impoverishment and social exclusion of women in both the global South and North.

The first feminist critiques of mainstream development scholarship and practice emerged in the 1970s. Pioneers such as Ester Boserup (1970) inspired a new wave of 'women in development' (WID) writings, which highlighted the pivotal contribution of women to economic life and the need to take account of women's economic roles in the formulation of effective economic development policies. WID analyses gained in visibility and acceptability in mainstream development discourse throughout the UNDW (1976–85). In doing so, WID perspectives stayed within a liberal modernization framework insofar as they questioned the exclusion and invisibility of women in development policy and practice but did not challenge the underlying assumptions of the mainstream development paradigm.

By the 1980s, the neo-liberal turn had permeated development discourses in the form of structural adjustment programmes (SAPs). Counter efforts to bring about a New International Economic Order (NIEO) more favourable to developing economies, led mainly by Third World governments, ultimately failed. Instead, SAPs, which required governments to cut spending and embrace market liberalization measures in exchange for development loans and assistance, became the hallmark of neo-liberal development policy. By the early 1990s, however, another shift was evident as there was a growing recognition in mainstream development circles of the human costs of SAPs, particularly their gender-specific detrimental impacts (Sparr 1994). Even international financial institutions began to question the efficacy of SAPs in achieving development goals. By the mid 1990s, while not explicitly supporting rights-based approaches to development (RBA), World Bank rhetoric shifted to acknowledge 'participatory development' and 'good governance' as relevant to the achievement of effective development (O'Brien et al. 2000, 26).

The GAD movement, which gathered momentum alongside the rise of SAPs, deepened the WID critique (Mitter 1986, Sen and Grown 1987). Shaped by Third World experiences, and inflected with socialist and radical feminist tenets, GAD approaches highlight the interplay of global capitalism, colonial/postcolonial relations of power and patriarchal practices in the continued subordination of women. Hence GAD analyses expose how unequal gender power relations – across public, private, social, economic, cultural and political arenas – obstructed women's social and economic empowerment. Importantly, GAD approaches problematize unequal South–North power differentials as fundamental impediments to sustainable and equitable development in the South. Given its roots in such far-reaching critiques of Western-centric and gender-biased liberalism, GAD scholarship and advocacy did not initially situate itself within a human rights or rights-based framework. The emergence of rights-based development discourse in the 1990s, however, opened up new possibilities for building bridges between development and human rights advocacy, especially between GAD and WHR streams.

Broadly speaking, rights-based approaches to development reject narrow economism and top-down models of development. Instead, the agency of individuals and groups is emphasized, both in envisioning the kind of development they want and in claiming the rights that enable people to achieve a decent standard of living and quality of life relative to others (Cornwall and Nyamu-Musembi 2004). As such, RBA are closely linked to ideas of 'human development', which prioritize the capabilities, agency and needs of people in development processes rather than the achievement of quantitative targets (Sen 1999, Sen 2004, Nussbaum 2001). In addition to a people-centred moral basis, however, proponents stress the potential of RBA to underpin accountability by promoting bottom-up participation and good governance (Cornwall and Molyneux 2006); facilitating the identification of specific 'rights and duty holders' (Tsikata 2004); and providing 'sanction, enforceability, targeted goals and structure' in development processes (Banda 2005, 274).

For most UN and bilateral agencies, and for international development non-governmental organizations, RBA are viewed as a progressive departure that complements people-centred human development discourses (Cornwall and Molyneux 2006). By and large, however, supporters of RBA have not moved beyond a rhetorical endorsement of rights. In part because of negative ideological associations with the former communist bloc and

NIEO critiques of Western hegemony, RBA proponents have generally avoided directly linking the realization of their vision to the implementation of binding human rights agreements, such as the ICESCR (Gideon 2006, Cornwall and Nyamu-Musembi 2004). Arguably, however, RBA will remain in the realm of rhetoric unless advocates take steps to utilize existing human rights standards and processes to promote economic and social rights. At the same time, optimism about the merits of RBA among many groups and NGOs has diminished in the resurgent 'conservative mood' that has characterized the global arena since the late 1990s and been exacerbated by the 'war on terror' (Cornwall and Molyneux 2006). In particular, the attempted co-optation of WHR discourse in justifying US/ UK-led invasions of Afghanistan and Iraq further strained the credibility of the human rights paradigm in the pursuit of political, social and economic gender justice in a global perspective. Any attempts to render RBA more effective, therefore, must address issues of political legitimacy as well as the gendered institutional and conceptual obstacles noted in the following section.

Disjuncture between development and human rights paradigms: gender dimensions

The disjuncture between mainstream development and human rights paradigms occurs on multiple levels – discursive, political, legal, institutional and so on. The Universal Declaration of Human Rights (UDHR) sets out a wide range of social and economic rights, including the right to food, shelter, education, healthcare. Further, it calls for an international social order conducive to the realization of all human rights (Article 27). Yet, in the decades after the UDHR was adopted, a human rights system emerged that actively marginalized economic and social rights and situated development outside its purview.

A variety of apparently gender-neutral explanations can be offered to explain the historical dominance of civil/political over social/economic rights and the exclusion of development concerns from the human rights arena. On one level, they mirror the ideological and political dominance of Western liberal powers in the international arena vis-à-vis former communist bloc countries and new postcolonial states. They also reflect the conceptual limits of international law discourses discussed in chapter 2. In particular, the primacy of state sovereignty militates against the creation of binding mechanisms that might underpin our 'cosmopolitan responsibility' to the populations of other states. Claims – now widely contested

– that economic and social rights are (1) more costly to uphold than civil and political rights and (2) not 'justiciable' and therefore not enforceable, also undermined efforts to strengthen economic and social rights as human rights.[1] Further, institutionally, the fact that the International Labour Organization (ILO) was in place almost thirty years before the UN was established provided an 'excuse' for the new human rights system to focus on areas of rights protection other than labour and welfare rights.

This marginalization of social and economic rights within mainstream human rights has gender dimensions that are rarely examined. In most societies, women are the ones directly responsible for meeting the basic needs (food, shelter, clothing, etc.) of family members and, importantly, for interfacing with the state and other agencies in order to access accommodation, health, education and other services. The enjoyment (or not) of social and economic rights, therefore, is a profoundly gendered issue. In this regard, the lesser priority given to the implementation of social and economic rights on a systemic level is also symptomatic of the diminished status enjoyed by women in general and their exclusion from agenda-setting and decision-making processes. For example, while the ILO has paid more attention to the gender aspects of its mission in recent years, the creation of most ILO standards has been driven by traditional trade union concerns and a primary focus on protecting the social and economic rights of male 'bread-winner' workers in formal-sector employment. Social and economic-security issues that affect women the most, for example, in contexts of informal sector employment or the provision of social care, have not featured on ILO agendas until very recently. This fragmentation of responsibilities, where the ILO addresses economic and social rights while the UN human rights machinery focuses on civil and political rights, therefore, has done little to challenge gender-blind understandings of economic and social rights.

While the World Conference on Human Rights (Vienna, 1993) endorsed more integrated approaches to human rights, subsequent challenges to advancing this agenda cannot be overstated as the hegemony of economic neo-liberalism deepens. Contemporary neo-liberal logic is pervasive and invisible. On a macro level, it discredits social and economic rights claims by associating them with excessive government spending, related inefficiencies, a lack of competitiveness and, ultimately, economic failure and poverty in the 'global market'. On a micro level, social and economic rights signify social parasitism, often through the construction of maligned gendered stereotypes such as 'welfare mothers'. The account of human rights acceptable within this vision of development, therefore, is generally silent on structural and gender inequalities or the responsibilities of states and the international community in eliminating them. Rather, neo-liberalism promotes a minimal state, one that provides political stability and underpins those rights most necessary to the operation of private enterprise, usually by formalizing the property rights of already privileged groups (Alston 2005, 780). Given such a legacy of state-centred, Western, class and gender bias in dominant rights discourses, proponents of alternative development paradigms have been understandably sceptical about the capacity of the existing international human rights framework to address substantive social and economic inequalities, especially in a context of deepening global inequalities. This means that proponents of RBA must be very clear about what they mean by 'rights' and not accept truncated, neo-liberal definitions. Equally, there is an onus on human rights advocates to demonstrate to progressive sceptics the transformative potential of substantive human rights in challenging social and economic marginalization on different levels.

Several recurring criticisms of RBA are made by development advocates in the Third World (Tsikata 2004). It is often pointed out that the legalistic and technocratic institutional apparatus of international human rights is generally inaccessible to grassroots organizers and associated more with the top-down imposition of policy than with participatory development. In addition, the focus on the state as the primary locus of accountability around human rights implementation is a source of particular scepticism. Dzodzi Tsikata notes that in the Third World, given the 'dismantling . . . of the state under structural adjustment, the proactive role . . . given to the state . . . is unrealistic' (2004). Moreover, on the face of it, a state-centric, rights-based paradigm does not appear to offer much scope for holding accountable international financial institutions, transnational corporations, Western governments or international NGOs for their role in perpetuating global inequalities and related denials of social and economic rights in the Third World. Further, confidence in the United Nations and the laws and standards it promulgates has been severely undermined as a result of the institution's perceived unwillingness and/or inability to challenge wealthy, powerful countries and apply the same standards of accountability to them as they do to poorer, less powerful nations. Finally, many in the Third World view RBA simply as another donor fashion and way for wealthy countries and international financial institutions to impose 'conditionalities' on aid and loans to developing countries while eschewing their own responsibility for bad development policies.

The implications of these critiques for GAD advocates who embrace RBA are addressed by Cornwall and Molyneux (2006). They argue that there is an onus on GAD advocates who seek to engage positively with RBA to contest the exclusions of traditional liberal rights discourse (along lines of gender, race, class, etc.) as well as the persistent gaps between agreed human rights standards and their implementation. In doing so, RBA proponents must persuade sceptics that such exclusions are not inherent to RBA but reflect biased interpretations that have been defined and imposed by dominant groups. Cornwall and Molyneux also flag as problematic the pivotal role of states in guaranteeing and delivering rights because it requires direct engagement by women's movements with states and the associated risks of marginalization and/or co-option.

Notwithstanding all of these challenges, feminist proponents of RBA focus on their transformative potential, particularly in situations where women 'experience the consequences of a lack of equal rights to men in [the form of] continuing gender-based discrimination, unequal and poor pay, high levels of violence, and exclusion from political arenas' (Cornwall and Molyneux 2006, 1175). Given that such conditions are daily realities for many women in many parts of the world, the central role of norms of gender equality and non-discrimination within RBA would appear to be particularly salient in the struggle to achieve GAD objectives. Reflecting this optimistic perspective, Joanna Kerr argues that RBA offer new opportunities to build constructive linkages between WHR and GAD streams of feminist advocacy. In this regard, she observes that GAD advocates increasingly 'recognise the link between laws and institutions that influence women's status . . . and the outcomes of development', while 'women's rights activists . . . are increasingly focusing on economic and social well-being' as core WHR issues (Kerr 2001). Sometimes referred to as GLAD (gender, law and development), this new approach – especially in Africa – has focused on 'changing laws on inheritance and property rights, particularly as they pertain to land . . . and challenging the restrictive interpretation of customary and religious laws' in a bid to remove structural impediments to women's full and equal participation in development (Banda 2005, 273).

Others are less optimistic about the common ground between WHR and GAD fields of advocacy and the benefits of closer links. While acknowledging the achievements of WHR advocates in 'injecting women's rights into the discourse of human rights', Tsikata echoes the concerns of many when she suggests that by focusing principally on contesting VAW and discrimination against women under customary laws, 'human rights feminism' shows that it is 'not particularly worried about the development paradigm and its implications for women' (Tsikata 2004). This interpretation, however, is somewhat short-sighted on a number of levels. First, it underestimates the interrelatedness of all rights in women's lives and how VAW and unequal access to economic and social resources (enforced by discriminatory laws – formal and customary) reflect not only individual violations but also structural injustices, which impede the advancement of alternative approaches to development. Second, Tsikata's critique discounts the strong links that already exist between WHR and GAD approaches, often based on a common recognition of the significance of VAW issues to both sets of agendas. Indeed, VAW became a priority issue of 'human rights feminism' largely in response to sustained mobilization by community-based women's organizations in the South and North, many of which were engaged in development advocacy and repeatedly identified VAW as an obstacle to women's participation in development programmes and a threat to their health and reproductive rights.

In the following sections, I highlight recent initiatives that contest the marginalization of economic and social rights, and the exclusion of development issues from human rights agendas, especially from a WHR perspective. In doing so, I underline evolving opportunities to use human rights standards and processes to seek economic and social rights and 'just development' for women.

Engendering economic, social and development rights

Despite persistent obstacles to reconciling human rights and development paradigms and advancing indivisible and gender-sensitive understandings of human rights, there have been many significant steps forward in recent years that signal the potential for further progress. This includes new advocacy initiatives and scholarship, as well as the development of international standards and new interpretations of existing standards. For example, the creation of new ILO protections, such as the Part-Time Work Convention (1994) and the Home Work Convention (1996), strengthen the human rights claims of women as workers in the global economy and reflect the growing importance of social and economic rights in an expanding international WHR framework. Since the 1990s, there has also been a steady flow of detailed recommendations from UN human rights treaty-monitoring bodies, which provide guidance to states and others on what is needed to achieve the substantive implementation of all human rights from a gender-equality perspective. In addition, the UN Development Fund for Women

(UNIFEM) has supported the development of innovative frameworks for integrating gender-sensitive budgeting processes with monitoring and measuring governments' compliance with their human rights commitments to women (Budlender and Hewitt 2004, Elson 2006). Such technical projects are critical to ensuring the translation of rhetorical commitments to WHR – especially social and economic rights – into policies that materially improve women's lives. Underlining this, former head of UNIFEM Noeleen Heyzer notes: 'Progress towards human rights entails monetary investment and a constant scrutiny of economic policies from a rights perspective. Accountability to women's rights needs to be translated into mobilizing the necessary resources to meet the commitments made by the ratification of CEDAW' (Elson 2006, 1). The very high-profile Realizing Rights: The Ethical Globalization Initiative (EGI), established by former UN High Commissioner for Human Rights Mary Robinson, also captures the spirit of the 1990s push to elevate the standing of social, economic and development rights in global policy debates.[2] Promoting gender equality as a cross-cutting theme, the EGI focuses on five critical areas of concern that reveal a particular vision of indivisible human rights within a broadly liberal frame: equitable trade, the right to health, humane migration policy, women's leadership and corporate responsibility.

The Montreal Principles[3] – an NGO-generated set of guidelines on implementing women's economic, social and cultural rights – are also indicative of the continuing high level of commitment among a broad base of NGOs to 'engendering' the indivisibility agenda articulated in the Vienna Declaration (1993). Further, the World Social Forum (WSF)[4] has become a recurring locus of activity for WHR advocacy with an economic and social rights emphasis. Building on the Montreal Principles, the women's working group of the Economic, Social and Cultural Rights Network (ESCR-Net),[5] for example, has played a coordinating role in bringing gender-conscious human rights perspective to WSF activities and debates. Similarly, complementary NGO campaigns, which expose the negative impacts on women of World Bank policies and international trade agreements, are examples of this stream of advocacy.[6]

One of the most important outcomes since the early 1990s, however, is a legacy of strong linkages among WHR, GAD and reproductive and sexual health advocates, forged in the context of lobbying initiatives at different UN conferences. As discussed in chapter 4, transnational feminist advocacy (TFA) around the International Conference on Population and Development (ICPD) (Cairo, 1994) is a good example of a concrete struggle for recognition of the indivisibility and interrelatedness of all human rights in women's lives, through a focus on reproductive health. These efforts deepened the links between the GAD and WHR streams of advocacy in a reproductive health movement that sought to frame reproductive and sexual health as human rights issues. The impact of these efforts is reflected in the ICPD Programme of Action (POA), which puts women as agents and rights bearers at the centre of population debates and clearly defines reproductive health as a human rights issue. The Millennium Project is the most recent large-scale UN exercise to mobilize international attention and resources around the issues addressed by the ICPD and other 1990s UN conferences. As such, it offers the latest round of opportunities and challenges to advancing RBA and WHR in particular. Recognizing its significance, the following section explores the strengths and weaknesses of the MDGs from a WHR perspective and considers the conditions necessary to capitalize on the transformative potential of the initiative.

The Millennium Declaration and Millennium Development Goals

After more than a decade of UN world conferences and review meetings, the Millennium Declaration and MDGs have emerged as the principal current locus of progressive UN activities in a post-September 11 world. The declaration was adopted by the UN General Assembly in September 2000. A reaffirmation of UN Charter principles, the declaration unequivocally endorses human rights as integral to the achievement of a 'peaceful, prosperous and just world' and calls on governments to 'strive for the full protection and promotion in all our countries of civil, political, economic, social and cultural rights for all'. The MDGs are the 'road map' subsequently drawn up by the UN secretariat to guide implementation of the declaration through 2015. They contain eighteen specific targets that are measured by forty-eight indicators in relation to eight priority aims:

1 eradicate extreme poverty and hunger
2 achieve universal primary education
3 promote gender equality and women's empowerment
4 reduce child mortality
5 improve maternal health
6 combat HIV/AIDS, malaria and other diseases
7 ensure environmental sustainability
8 develop a global partnership for development.

Attitudes to the MDG process vary from 'great scepticism to energetic endorsements' (Barton 2004, 3). Much has been written about the limitations of the MDG framework (Alston 2005, Barton 2004). Many are concerned that it heralds a return to a narrow, linear and positivist approach that fails to address the structural roots and gender dimensions of the problems being tackled (Barton 2004, 3; Antrobus 2004b, 14; Morales 2004, 24). Human rights advocates worry that the failure to frame the Goals explicitly in human rights terms takes pressure off governments to fulfil the more comprehensive human rights standards and programmes of action that they are also obliged to implement (Symington 2004, 16). Clearly, exceptional efforts are needed by governments, relevant agencies and advocates to integrate human rights and MDG-monitoring processes. The challenges to achieving this are considerable, however, and there is little evidence of it happening so far. A survey of national MDG reports up to 2004, for example, reveals very few references to human rights ideas and standards (Alston 2005, 760), and practice continues to be characterized by a 'limited convergence between the agendas of those dealing with the MDGs and those dealing with human rights' (p. 761).

Ironically, the MDG framework has also been criticized for its implicit failure to endorse the indivisibility of all human rights by underplaying the role of political and civic participation as constitutive elements in the generation of people-centred 'human development' and bottom-up participation in human rights promotion (Alston 2005). The burden that the Goals impose on states is also a cause of concern. Many commentators call into question the feasibility of expecting Third World states to achieve the Goals at a time when their effectiveness and resources are being eroded by privatization and globalization pressures, while the power of unaccountable non-state actors such as transnational corporations increases (Alston 2005; Abeysekera 2004, 6; Antrobus 2004b, 14). Linked to this point, GAD advocates have strongly criticized the MDG framework for its failure to acknowledge explicitly the many ways in which neo-liberal development and trade liberalization paradigms have actually 'served to halt and reverse progress toward the achievement of [the Goals]', especially in women's lives (Antrobus 2004b, 14). Others fear that the MDG process is simply another top-down fad that will redirect and consume scarce resources without producing the in-depth understanding and action necessary to overcome the obstacles to achieving the Goals (Alston 2005).

Gender critiques of the MDG framework

In addition to the concerns already noted, WHR and GAD advocates have highlighted the minimalist and relatively weak gender-specific provisions of the Goals.[7] Only one goal explicitly deals with the status of women per se in its call to promote gender equality and empower women (MDG3).[8] In contrast to the hundreds of strategic actions enumerated in the Beijing Platform for Action (BPA), and the far-ranging scope of the obligations created by the UN Women's Convention, MDG3 seems very inadequate. Feminist commentators have particularly criticized the exclusion of reproductive health as a core goal (Antrobus 2004a, Corrêa 2005). Building on alliances formed around the ICPD and the Beijing Conference, feminist advocates working at the intersection of women's health, human rights and development sought the inclusion of reproductive health as one of the international development targets in the years running up to the adoption of the Millennium Declaration (Freedman 2003; Corrêa 2005). At the last minute, however, conservative forces rallied successfully to remove all references to reproductive health. In the end, only MDG5 contains an explicit reference to women's health – to 'improve maternal health' with a target of reducing maternal mortality rates by 75 per cent between 1990 and 2015. This outcome is a reminder that, despite decades of mobilization by women, and many hard-won commitments from governments to remedy gender-based discrimination and inequalities, rights-based approaches to reproductive and sexual health continue to be resisted and contested, and the gains secured in Cairo and Beijing in this area are constantly at risk of erosion.

Despite its many shortcomings, WHR and GAD advocates have opted to engage actively with the MDG initiative for a number of pragmatic and substantive reasons. More than a decade of efforts to implement the BPA and other agreements have been met by a chronic lack of political will and resources. In this regard, the clear focus and deadlines of the Goals have certain merits. More generally, most GAD and WHR proponents appreciate the strategic importance of engaging with the MDG framework because it will continue to be the main focus of development policy and resource mobilization through 2015. Others are optimistic that the ongoing, high-level attention paid to achieving MDG3 and the other Goals offers genuine opportunities to challenge the gender inequalities that lie behind failures to achieve the Goals. On a substantive level, the MDG process is currently the most significant locus of efforts to reconcile development and human rights paradigms and to advance the indivisibility agenda (Alston

2005). It is important to ensure the inclusion of WHR and GAD perspectives in this process. The questions to be addressed, therefore, are, as Philip Alston states: 'How can the MDG process be made more human rights friendly? And how can human rights standards and procedures be mobilized so as to enhance the effectiveness of the MDG initiative?' (Alston 2005, 800).

Here, I am concerned with answering these questions from a gender perspective. Recognizing that 'private' processes of social and biological reproduction are at the heart of most of the Goals (Antrobus 2004b), a WHR approach begins with the premise that gender power relations and their implications for women's equality and human rights are integral to the tasks of monitoring and achieving the Goals. More specifically, it identifies the gender-specific, human rights dimensions of each goal and explores ways of bringing existing human rights standards to bear in their implementation and vice versa. Arguably, if the Goals are viewed through a WHR lens and the MDG3 is understood as a cross-cutting goal, the international focus on implementing the Goals has considerable transformative potential.

Before exploring in more detail what it means to apply a WHR approach to particular Goals, it is important to flag some of the core principles that define non-oppressive transnational advocacy in this field. Mahmoud Fathalla cogently identifies 'three hard lessons' gleaned over more than a decade of advocacy in the reproductive health field, which also serve as basic tenets of any viable WHR project (Fathalla 2005, 136). In addition to the imperative of using a human rights perspective in planning and implementing the Goals, these are that 'the voices of women should be heard and respected [and] solutions from the North should not be imposed on the South' (p. 136). In tandem with these principles of emancipatory cosmopolitan feminist practice, proponents of greater links between human rights and MDG frameworks must continue to contest the conceptual boundaries of mainstream human rights and develop alternative, gender-sensitive understandings, especially around ideas of accountability. This means raising questions about the roles and responsibilities not only of the principal or home states, but also of third-party states, international organizations and non-state actors, in impeding or promoting enjoyment of social and economic rights, and ultimately achievement of the Goals.

The concept of accountability is the most frequently cited benefit of RBA. However, especially in relation to social, economic and development rights, there is little consensus or clarity around what this means in practice. Within the formal/legal human rights system, accountability mechanisms have generally relied on 'naming and shaming' states in response to their active commission of violations of civil and political rights. Arguably, legalistic, confrontational and state-centred modes of accountability are less relevant in efforts to ensure the 'progressive realization' of social, economic and development rights. This is especially so when a state's resources are extremely limited and global economic and trade policies serve to deepen debt and poverty. Hence, any human rights claims or calls for action that arise around failures to meet the Goals must be contextualized vis-à-vis wider, global inequalities.

Addressing the limitations of a state-centric 'name and shame' approach, Lynn Freedman argues that processes of 'constructive accountability' are more appropriate in the context of the MDG initiative, whereby the primary purpose is to build the capacity of governments, communities and civil-society organizations to create conditions under which human rights can be realized for everyone (Freedman et al. 2005). The idea of 'constructive accountability' fits well with feminist methodologies that favour dialogue, participation and partnership. In taking this approach, however, it is vital to avoid the open-endedness and inaction usually associated with the obligation of 'progressive realization' of social and economic rights. One way to counter these limitations is to require governments, on an ongoing basis, to formulate 'concrete, deliberate and targeted' actions, to ensure 'relevant budget allocations', and to prioritize particular interventions as circumstances demand (2005).

This is not to say that formal/legal modes of accountability should not be features of RBA. Indeed, there is growing discussion of the need to develop and apply binding (rather than purely voluntary) human rights accountability mechanisms to the actions of non-state and private actors, such as transnational corporations or private companies that are engaged in the provision of services previously provided by states, including health, education, security and so on (2005). Another key question in rethinking traditional state-centred accountability focuses on the specification of when and how other countries and the international community have a 'legal' duty to act to achieve the Goals in a particular jurisdiction and can be held accountable for failures to do so. For example, Philip Alston argues that the first six goals at least can be considered part of international customary law whereby there is an obligation to act to achieve the Goals on a par with obligations to abolish slavery or stop genocide (Alston 2005). Similarly, in the context of MDG5, for example, human rights advocates should explore how international human rights law can help to define 'the complicity of wealthy countries in the crisis affecting health today . . . and shape a norm of obligation on which claims for action by international actors can be based' (Freedman et al. 2005, 100).

With this context in mind, I turn now to consider specific MDGs from a gender perspective, and discuss the ways in which advocates are applying WHR analyses to the achievement of the Goals. A comprehensive analysis of all the Goals is beyond the scope of this chapter. Instead, to illustrate the main elements of a WHR approach to the MDG process, I focus on two of the goals: to promote gender equality and women's empowerment (MDG3) and to improve maternal health (MDG5).

MDG3: promote gender equality and women's empowerment

The one official target attached to MDG3 (Target 4) centres on the elimination of gender gaps in education. The four indicators chosen to measure progress in achieving Target 4 focus on female-to-male literacy ratios and the proportion of women's participation in formal education, non-agricultural waged employment and national politics. In doing so, in the absence of vigilant women's movements, official accounts of achievement of MDG3 will privilege limited (albeit important) outcomes in the public sphere and avoid scrutiny of obstacles to gender equality in the private sphere. In this regard, the MDG framework lags behind established international standards, which increasingly recognize that events and patterns in the private sphere – including VAW and the discriminatory distribution of household burdens and resources – constitute major obstacles to the achievement of gender equality and WHR. From this perspective, there is a compelling argument to include 'domestic violence' and 'time use', for example, as indicators of progress on MDG3 (Antrobus 2004b). Even within the confines of Target 4, it is not difficult to demonstrate that women and girls who are marginalized, over-burdened with caring responsibilities, or subject to abuse in households and private life have greatly diminished chances, relative to men and boys, of accessing formal education, waged employment and political power. Feminist analyses of the MDG process, therefore, keep a spotlight on the ways in which discriminatory practices in private constitute major obstacles to achieving MDG3 in public. In doing so, they also underline how the transformation of patriarchal power relations and the realization of MDG3 are inseparable processes.

A growing body of international human rights law reflects this understanding of gender relations and has much potential to strengthen the

MDG process. Since the 1990s, gender analyses challenging the structural sources of inequality, the unequal impact of the public–private divide, and the interdependence of all rights are increasingly shaping international 'soft law' (exemplified by the BPA and similar conference outcome documents), as well as evolving legal interpretations issued by human rights treaty-monitoring bodies. These developments are very relevant both to achieving MDG3 and to the gender-sensitive implementation of all the Goals. Since the early 1990s in particular, the committee overseeing implementation of the Women's Convention (CEDAW) has led the way in clarifying the obligations on states to take active steps to eliminate discriminatory gender roles and stereotyping in both private and public life, on the premise that patterns of gender inequality in the two spheres are inextricable.[9] General recommendations formulated by the CEDAW committee elaborate in careful detail how the public–private divide operates to construct, perpetuate and render invisible gender inequalities and discrimination against women, and the steps necessary to counter these patterns. Most notable in this regard are the committee's in-depth analyses and recommendations on temporary special measures (General Recommendation No. 25, 2004), VAW (General Recommendation No. 19, 1992) and equality in marriage and family relations (General Recommendation No. 21, 1994).

The Women's Convention and its monitoring committee's recommendations form a major piece of the WHR framework that can be drawn on to deepen understanding of what is required to achieve gender equality and empowerment across all of the Goals. Moreover, there is obvious scope from a bottom-up, advocacy perspective to link closely NGO activities around CEDAW reviews of states' implementation of the Women's Convention on the one hand, and MDG monitoring on the other. In particular, the actions needed to achieve substantive compliance with the Women's Convention's requirements on equality in political and public life (Article 7), education (Article 10) and employment (Article 11) are the same actions that will register positive gains in official MDG3 indicators in these areas. Moreover, the committee's recommendation on equality in political and public life (General Recommendation No. 21, 1997) is part of an evolving WHR framework that can be used to evaluate progress and flag actions necessary to achieve much-needed increases in the 'proportion of seats held by women in national parliaments' (MDG Indicator 12). Approached in this way, the MDG monitoring process can be more than a superficial accounting exercise and becomes instead a mechanism to highlight real deficiencies and prompt remedial action. At the same time, linking the two processes will also enhance the impact of CEDAW monitoring by tying it to a timely moral consensus around achieving the MDGs.

Importantly, evolving gender-conscious interpretations of other human rights treaties are also relevant to monitoring progress on MDG3 and the other Goals. The recommendation on the 'equal right of men and women to the enjoyment of all economic, social and cultural rights' issued by the UN Committee on Economic, Social and Cultural Rights (CESCR) in 2005, for example, makes clear that ending women's inequality is integral to the substantive implementation of the ICESCR. This puts an onus on states to transform discriminatory practices in both private and public contexts as part of their obligation to ensure the equal enjoyment by men and women of social, economic and cultural rights. The CESCR's interpretation of what states must do to achieve equal rights with regard to the 'protection of the family' (ICESCR Article 10), for example, is especially important given that this provision is often the locus of conservative pressures to limit women's equality. In particular, it builds on the work of CEDAW in recognizing that gender-based violence is a form of discrimination that inhibits the ability to enjoy rights and freedoms, including economic, social and cultural rights, on a basis of equality and calling on States Parties to 'provide victims of domestic violence, who are primarily female, with access to safe housing, remedies and redress for physical, mental and emotional damage' (CESCR 2005). Very significantly, the comment recognizes that the ICESCR creates *immediate obligations* on states to act and, in doing so, reflects a clear departure from the 'progressive realization' mode usually applied to social and economic rights in mainstream human rights discourse. These efforts, which strengthen the effectiveness of economic, social and cultural human rights obligations, are directly relevant to achieving the MDGs. They highlight important ways in which critical human rights thinking and practice can be used not only in efforts to achieve MDG3 but also to insist on sensitivity to WHR in the realization of all MDGs.

MDG5: improve maternal health

The ICPD prompted a well-documented backlash against the further elaboration of rights-based approaches to reproductive and sexual health (Petchesky 2003, Buss 2004). In this context, reproductive health advocates were deeply disappointed but not surprised by the initial narrow framing of the fifth MDG (MDG5)[10] – to 'improve maternal health' – and its targets and indicators (Crossette 2005, Antrobus 2004b). Nevertheless, they also recognized that 'actions to promote sexual and reproductive health and rights will need to play a central role [in the realization of MDG5] – both as a matter of good evidence-based public health policy and as a matter of human rights' (Freedman 2003, 99). For these reasons, since 2000, reproductive health and rights advocates have engaged extensively with the MDG process and used it to highlight once more the imperative of addressing the myriad structural inequalities that are implicated in poor maternal health (Freedman et al. 2005, 36; Germain and Dixon-Mueller 2005; Fathalla 2005). The results of these efforts are most evident in the analyses and recommendations of the Millennium Project Task Force on Maternal Health and Child Health (Freedman et al. 2005). As such, the report captures an important moment in the evolution of an indivisible vision of WHR directed at achieving the Goals and ensuring women's reproductive and sexual health.

The report of the Millennium Project Task Force on Maternal Health and Child Health, among all of the outputs of the Millennium Project, is especially emphatic in its assertion of the pivotal role of a commitment to 'equity and human rights' in the achievement of all of the Goals, particularly those focused on health. This entails recognizing health as an intrinsic good and constituent of human dignity and human capability, as well as a pre-requisite for economic development (Freedman et al. 2005, 19). Moreover, it demands an understanding of the health system as a 'core institution' for reducing poverty and for promoting participative development and democratic practice and a culture of respect for human rights (p. 15). In reality, however, 'abusive, marginalizing or exclusionary treatment by the health system has come to define the experience of being poor' in most countries (p. 11). It follows that MDG5 (and MDG4, which seeks to combat HIV/AIDS and other diseases) cannot be achieved without the transformation of health systems. Documenting and understanding disparities in health status and the utilization of healthcare, along lines of gender, 'race', socio-economic background, geographic location, etc., is a key step towards such a transformation. Very significantly, the task force report insists that 'to effectively move from a research-oriented agenda for meeting the Millennium Development Goals as true development goals, we need human rights' (p. 32). It continues: 'Human rights is ultimately about identifying the workings of power that keep unacceptable situations as they are and then using . . . a growing set of rights-based practices to demand, implement and ensure the rearrangement of power necessary for change' (p. 32). A human rights approach to healthcare, therefore, begins with a recognition of the entitlements of people (as expressed in various international human rights standards) to have 'access to healthcare or to the social and environmental conditions that make good health possible' (p. 34) and, importantly, to be able to claim those rights. Equally, it fore-grounds the obligations and accountability of states, and of health authorities and healthcare providers at every level, to 'respect, protect and fulfill' these entitlements (p. 34). More specifically, a WHR-based approach to achieving MDG5 (and MDG4) means 'paying attention to individual dignity and autonomy; to the right to make decisions free from [public or private] coercion, violence and discrimination; and to broader questions of equal access and social justice' (p. 44). Moreover, it requires that the indica-tors used to measure progress in accessing services 'focus on the user of those health services, their needs . . . and the ability of the health service to meet those needs' (p. 135). From this perspective, current official indica-tors to measure progress on MDG5 (maternal mortality rate and proportion of births attended by skilled professionals) are very deficient. To ensure a user-centred, human rights-based approach, the Task Force recommends adding new indicators to measure progress on MDG5, including the pro-portion of women's personal family planning desires or preferences that are satisfied, the adolescent fertility rate and the prevalence and outcomes of unsafe abortion (p. 136).

The efforts of reproductive and sexual health and rights advocates have had a discernible impact on the MDG process. The idea that 'universal access to reproductive health services, including family planning and sexual health, is required for the achievement of the MDGs', is now accepted by all the relevant UN health and development bodies and is widely reflected in outputs of the Millennium Project (Germain and Dixon-Mueller 2005). Putting this understanding into action, however, requires strong political leadership and concomitant commitments of resources, both of which are in scarce supply in the prevailing climate of backlash. Nonetheless, as one very experienced reproductive health advo-cate put it, 'the genie of human rights is out of the bottle and is not about to go back in' (Corrêa 2005, 11). Moreover, in the context of negotiations at the 2005 World Summit, which convened to review progress on the Goals, this enabled a 'much stronger political platform for social transfor-mation even if it is under fire from conservative political forces' (p. 12).

Complementing this advocacy work, recent gender-conscious interpre-tations of formal/legal human rights standards also have the potential to strengthen the human rights basis of the MDG process. Some of these have particular relevance to tackling obstacles to achieving the health-focused

Goals. Especially notable in this regard is the Human Rights Committee[11] recommendation on achieving 'equality of rights between men and women' in implementing the International Covenant on Civil and Political Rights (ICCPR) (General Recommendation No. 28, 2000). In a significant departure from traditional definitions of civil and political rights, the Committee calls on States Parties 'to put an end to discriminatory actions, both in public and private sectors, which impair equal enjoyment of rights' (Paragraph 4). Towards this end, it requests governments to include in their reports to the committee information on restrictive access to abortion, forced abortion, forced sterilization and female genital mutilation, as well as on rape and domestic violence. Bearing in mind the caveats noted above about the relative usefulness of 'constructive' versus 'confrontational' modes of accountability, this development is most salient where state policies on reproduction involve coercive or prohibitionist practices that inflict great hardship on women and foster highly discriminatory health service provision.

Conclusion

This chapter has explored the contested terrain at the interface of human rights and development from a WHR perspective. I have highlighted historical gaps between the two fields – in terms of underlying concepts, political and ideological influences, institutionalization and practical approaches. The renewed commitment to advancing an integrated vision of universal human rights expressed in the Vienna Declaration and Programme of Action opened up fresh possibilities for transformative links across critical human rights and alternative development advocacy. While the obstacles to real and substantial progress along this road are numerous, discounting the transformative potential of RBA at this juncture is premature. Much more dialogue is needed among development and human rights advocates to explore common goals and to develop common analyses and mutually beneficial strategies.

Scepticism about the legitimacy of human rights discourse and what it can contribute in the struggle for alternative models of development is justified and necessary. Indeed, a critical, action-oriented approach to mainstream human rights thinking and practice is integral to the process of transforming human rights discourse and retaining a focus on its radical promise. Many critics of RBA, however, tend to assume that human rights discourse is monolithic and that it invariably expresses hegemonic interests. In doing so, they overlook and even undercut significant counter-hegemonic efforts by human rights advocates who seek to move social and economic rights from the margins to the centre of human rights concern. Moreover, dismissing the links between bottom-up human rights advocacy and promoting alternative development paradigms concedes too much to regressive forces – locally and globally – that have vigorously contested the strengthening of human rights provisions since the early 1990s, especially as they apply to women.

In this chapter I have underlined some of the recent gains made that are laying a foundation for more effective protection and promotion of social and economic rights in a context of globalization. In large part, these are being driven by sustained TFA to carry forward global commitments to WHR, especially those agreed at Vienna, Cairo and Beijing. As illustrated by this chapter, leaders in the transnational movement for reproductive and sexual health rights are playing a pivotal role in linking WHR and GAD advocacy in the context of the Millennium Development Project. This is most evident in efforts to integrate human rights principles and practice into MDG monitoring processes, most particularly in relation to gender equality and WHR as cross-cutting norms. At the same time, there has been a steady accretion of quasi-legal developments from within the human rights machinery – most notably in the form of recommendations issued by human rights treaty monitoring bodies. These are providing an increasingly firm 'legal' basis and new tools to bolster advocates' efforts to transform the idea of indivisible and interrelated human rights into substantive outcomes.

Nonetheless, active proponents of the indivisibility of human rights are still a minority in the human rights world and many more progressive human rights advocates must prioritize economic and social rights to bring about a real paradigmatic shift, wherein political and civil rights are no longer seen as the only 'real' human rights. This agenda will not be advanced without external, broad-based pressure to do so. Moreover, the gender sensitivity of this shift depends upon the active participation of both WHR and GAD advocates in incorporating bottom-up, critical human rights practice in development agendas and pressing for recognition of the interrelation of all rights in other spheres of human rights activity.

7

Fundamentalisms and Women's Human Rights

Introduction

In tandem with the emergence of a traditional movement for women's human rights (WHR), the past three decades have also seen the proliferation of fundamentalist political projects that actively resist and obstruct the promotion of women's equality and rights. The story of transnational advocacy for WHR, therefore, is incomplete without a discussion of the nature and methods of fundamentalist projects in local and global contexts. This is especially important given the role of fundamentalist forces in leading the backlash against implementation of WHR commitments, particularly those agreed at the International Conference on Population and Development (ICPD) (Cairo, 1994) and the Fourth World Conference on Women (FWCW) (Beijing, 1995). In taking a critical stance on all forms of fundamentalism as political projects, however, I do not dispute the positive role that religious belief and practice can play in people's lives and communities. Rather, my concern is to highlight the gender-specific implications of fundamentalist projects that use the political and legal infrastructure of states and, more recently, the United Nations to promote particular understandings of religious beliefs and practices in public and private domains and to bring (global) public policy in line with particular religious values regardless of the beliefs of the people affected. I especially want to foreground the responses of women's movements to such projects in local and global contexts where fundamentalist projects have become influential and, in doing so, identify core tenets of anti-fundamentalist feminist praxis.

The term 'fundamentalism' is problematic. It was first used as an affirmative self-designation by protestant groups in the United States of the late nineteenth century (Freedman 1996). Today it is used mainly in the West to signify irrational and violent forces in Islam. Particularly evident in a pervasive 'moral panic' in the West that reduces the question of women's human rights and religion to one that applies only to Islam, this worldview casts Islam as inevitably at odds with 'Western values'. In Feminist scholars have noted how, especially in the context of Europe, the 'veiled Muslim woman' is invoked instrumentally as confirmation of the incompatibility of 'backward/fundamentalist Muslims' and 'progressive/secular Europeans' (Scott 2007). This ignores how Christian religions are intertwined with the state to varying degrees in most European countries (Klausen 2005) with consequences for WHR on a variety of levels. At the same time, growing research (especially by Muslim and non-Western scholars) continues to problematize the negative impact on women of rising religious traditionalism globally and the instrumental use of religion/culture to discredit promotion of gender equality and WHR in 'non-Western' contexts (Shaheed 1989, 1995, 2001, 2008; Othman 2006; Narayan 2000; Hom 1992). These developments pose complex challenges for conceptualizing and operationalizing WHR in multicultural and cross-cultural contexts – where recognition of women's differences, and respect for cultural diversity and religious freedoms, are also central concerns.

This chapter is primarily concerned with exploring the particular challenges to the promotion of women's human rights posed by 'fundamentalist' forces, which operate in all religious traditions and cultural contexts. From this perspective, it is important to continue naming and challenging the phenomenon of fundamentalism in its changing forms. In doing so, however, the term 'fundamentalism' must be used critically and be consciously unlinked from the many false binaries that constitute the West's view of Islam, and the global South more generally, as 'backward' and ungovernable, and, therefore, legitimate targets for the imposition of 'civilizing' Western agendas (Said 1978). Using the plural term 'fundamentalisms' contests this worldview and signals recognition of the heterogeneity of fundamentalist projects, which exist across all religions and regions. In recent decades, however, fundamentalist Christian and Islamist movements have had the most dramatic and extensive impact in women's lives.

The United States, in particular, has seen major growth in the political influence of the Christian fundamentalist lobby since the Reagan era. This is reflected most strikingly in the 'gag rule' – recently rescinded by US president Barack Obama – which had prohibited primary and family-planning healthcare programmes in countries that receive US federal aid from providing information and counselling on abortion services, even if this work was funded from a separate financial source.[1] Similarly, fundamentalist Christian agendas have disproportionally shaped US international policy on HIV/AIDS prevention, which in recent years promoted abstinence from sexual activity rather than condom use as its primary strategy (Susskind 2005). This has catastrophic implications, especially where power differentials make it impossible for many women and girls to enforce 'abstinence', even if this was their preference. Within the USA, despite a modest global trend in favour of easing restrictions on access to abortion services, new laws disproportionately affecting poor and young women have been introduced to restrict access to abortion (CRLP 2005, 6). Catholic influence on national law and policy is also reasserting itself in some countries, especially in Latin America. Recently, for example, El Salvador and Nicaragua joined Chile by introducing total bans on abortion regardless of risks to the life of the woman or whether the pregnancy is a result of a crime.[2] I will return to these trends again in the context of global efforts to secure recognition of reproductive and sexual rights. For the moment, I note these examples of the growing influence of Christian fundamentalism to underline the heterogeneity of fundamentalisms and caution against equating fundamentalism with Islam, as is often the case in mainstream discourses on the topic.

While much anti-fundamentalist feminist advocacy has a significant transnational dimension, it is important to note that the bulk of efforts by women's movements to counter fundamentalist forces originate in and/or are led by women who are living in situations directly affected by fundamentalist forces. Indeed, since the 1970s, well before Huntington's idea of the 'clash of civilisations' (1993) was popularized in the aftermath of the September 11 attacks, women's movements around the world have been at the forefront of efforts to defend precarious rights commitments and emerging democracies against burgeoning fundamentalist forces. In doing so, anti-fundamentalist feminist praxis necessarily engages with two key areas of contestation in mainstream human rights discourse. The first is the tension between universal rights claims and respect for cultural specificity and the need to articulate the conditions under which women's rights and gender equality are upheld or not within this nexus. The second concerns the particular challenges involved in simultaneously deepening gender and other critiques of mainstream human rights, democracy and the 'rule of law', while also using them to contest fundamentalist forces. Ultimately, I argue that the responses of women's movements to fundamentalist forces discussed in this chapter demonstrate the imperative of retaining a commitment to the universality of human rights, democracy and the rule of law – albeit as contested categories – from bottom-up, transformative, feminist standpoints.

To contextualize this discussion, it is important to note the common methodologies and transnational links of the feminist advocates and researchers whose work and analyses I draw on in this chapter. Most significantly, all have ongoing associations through the international solidarity network Women Living under Muslim Laws (WLUML).[3] A primary objective of the WLUML network is to expose the myth of a single, homogeneous Muslim world. This is achieved primarily by documenting and disseminating gender-specific information and analyses on the wide variation in interpretation and practice of Muslim laws affecting women across different contexts. In doing so, WLUML demonstrates that religious dictates are not timeless truths but, like all cultural practices, expressions of particular historical and social conditions and power relationships. The knowledge gained and exchanged through this comparative approach enables women to question the use and misuse of religion and religious arguments to discriminate against and limit the freedoms of women relative to men in the same communities. Moreover, it draws attention to the common features of all fundamentalist movements as anti-democratic political projects seeking to control public and private life, wherein the subordination of women is a pivotal strategy and goal.

Through its work, WLUML is committed to generating situational analyses rather than 'one size fits all' solutions to the complex issues it addresses. At the same time, however, the vast documentation and commentary generated under the auspices of WLUML since the mid 1980s reveal an unambiguous commitment to defending WHR across all regions and cultural traditions, albeit from a contextualized standpoint that is highly critical of mainstream human rights discourse. Anti-fundamentalist feminist initiatives, exemplified by the work of WLUML members, therefore, have at least two dimensions. On one level, they directly challenge fundamentalist projects because of their treatment of women. At the same time, they are constitutive players in wider struggles to advance critically interpreted human rights, democracy and the rule of law. Here, I consider the links between both dimensions of anti-fundamentalist feminist advocacy. In doing, so I highlight the gendered impacts of fundamentalist forces in specific contexts and the responses of locally situated feminist critics and activists in challenging them.

The next section begins by highlighting important commonalities – origins, key features and methods – in the rise of fundamentalist projects. This is followed by a discussion of the damaging interplay of cultural relativist arguments coming from both the traditional Western 'left' and the fundamentalist 'right' – especially regarding contemporary responses to 'the Muslim headscarf' in the West. The remaining sections illustrate how the wider debates informing this chapter have played out in particular national contexts as well as at the transnational level. Specifically, I draw on examples from Bangladesh, Malaysia and Nigeria, which have seen a rise in the political influence of fundamentalists from the 1970s, 1980s and late 1990s, respectively. In this context, I also consider feminist quandaries about the limits and advantages of negotiating within fundamentalist structures and logic. Finally, I return to the global policy arena to consider the operation of fundamentalist forces in UN forums since the mid 1990s and the implications of these developments for advancing WHR agendas in the early twenty-first century.

Fundamentalist projects: origins, features and methods

The specific forms that fundamentalism takes vary from context to context; however, it is possible to make some general points about the roots, key features and methods used. In particular, as already noted, it must be emphasized that fundamentalist projects are not about religion per se. Rather, they are deeply political projects that mobilize around religious, ethnic and/or nationalist visions and identities in the pursuit of wider power and influence (Shaheed 2001, Yuval-Davis 1997). Fundamentalist movements tend to emerge in situations of rapid social change. Around the world, processes of decolonization, national independence, modernization and globalization have generated a 'bewildering pace of change' and a need to construct new histories and (re)create identities and ways of belonging at the individual, community and national level (Shaheed 1989, 4). In the global South, most fundamentalist initiatives have roots in a legacy of Western 'colonisation and hegemonic rule and control' (Shaheed 2001, 3). After the initial optimism prompted by decolonization processes in the 1950s and 1960s, disillusionment set in as it became clear that none of the available paradigms – nationalism, capitalism or communism – could meet most people's material, social and spiritual needs (Imam and Yuval-Davis 2004).

Another period of positive expectations at the end of the Cold War also gave way to scepticism as the hegemony of neo-liberal globalization produced widening global inequalities and the events of September 11, 2001, were used to justify a reassertion of unilateral global politics and many examples of a flagrant disregard for human rights in the name of the 'war on terror'. Disenchantment has been reinforced at the local level as many governments failed in their obligations to meet the most basic human rights of their populations, including adequate food, water, shelter, healthcare and education (2004). Furthermore, the corruption and repressive practices of many governments also eroded people's belief in the 'modernization' project (2004). Under such conditions, fundamentalist leaders often appear to offer meaningful alternatives. Moreover, as noted earlier, the spread of fundamentalisms is not limited to the global South or to minority communities in the 'developed' world. Christian fundamentalist movements in the USA and other ultra-right nationalist movements throughout the West are also symptomatic of the 'need for defensive identity communities' in the face of globalization and rapid social change (2004).

Fundamentalist projects generally share the following defining features: (1) they are an expression of identity politics where religion is a primary locus of identity; (2) unequal gender relations and the control of women are core agendas; and (3) they seek to use the law and state institutions to achieve their ends. Regarding the first point, in situations where religious practices are already integral to everyday life, fundamentalist leaders, mobilizing around ethno-religious identity, are well positioned to gain a political foothold. In the context of internal power struggles in postcolonial situations, Shaheed explains the dynamic as follows: 'Religion provides a useful vehicle through which the losers can express their alienation and antagonism vis-à-vis the ruling elites, who in ex-colonial states are condemned not for being exploiters but for *being Westernized*. Alternatively, religion can be the vehicle adopted by an emerging class that, having gained economic status, is making a bid for political power' (Shaheed 1989) (my emphasis). In these processes, fundamentalist leaders claim the monopoly on the authentic and definitive version of collective identity and set about imposing this vision on the wider community, often extending beyond the immediate constituency they claim to represent (Imam and Yuval-Davis 2004). Ironically, while promoting a vision of fixed and timeless cultural values and identities, the actions of fundamentalist leaders exemplify the fluidity of culture as they purposively seek to introduce new and often alien practices in the name of reviving a community's supposedly lost traditions. In the context of Malaysia, for example, Othman notes that 'the imposition and importation of Islamic fundamentalist ideology and practices is also coterminous with the delegitimation of Malay . . . traditions . . . [that are being] gradually replaced by . . . politicised versions of an Arabised Islamic identity' (Othman 2006, 343).

Further, as the above quote from Shaheed suggests, fundamentalists in the global South often present their worldview as an antidote to all that is problematic with modernity and Western hegemony. However, in reality, 'they are far from being pre-modern' and make astute use of the modern state, new media and advanced technologies (including military technologies) to promote their project (Imam and Yuval-Davis 2004). Importantly, problematizing the imposition of monolithic cultural identities in this way does not in any way undermine the validity of self-ascribed cultural/group identity or the human rights claims of groups that are subject to discrimination and abuse on the basis of that identity. Rather, it highlights the imperative of viewing all cultures as complex and changing. As such, they must be seen as sites of *internal* contestation and struggle and not solely loci of resistance vis-à-vis oppressive *external* hegemonic forces.

The second defining feature of fundamentalist projects is their focus on gender relations and the control of women. Whether they invoke traditionalist Muslim, Christian, Jewish or Hindu precepts, the collective identity and vision of the 'good life' envisaged by fundamentalist leaders inevitably demands a subordinate role for women in relation to men. In particular, religious fundamentalisms entail an explicit preoccupation with controlling sexuality – especially women's sexuality, which is constructed as dangerous and the root of social chaos and disorder. As Norani Othman notes, fundamentalist movements target 'first and foremost women – women's rights and status in the family and society – and woman's body' (2006, 341). Fundamentalisms that mobilize around a confluence of religion and ethnicity doubly construct women as the principal bearers of culture and locus of collective identity. The detrimental impact on women of this symbolic logic is demonstrated most graphically when women's bodies literally become the battleground in ethnic conflicts. Under such conditions, sexual violence and forced pregnancy are used as strategies of military conquest or genocide, for example, in conflicts in the Former Yugoslavia, Rwanda or, more recently, in Darfur.

Using the law to bolster gender inequalities and undermine democratic freedoms is the third defining feature of fundamentalist forces. Feminist observers of rising fundamentalisms over more than twenty years have identified several warning signs of their growing grip in any society.[4] These include:

- changes in family laws that diminish women's rights in relation to marriage, divorce and child custody;
- imposition of new laws, dress codes and gender segregation requirements designed to control women's sexuality, reproduction and freedom of movement;
- new limits on progressive media; and
- restrictions on freedom of association, especially in relation to the activities of women's and human rights organizations.

Where Muslim fundamentalist forces gain power, Muslim or Sharia laws are introduced or strengthened and policed by state and/or non-state actors with differing levels of intensity. Over the past three decades, this trend has been evident in a wide range of countries – some formerly secular and/or democratizing states – including Afghanistan, Algeria, Bangladesh, Chechnya, Egypt, Iran, Iraq, Malaysia, Nigeria, Pakistan and Sudan. Legislative 'reform' is another mechanism used to spread fundamentalist ideologies across countries/regions. In South Africa and Mauritius, for example, 'advisers' from other Muslim states were brought in to help draft new laws to regulate the Muslim community in ways that are detrimental to women's rights (WLUML 1997, 10). Within a normative framework of Western multiculturalism, there has also been growing pressure from minority Islamist communities in the United Kingdom and other Western democracies to accommodate customary and religious practices that potentially open the door to parallel legal systems that erode women's equality and human rights more generally. In addition, as noted earlier, the Christian fundamentalist movement in the USA has expended enormous resources lobbying for increasingly restricted access to abortion. For example, a proposed 'Teen Endangerment Act', if passed, could jeopardize the safety of girls and young women by requiring parental notification and criminalizing friends and other relatives who attempt to assist a young woman to obtain an abortion (CRR 2006).

In addition to using mainstream and parallel legal systems (as well as international flows of money and arms), fundamentalist projects every-where use a variety of more subtle methods to strengthen their position. In particular, many actively seek to meet the social needs created by the absence of state services in order to gain support among increasingly marginalized sections of the population whose governments must conform to austerity measures imposed by international financial institutions (WLUML 1997, 10). Significantly, fundamentalist movements often cultivate women supporters (p. 10). As a result, it is important to be clear about the line between feminist advocates (including those who work within a religion) and fundamentalist women (who often describe themselves as supporters of women's rights). While both groups of women are 'activists', the dividing line is in the endorsement or rejection of gender inequality and support for governance based exclusively on religious principles rather than human rights and equality. Moreover, because many fundamentalist leaders are skilled in the use of a human rights discourse to express their claims, it is especially important to look closely at who their partners are on the ground in order to assess their credibility in terms of a basic commitment to democratic governance and to women's equality and human rights.

Cultural relativism and fundamentalist politics

The nexus of relativist multiculturalism and fundamentalist politics creates particular challenges for proponents of WHR, especially in the context of the 'war on terror'. Fundamentalist politics feeds on the relativist logic explored earlier in this book. It construes human rights solely as a Western-defined paradigm that promotes atomistic individualism and undermines non-Western cultures and values – not least by lending support to feminism. At the same time, Western multicultural politics of the 'left' also endorses forms of cultural relativism. This confluence of rising fundamentalisms, crude hegemonic Western responses that demonize Muslim cultures, and counter-hegemonic multiculturalism can be inimical to promoting and protecting WHR.

The US–UK-defined 'war on terror' paradigm is infused with gendered and racialized perceptions prevalent in the West, which equate Islam with fundamentalism and 'terrorism'. This makes Muslim and other minorities more vulnerable to intolerance, discrimination and state-sponsored abuses of human rights, especially in the West (Fekete 2004). In addition to affecting women as members of targeted minority communities, these trends have wider gender-specific implications. For example, minority women are generally the ones who engage directly with the mainstream population on a daily basis (for example, around accessing housing, education, healthcare and other services) and, therefore, bear the brunt of discrimination against their wider community. Further, in situations of heightened tension between minority and majority communities, minority women who are experiencing abuse within the family or community are extremely unlikely to seek assistance if they fear they will be stigmatized for betraying the community and/or that they or their abuser will be subject to maltreatment by the authorities.

Against this backdrop, multiculturalist positions, ostensibly aiming to redress harms caused by imperialism and contemporary forms of racism and xenophobia, must be carefully scrutinized. Gita Saghal, for example, has critiqued multiculturalist British policy, which initially allowed many social policies to be determined by conservative male community leaders. In response to secular Asian feminist pressure to address crimes against women in these contexts (especially forced marriage), British politicians and policy-makers, still operating within a particular multicultural frame, looked for religious arguments (Hindu, Sikh, Muslim) to justify legal and policy interventions against forced marriage. In doing so, however, Saghal argues they 'resorted to developing support amongst the very people [they] wanted to criticise, and thereby helped increase their hold over "their" communities' (Saghal 2004, 58).

Another example is found in the renewed preoccupation in Western societies with the issue of Muslim women wearing headscarves or not, and the ways in which some leaders on 'the left' are keen to be seen supporting Muslim women's freedom to wear different forms of veiling. Blatantly intolerant and xenophobic responses from the extreme right are the easiest to rebut in human rights terms. Responses from the progressive left of the political spectrum to the current moral panic around 'the Muslim headscarf' can also be problematic, albeit in other ways. Western proponents of the right of Muslim women to wear a form of head covering generally operate within liberal logic that uncritically presumes the act of wearing a headscarf to be a voluntary expression of a woman's personal identity. Alternatively, they espouse a communitarian logic that treats the issue as an organic expression of cultural or religious collective identity. In the first case, the universe of culture is treated as a special category of the private sphere – except the usual liberal alarm bells about the possibility of harms caused to individuals by the exercise of arbitrary power fail to be raised. In the second case, the culture of 'others' is constructed as timeless and immutable, usually at the expense of women's agency, in ways that, arguably, are 'naïve and ultimately . . . racist' (Winter 2006, 386).

This is a complex terrain, so each 'Muslim headscarf' situation needs to be considered separately in context. However, some general points apply. First, prohibitionist responses to different forms of head or body covering are clearly at odds with the human rights principle of freedom of expression (including, but not necessarily, religious expression). As Norani Othman notes: '[W]hether there exists a ruling to force women to cover or to prevent them from donning a head covering . . . the impact on their human rights is still the same in that it takes away the right . . . of a Muslim woman to choose for herself' (2006, 342). The second point implicit in Othman's statement, however, is that progressives who defend women's freedom to cover their heads or bodies must also contest coerced 'veiling' and seek to articulate the conditions of respect for human rights under which the choice to wear various forms of head and body covering or not is indeed 'free'. As one WLUML advocate notes: 'When Muslim women in the West raise their voices in support of the hijab and proclaim their right to wear it, they must also acknowledge the reality of the oppression faced by those Muslim women who refuse to wear it' (Zakaria 2006). While wearing a veil can be a benign choice and/or a positive signifier of identity vis-à-vis a dominant or hegemonic culture, frequently the actual choice that women face is between wearing some form of veiling, being confined to their homes, and/or risking social censure, harassment or violence at the hands of extremists inside or outside of their families. This experience is cogently captured by the author of the Riverbend blog,[5] which documents life in war-torn Iraq from a young feminist's perspective, including the impact of new forms of fundamentalism:

> Females can no longer leave their homes alone. Each time I go out, [my brother] and either a father, uncle or cousin has to accompany me. It feels like we've gone back 50 years. . . . A woman, or girl, out alone, risks anything from insults to abduction. . . . [B]efore the war, I would estimate (roughly) that about 55% of females in Baghdad wore a hijab or headscarf. IIijabs do not signify fundamentalism. That is far from the case – although I, myself, don't wear one, I have family and friends who do. The point is that, before, it didn't really matter. It was my business whether I wore one or not – not the business of some fundamentalist on the street. (Riverbend 2003)

By side-stepping the coercive conditions that often mediate gendered religious practices such as wearing Muslim headscarves, and by failing to comprehend the nuanced perspectives of feminist Muslim voices in relation to this and similar issues, Western cultural relativist positions effectively undermine women's counter-fundamentalist initiatives in contexts where fundamentalist politics are gaining ground. Cultural relativist arguments from global South perspectives draw on a similar gendered logic. They rely on a false dichotomy that permits only two possibilities: the defence of authentic local culture or the neo-imperialist imposition of Western values and agendas. Within this logic, which is at the heart of contemporary Islamic fundamentalist projects, internal dissent is not simply absent but impossible as critical voices are instantly dismissed as 'Westernized' betrayers of Islam and local culture (Mukhtar 2003; Shaheed 1989, 2). This disingenuous position denies the agency and 'belonging' of locally situated dissenting political actors who both (1) articulate human rights claims in their own contexts *and* (2) firmly reject the imposition and false universalization of human rights values from various dominant standpoints, internally and externally. The following section explores examples of women's movements that embody this dual perspective in the effort to resist fundamentalist projects. In doing so, they foreground the similar origins and strategies of fundamentalist movements in different locations. Equally, they highlight common ground between local anti-fundamentalist feminist movements and wider, transnational feminist struggles to re-envision human rights, democracy and the rule of law.

Feminist resistance to fundamentalisms

In this section I draw on three contexts where Muslim fundamentalist forces have become central to national politics in recent decades. These are Bangladesh, Malaysia and Nigeria, all of which have seen a rise in the political influence of fundamentalists from the 1970s, 1980s and late 1990s, respectively. In each case, fundamentalist leaders have sought to use the state to impose their version of Islam and morality on as wide a population as possible. Women pay an especially high price in these processes, which challenge the basic principles of democracy and the rule of law, including recognition of equality regardless of gender, race, religion and so on; the separation of church and state; and freedom of association and expression. Countering the rise in fundamentalist forces, however, significant feminist movements have also emerged in each case. These provide a window on feminist modes of resistance to fundamentalisms and how they relate to international human rights discourse and TFA.

In Bangladesh, fundamentalist forces initially gained a political foothold under conditions of weak democracy. While an explicit commitment to secularism in the 1972 Bangladesh Constitution posed an obstacle at first, the entry of fundamentalists into political life was ultimately enabled by 'a history of military dictatorships and fragile democracies' (Amin and Hossein 1994–5, 1338). In particular, successive military governments played 'the religious card' to win popular support (p. 1339) and introduced a series of constitutional amendments that effectively brought about the Islamization of the constitution (p. 1348). Significantly, however, despite these gains at the constitutional level, fundamentalist ambitions for wider influence were curtailed by counterforces, including development NGOs whose activities in rural areas revolved around women's empowerment (Amin and Hossein 1994–5, 1339; Guhathakurta 2003).

Indeed, the growing visibility of women in community development and employment, and new assertions of women's reproductive rights following the ICPD (Cairo, 1994), prompted fundamentalist leaders to target single women who were deemed to have violated social and moral norms. Exploiting fears of social change and disorder, they began to use traditional courts (*shalish*) to issue *fatwa* accusing women of 'adultery' and sentencing them to stoning, caning or burning (Amin and Hossein 1994–5, 1340). It is important to note that these developments were not a revival of traditional practices but a new departure. By trying and convicting women for acts that are not criminal offences under Bangladeshi law and by imposing punishments not sanctioned by the state, the 'shalish authorities . . . stepped far beyond their traditional bounds' of mediating family or land disputes and responding to petty crime (p. 1340). It is also significant that after an initial focus on repressing women's sexual and reproductive autonomy, fundamentalist attacks shifted to the staff and beneficiaries of development and healthcare projects and secular schools attended by large numbers of girls. These developments demonstrate how fundamentalist rhetoric around defending cultural and religious integrity serves to justify aggressive attacks on women, erode respect for principles of the freedom and equality of individuals and their right to fair and equal treatment under the law, and obstruct the development of civil-society participation and other manifestations of bottom-up democratization.

Norani Othman similarly highlights how women are the main losers in the ongoing wave of Islamization in Southeast Asia. While Sharia law has been a feature of most Muslim societies, she notes that recent decades have seen the introduction of 'more and more Muslim laws that are retrogressive for women' (Othman 2006). In Malaysia, the process began in the 1980s when the National Front coalition government led by Mahathir Mohamad endeavoured to win the support of the majority Muslim population and keep the more radical Islamist party, the Pan-Malaysian Islamic Party (PAS), out of power. A process of systematic administrative and legal reform ensued, which put over 100 Islamic scholars at the centre of federal policy-making mechanisms. At the same time, the Sharia judicial and legal system was strengthened and extended to the detriment of women (p. 344). In particular, 'polygamy and divorce have been made easier for men' and, increasingly, women who have been 'divorced, abandoned, beaten up or neglected by their husbands . . . complain of injustice and discrimination in their search for redress through Malaysian Sar'iah courts' (p. 344). In response, Othman argues, feminism in Malaysia must be a two-tiered struggle against gender discrimination and oppression emanating firstly from 'secular patriarchy' and, secondly, from more recent manifestations of 'Muslim patriarchy' (p. 347).

Importantly, Othman argues that the women's movement in Malaysia must directly address the impact of fundamentalist politics on the integrity of constitutionalism and respect for human rights and democracy. When fundamentalist forces permeate state power, breaches of religious or moral ethics, as determined by local religious leaders, are treated as 'criminal behaviour', while state-sponsored or self-appointed vigilantes use violence to enforce the new codes of behaviour (Othman 2006, 346; Imam 2003). For Othman, a more participatory democracy is vital to contesting this slide into the arbitrary exercise of power which has been so detrimental to women. She notes that in Malaysia a 'pernicious state of silence' – flowing from the fear of being labelled anti-Islamic – has prevented politicians and the general population from challenging fundamentalist politics and has created a political environment characterized by the absence of open discussion, debate and participatory decision-making. This confluence of identity politics and the erosion of constitutionalism enabled the retrogressive Shariah Criminal Offences Act to be adopted by fourteen states without any protest or discussion – not because people were in favour of the Act but because they were afraid to speak out against it (Othman 2006, 346). Reflecting a feminist reading of An Na'im's cultural legitimacy thesis (CLT), Othman urges Muslim women to reflect critically on the role of 'Islamic knowledge' in 'reclaiming the space for substantive democracy and justice' and to find a 'language of protest and resistance to religious and state authoritarianism' (p. 347). Moreover, she stresses, the extent to which 'internal debate among Muslims can help to . . . re-constitute women's rights and gender equality in Islam *depends on the democratic space* . . . that exists in Muslim societies' (p. 352) (my emphasis).

Ayesha Imam's account of Islamization in Nigeria from 1999 onward reveals a similar pattern. Widespread disillusionment caused by the failure of 'independence and the nationalist promises', corruption in politics and the judiciary, and 'poverty and social problems exacerbated by the World Bank structural adjustment programs' (Imam 2003, 22–3) prompted a turn to identity politics. This created new openings for the religious right to influence disproportionately the tone and direction of the civil political culture. State governors, mainly in Muslim majority states, fearful of appearing 'anti-Sharia', moved quickly to extend the reach of Sharia law beyond its traditional confines of marriage and family life to criminal justice. This precipitated a proliferation of cases of women sentenced to death by stoning for 'adultery' by local Sharia courts, with the case of Amina Lawal being the best known internationally. Imam's organization BAOBAB for Women's Human Rights played a lead role, taking successive appeals through Sharia courts on behalf of Lawal, culminating in 2003 in Lawal's conviction being overthrown by the Katsina State Sharia Court of Appeal.

Also employing a version of the CLT, Imam defends BAOBAB's legal strategy of working *within* the Sharia system as part of a process of internal critique: 'If we only criticize from the outside, it doesn't do anything for the victim of the charge. If we go to court and win an appeal, it demonstrates that the victim should never have been charged . . . We must establish that even when abuses are perpetrated in the name of Islam, they can and must be challenged' (Imam 2003, 23). Other critics of Islamization in Nigeria, however, highlight the dangers of this approach. They argue that battles won within the Sharia courts to date have had little impact beyond the individual cases and have not helped the 'vast majority of women who still live under imminent threat of the Sharia legal system' (Ewelukwa 2003, 25). Echoing Othman's argument, such critics urge instead the pursuit of legal cases that explicitly challenge the constitutionality of aspects of Sharia penal legislation in order to establish precedents with wider applications (p. 25). In addition, they underline the imperative of proactively reasserting universal human rights principles that are 'absent in Sharia', especially that of 'equality between men and women and between Muslims and non-Muslims' (Mukhtar 2003, 26). Mahnaz Afkhami makes a related point when she questions the possibility of combining Islamic and feminist principles: 'I call myself a Muslim and feminist. I not an Islamic feminist – that's a contradiction in terms' (Moghadam 2002, 1152). Similarly, regarding Iran, Valentine Moghadam notes that: 'Any reform movement . . . that takes for granted the legitimacy and permanence of an Islamic state and of Qur'anic edicts is at best a very limited project and at worst a way of legitimizing the Islamic legal, political, and moral framework (p. 1151).

These criticisms express very valid concerns and highlight strategies that are vital to pursue. However, in taking these critiques on-board it is important not to overstate the either/or choice vis-à-vis working inside/outside Islam and the Sharia system. Doing so potentially misses a compelling aspect of Imam's argument: the critical importance of paying attention to process and 'doing human rights' in ways that are sensitive to local contexts, while also maintaining a commitment to the realization of universal human rights. BAOBAB – a frontline legal literacy and support organization and part of the international network WLUML – coordinates a wide range of activities and campaigns with local groups to make people aware of 'women's rights whether in Muslim, secular or customary laws or in international human rights conventions' (Imam 2003, 23). As such, the work of BAOBAB illustrates a bottom-up, critical and ultimately transformative approach to human rights. Imam explains that the organization does not simply focus on 'legal texts, but on ways in which people can actualize rights acknowledged in them' (pp. 23–4). Further, she argues: 'If people don't recognize rights at an everyday level, then international rights treaties and covenants are dead letters. People must say, "that's our right and we are going to do something to get it"' (p. 23). In this process, Imam acknowledges that international campaigns are often very helpful to local causes but cautions against the potential of external influence to produce a backlash that could inhibit local ownership of human rights values. She also highlights the fact that international human rights law is deficient in many ways and that the development of rights discourses from the global to the local is always a work in progress. This critical approach to human rights should not be construed as a relativist stance. Imam notes that Muslims have helped to craft contemporary human rights thinking and insists on 'being able to reclaim and contribute to international human rights discourse rather than allowing it to be seen as only western' (p. 23). Hence, the end goal is not to bolster relativist readings of human rights but to foster 'true universalization', which Imam believes calls for 'all organisations and activists . . . [to] work together, respecting diversity, while developing solidarity and common understanding of principles, and not just assuming it' (p. 24).

The following section turns to the global arena where international human rights standards are ultimately negotiated and agreed (or not). In particular, it highlights how fundamentalist forces have moved into the global policy arenas since the ICPD and FWCW, and the major challenges they pose to safeguarding WHR around the world – in principle and in practice.

Fundamentalist agendas at the United Nations

In the global arena, the norm-setting UN conferences of the 1990s and their follow-up meetings became prime targets of highly coordinated fundamentalist campaigns seeking to roll back or prevent the further development of WHR agendas, most particularly in the realm of reproductive and sexual rights and recognition of non-traditional family formations. The unprecedented alliance of the Vatican, the US Christian right,[6] and sympathetic states (Egypt, Iran, Pakistan, Libya, Sudan and others) against WHR agendas in UN forums has been well documented and analysed by academics and activists alike (Buss 2004, Petchesky 2003, Druelle 2000, Nankani n.d., Stephenson 2005). This coordinated backlash began to gather momentum after the Vatican and US Christian fundamentalist leaders became aware of the magnitude of the global movement for WHR and its impact at the World Conference on Human Rights (Vienna, 1993) and preparatory meetings for the ICPD and the FWCW. In Cairo, the Vatican vigorously – but, ultimately unsuccessfully – opposed applying a human rights framework to reproductive health, seeing it as a step towards a global right to abortion (Buss 2004, 63). Similarly, in Beijing, fundamentalist alliances resisted further elaboration of commitments to reproductive rights and the introduction of text prohibiting discrimination on the grounds of sexual orientation (Bunch and Fried 1996).

After Beijing, the scope of the fundamentalist agenda widened to oppose an array of measures that threatened 'traditional' patriarchal and heteronormative social structures (Petchesky 2003, 37). Hence, at the five-year UN meetings to review implementation of the Cairo and Beijing programmes of action, and at the Children's Summit (2002) (the UN General Assembly Special Session (UNGASS) on Children), fundamentalist actors united across religions, countries and regions to oppose language that explicitly or implicitly appeared to endorse: (1) access to legal abortion; (2) reproductive or sexual autonomy on the part of women and/or young people, including in regard to protection against HIV/AIDS; (3) family formations other than the male-headed, heterosexual, nuclear family; and (4) the extension of concepts of reproductive and sexual health to adolescents or to gay and lesbian people (Petchesky 2003). As highlighted earlier, the UN ten-year progress reviews on implementation of Cairo and Beijing commitments saw the rehearsal of similar battles. Post-September 11, the global climate was increasingly characterized by US unilateralism and a disregard for international norms. The zealousness of the Bush administration exemplified in the 'gag rule' and the USA's persistent opposition to 'new rights', and to reproductive and sexual rights in particular, ensured that these events did little to strengthen the political will of world governments to implement global commitments to gender equality and human rights.

The confluence of fundamentalist forces in contesting sexual rights was also evident at meetings of the UN Commission on Human Rights (UNCHR) in 2003 and 2004 when a resolution on sexual orientation was debated. Introduced by Brazil in 2003 (supported by the EU, Canada and Australia), the resolution called on governments to recognize sexual-orientation-based discrimination as a violation of human rights and to take actions to eliminate it. The resolution was strenuously opposed by the Vatican and the Organisation of the Islamic Conference (OIC)[7] countries, particularly Pakistan, Malaysia, Saudi Arabia and Bahrain, as well as by Zimbabwe and others, and further discussion was deferred to 2004. In 2004, however, Brazil did not resubmit the resolution for debate due to intense pressure from the OIC, the Vatican and the US Christian right

(Obando 2004). In addition to bitter debates on reproductive and sexual rights, the global consensus that violence against women (VAW) is a violation of human rights was also called into question at a session of the UN Commission on the Status of Women (CSW) in 2003. At that meeting, Iran and Egypt objected to a call on governments to 'refrain from invoking any custom, tradition, or religious consideration to avoid their [human rights] obligations' to eliminate VAW (Merry 2006, 26).

These examples of the backlash against WHR, following the successes of Vienna, Cairo and Beijing, reveal much about the complex and shifting nature of fundamentalist forces and their key players on the global stage. They forge alliances across NGO and state lines, across religions and religious denominations, and across countries and regions in ways that rarely, if ever, occur around other global policy issues where gender relations are not (ostensibly) at stake. This extraordinary display of unity begs many questions. What is it that unites disparate fundamentalists – Protestant, Catholic, Muslim and others – across the North and South, from the poorest to the richest nations? They unite in their intense opposition to women's empowerment, to reproductive and sexual rights, and to the radical transformation of gendered power relations that recognition of such commitments implies. This sobering insight underlines how the struggle against fundamentalisms and the fight for gender equality and WHR are inextricable.

Conclusion

While the precise character and expression of fundamentalist projects differ from context to context, this chapter illustrates how they share common goals and use similar strategies to achieve their ends – whether at the national or international level. This includes broad-based mobilization around, and enforcement of, supposedly authentic and homogeneous religious (and ethnic) identities; targeted efforts to 'reform' secular law or to inculcate customary / religious laws; and the use of political power to infuse public and private life with religiously framed values and practices. Moreover, like their counterparts in progressive social movements, fundamentalists increasingly cooperate in highly coordinated transnational networks of like-minded groups, despite an otherwise ideological stance against globalist values (Buss 2004, 58). Most importantly, however, fundamentalist projects share an intense preoccupation with policing gender roles, sexual behaviour and 'the family' in ways that are inherently at odds with the gender equality and WHR norms. Hence, women's lives and women's movements – and lesbian, gay, bi-sexual and trans-gendered (LGBT) people and movements – locally and globally, necessarily constitute a *primary battleground* for fundamentalist projects in their pursuit of social, political and legal power to transform societies according to religiously framed constructions of 'the good life' and 'the just society'.

At the start of this book, I offered an account of emancipatory cosmopolitan feminism as the normative and analytical framework that runs through my analysis. The examples of fundamentalist politics in action explored in this chapter confirm the salience of such a cosmopolitan feminist framework in resisting the corrosive impact of fundamentalisms – both in seeking to deny the rights and dignity of women and other targeted groups and in displacing democratically grounded understandings of the 'rule of law'. The law in its many forms comes into focus as a site of struggle that local and global women's movements cannot avoid if they are to effectively counter fundamentalist influences. In doing so, however, as Othman notes, they must contest both 'secular patriarchy' (i.e. falsely universalized, top-down, secular 'rule of law') and 'Muslim patriarchy' (i.e. imposed customary or religious law) (Othman 2006).

Meeting this challenge, the cosmopolitan feminist resistance to fundamentalist forces, illustrated by the examples explored in this chapter, maintains a focus on the radical promise of the 'rule of law'. That is, they promote an understanding of the rule of law that is grounded in respect for formal *and* substantive equality and a practical commitment to realizing all human rights, locally and globally. Moreover, this critical understanding of the law – as a site of contestation and potentially emancipatory action – presupposes the bottom-up participation of progressive civil society in realizing the transformative potential of the law, especially international human rights. In this regard, women's movements at the forefront of battling actual fundamentalisms, especially from Southern perspectives, constitute a particularly comprehensive, practical critique of truncated understandings of democracy, human rights and the rule of law. Not only do they contest secular and fundamentalist patriarchal constructions of the law as noted above, but they actively deconstruct Western-centric interpretations that reproduce oppressive North–South binaries.

Such women's movements are keenly aware of abuses of international law and global norms by Western powers and the insidious promulgation of anti-Islamic and racist thinking in mainstream global security and rights discourses. Yet, they have been most vocal in the call for 'moderation and adherence to principles of international human rights and humanitarian law and standards' in dealing with the September 11 attacks

(Abeysekera 2001). This cosmopolitan position is informed by a firsthand understanding, in contexts of aggressive fundamentalist projects, of the inextricable links between: (1) local feminist struggles to reclaim/renew democracy and the 'rule of law' as integral to pursuing substantive gender equality and WHR; and (2) global women's movements' efforts to critically redefine international law and global norms from gender and other previously marginalized perspectives. In comprehending and acting on these links, strong local women's movements and TFA come into focus not simply as targets of fundamentalist forces but as absolutely essential to halting their influence and to building emancipatory models of democracy and the rule of law.

8

Conclusion

This book has put a spotlight on the varieties of UN-oriented transnational feminist advocacy (TFA) that have emerged in recent decades and that continue to be vital in advancing our understanding of gender and global issues in the twenty-first century. Unfortunately, gender inequalities and threats to women's human rights (WHR) are stymieing the life chances of women and girls in all regions. With few exceptions, persistent gender pay gaps and economic insecurities, chronic under-representation in decision-making and public life and multiple forms of violence against women (VAW), from domestic violence to trafficking, constitute the lived realities of too many women. Further, these underlying inequalities are exacerbated and exploited in contexts where conflict, religious fundamentalisms and economic or environmental crises take hold. Given the global scope and range of the gender inequalities that prevail, it would seem that there is a place for 'global feminism' and a clear need for a global WHR movement to press for the transformations necessary to advance gender justice in the widest sense.

Yet, throughout academia and in mainstream discourses in general, many claim that we live in a 'post-feminist' era. For some, this is because they believe that there have been genuine improvements in women's legal, economic and social status and that it is up to individual women to make the most of these changes. For others, the assertion that we live in a post-feminist era stems from the idea that even in places where women's status is not equal to that of men, it is usually explained with reference to non-Western 'culture' wherein it is supposed that (Western) 'feminism' has no relevance. In academic contexts, acceptance of the post-feminist story generally flows from the postmodern philosophical quandary created by the recognition that the modernist subject, invested with reason and agency, no longer 'exists'. Each of these positions poses particular challenges to those of us who wish to defend a commitment to emancipatory feminist political theorizing and practice in a globalizing age. Throughout this book I have sought to explicate a model of cosmopolitan feminist engagement that responds to these and other positions that are sceptical about the prospects for a non-oppressive 'global feminism'.

Since the 1970s, 'Feminism' as a political and academic project in all regions of the world has been rightly challenged by successive waves of 'internal' critics who have called to task influential feminist thinkers and actors of the day for their failures to comprehend the central importance of differential power relations among women vis-à-vis 'race', ethnicity, class, socio-economic status, global inequalities, age, sexuality, ability / disability and so on. Feminist theorizing has largely responded by retreating progressively from the notion of 'Feminism' as a philosophical or political project, except in its plural, particular or strategic configurations. This is positive insofar as it underpins constant vigilance against false universalization from hegemonic perspectives, and ideas that all women are oppressed in the same way or that they automatically share common values and agendas. This position, however, is also unnecessarily limiting in that it closes off theorization of the practical conditions for the emergence of non-oppressive global feminism. The latter begins with an acceptance that there are persistent structural forces at work worldwide that disadvantage women and girls in gender-specific ways. However, such patterns of gendered marginalization and disadvantage are experienced very differently according to our location in the global political economy and across lines of class, 'race', ethnicity, sexuality, disability and so on. I have argued that this recognition opens up the possibility of, and underlines the necessity for, feminist dialogue across multiple boundaries as the basis for solidarity and collective action. The question is, what kind of dialogue, solidarity and action, and from whose perspective? A core contention of this book is that de-centred, bottom-up, critical engagement with human rights norms and mechanisms is integral to promoting and sustaining non-oppressive feminist dialogue, solidarity and action in the cosmopolitan tradition.

International human rights law (like all law) is socially constructed and a site of struggle and contestation. Although it is motivated by a commitment to a 'universal' norm – recognition of the equal worth of all human beings – actual human rights agreements are inevitably contingent. That is, they reflect prevailing power relations, along lines of gender, geo-politics, culture and so on. The exercise of hegemonic power, however, is not the full picture. Existing human rights agreements – with the Universal Declaration of Human Rights (UDHR) being a prime example – frequently bear the stamp of moments of resistance that contest false universalization and unsettle dominant notions of what constitutes human rights and whose rights matter, and under what conditions. While the overall orientation of international human rights discourse since the inception of the UN has been shaped deeply by hegemonic Western, neo-liberal, male biases, the accounts of feminist interventions highlighted throughout this book underline the potential to disrupt dominant trajectories and create spaces where marginalized actors can achieve meaningful shifts in the exercise of power. This critical view of human rights is at the heart of the overarching cosmopolitan feminist framework that shapes this book. Illustrating this perspective, I have highlighted the pivotal contributions of women's rights advocates – from the global South as well as from the North – in creating a range of new standards that have enshrined principles of sex-based equality and non-discrimination in international law. Most importantly, however, I have sought to show the ways that WHR advocacy has elabo-rated what it means to realize such 'universal' principles in the lives of 'particular', differently situated women. Undoubtedly, yawning gaps persist between global norms and local implementation. A major tenet of my argu-ment, however, is that sustained, bottom-up advocacy by women's NGOs and networks and other supporters of WHR is indispensable to bridging the gaps.

In this context, the UN Decade for Women (UNDW) (1976–85) and the UN world conferences of the 1990s played a formative role in making the UN more accessible as a site of critical feminist engagement and in encour-aging the unprecedented development of women's organizations and networks globally. In particular, during this time we saw the emergence of critical, bottom-up approaches to formulating and implementing interna-tional law – wherein WHR advocacy has played a leading part. Important examples discussed in this book include the reinvigoration of the Convention on the Elimination of All Forms of Discrimination Against Women (CEDAW) (1979) since the 1990s, as well as highly effective campaigns to achieve recognition of VAW as a violation of human rights, to define sexual violence as a war crime and a crime against humanity, and to bring about the adoption of Security Council Resolution (SCR) 1325 calling for the protection of women in conflict situations and their full inclusion in peace-building and post-conflict reconstruction.

While WHR campaigning since the 1990s consistently highlighted the full range of human rights concerns affecting women, more than any other issues VAW and reproductive and sexual health (RSH) have come to signify the 'new' WHR agenda. Of these two sets of issues, however, much greater inroads have been made around the inclusion of VAW on interna-tional agendas. While this undoubtedly reflects the impact of WHR advocacy, it also indicates a degree of receptiveness within the mainstream human rights community to the issue, a receptivity that flows from well-established norms that condemn egregious acts of physical violence (outside of war). Securing recognition of RSH as a part of 'human rights' is an even more demanding leap. It further extends ideas of self-determination and bodily integrity into arenas where women have long contended with powerful patriarchal forces that seek to enforce contrary positions. Equally challenging, it calls for a proactive understanding of the 'right to health' that is at odds with the current, globally pervasive ideological commitments to privatization and the minimal state. Moreover, almost immediately after the 1993 UN World Conference on Human Rights in Vienna, a backlash began to take shape in UN forums whereby conservative states and traditionalist civil-society actors worked in concert to block advancement of WHR agendas, and efforts to promote reproductive and sexual rights in particular.

Notwithstanding the backlash evident throughout the UN 'plus Five' and 'plus Ten' processes, however, TFA still secured some very positive outcomes in the area of gender, conflict and peace. As noted, successful campaigns targeted the International Criminal Court (ICC) and the Security Council to produce important new commitments aimed at ensuring 'justice' vis-à-vis wartime crimes against women and the comprehensive inclusion of women in post-conflict transformation. While these gains are very significant on many levels, I argue that they are best understood as part of a political process to contest and constitute global legal norms in ways that underpin WHR, and not primarily as avenues to seek 'justice' for individual women. More generally, feminist critics of the use of law in conflict-affected settings must remain vigilant in exposing gender biases in determining what counts as conflict-related harms and in advancing ways and means to eliminate such biases in both formal and informal modes of dealing with past abuses. At the same time, it is necessary to continue to expand the horizon of justice in post-conflict transitions beyond dealing with particular abuses during conflicts.

In this context, women's movements possess a potentially very useful tool in the form of Security Council Resolution 1325, one that could be used by them to capitalize on the transformative opportunities opened up by post-conflict and transitional moments. This potential is undercut, however, by the frequency with which women – whose informal political engagement often plays a key role along the path from conflict to peace negotiation – are marginalized in post-conflict (or post-peace agreement) politics and are expected to resume traditional and subordinate roles. This pattern is discursively and materially (re)produced by the pervasive uncritical acceptance of the gender-biased models of minimal, formal and/ or consociational models of 'democracy' as the end goals of transition. This hegemonic transitional perspective means that structural inequalities, which disproportionately disadvantage women and obstruct their full and equal political participation, are ignored. Further, the failure to recognize the pivotal importance of informal, broad-based civic engagement in underpinning sustainable and transformative peace is deeply gendered; it structurally enforces the invisibility of women as political actors and fosters the trivialization of gender concerns in the post-conflict contexts. Furthermore, the systemic exclusion of women from the exercise of power is deepened by a widespread willingness – among progressives and conservatives alike – to allow gender equality to be ignored or traded in an effort to signify deference to the 'cultural' claims of one or another of the conflicting parties. In such contexts, SCR 1325 in isolation cannot address deep-seated gender inequalities, which are produced by and reflected in legal, political, social, economic and cultural practices, institutions and identities. Rather, its radical promise can be tapped only if it is understood as one element in the panoply of international commitments to WHR within a framework of bottom-up participation and commitment to deepening democratic practice.

While there is a consensus that we now have greater recognition of certain WHR concerns, especially VAW and the situation of women in conflict-affected contexts, it is less clear what progress has been made to render meaningful the idea of the 'indivisibility' of all human rights in women's lives. Exacerbated by the hegemony of neo-liberal globalization, there is justifiable scepticism about the very compatibility of established human rights practice with struggles for alternative models of development and whether the prioritization in established human rights discourse of narrow civil and political rights over economic and social rights can ever be overcome. In response, I have underlined some recent positive developments that are slowly laying a foundation for more effective protection and promotion of social and economic rights in a context of globalization. In large part, these have been advanced by advocacy to carry forward commitments to WHR agreed at the UN World Conference on Human Rights (Vienna, 1993), the International Conference on Population and Development (ICPD) (Cairo, 1994) and the Fourth World Conference on Women (FWCW) (Beijing, 1995). In particular, leaders in the transnational movement for RSH rights are playing a pivotal role in linking WHR and gender and development (GAD) advocacy in the context of the UN Millennium Project and the Millennium Development Goals (MDGs). At the same time, human rights treaty-monitoring bodies have generated many new recommendations that offer an increasingly firm, 'legal' basis to bolster efforts to translate the idea of the indivisibility of human rights into substantive measures (for example, in the realm of healthcare). Proponents of the indivisibility of human rights, however, are still a minority in the human rights world and many more progressive voices must prioritize economic and social rights in order to bring about a real paradigmatic shift, wherein political and civil rights are no longer seen as the only 'real' human rights. Further, the inclusion of women and gender perspectives in this shift demands the active participation of both 'women's human rights' and 'gender and development' advocates in incorporating bottom-up, critical human rights practice in development agendas and insisting on recognition of the interrelation of all rights in other spheres of human rights activity.

Finally, religious extremism and fundamentalisms in the twenty-first century continue to pose massive challenges to supporters of WHR across all regions and religions – whether Christian, Jewish, Hindu or Muslim. I have highlighted the common purpose and methodologies of all fundamentalist political projects, especially in the ways that they seek to (re)assert control over women's day-to-day lives. This includes broad-based mobilization around supposedly authentic religious (and ethnic) identities, law reform and the use of political power to infuse public and private life with religiously framed values and practices. In contexts of resurgent religious extremism, women's lives and women's movements, and lesbian, gay, bi-sexual and trans-gendered (LGBT) people and movements constitute a core battleground for fundamentalist projects that use social, political and legal power to transform societies according to particular interpretations of religious doctrine in the coercive constructions of 'the good life' and 'the just society'. In this context, women's movements battling Muslim fundamentalist projects on the ground offer a particularly salient practical critique of truncated Western-centric understandings of democracy, human rights and the rule of law. In doing so, they exemplify an emancipatory cosmopolitan feminist perspective. This means actively contesting patriarchal constructions of (Western) secular *and* of fundamentalist religious law *and* rejecting oppressive, Western-centric configurations of 'Islam' and the Third World 'other'. By occupying this position, strong anti-fundamentalist women's movements come into focus not only as targets of fundamentalist forces but as key to countering religious extremisms and engendering accountable, bottom-up democratic practice linked to critically revised accounts of human rights norms and the 'rule of law'.

Is it possible to be optimistic about the prospects for transformation, given the myriad forces working against the substantive realization of WHR in a context of globalization? I can say that I am optimistic because, wherever there is oppression of any kind, you will find women taking action to protest and seek change. Some recent examples include: women's organizations marching in Zimbabwe (despite state violence against them) to demand progress on power-sharing talks; the outspokenness of Iranian feminist human rights activist and Nobel laureate Shirin Ebadi, which has prompted the Malaysian government to ban her from giving a public lecture in Kuala Lumpur; the efforts of women's local NGOs in Haiti (supported by the New York-based organization MADRE) to lead relief efforts to meet the needs of victims of the latest hurricane catastrophe there; a call by a coalition of feminist lawyers in the United Kingdom working with MPs for the modernization of the UK's abortion laws to remove arbitrary obstacles to women's reproductive health decisions. These are just a few illustrations of the different moments of contemporary 'global feminism' – understood not as a single centralized movement pursuing a universal agenda, but as a critical perspective grounded in a practical commitment to seeking gender equality and WHR in ways that resonate with local contexts and the priorities of local women's movements. Such an open-ended, cosmopolitan commitment is at the heart of all sustainable efforts to seek women's human rights in an age of globalization.

Notes

Chapter 1 Women's human rights advocacy

1 The term 'postcolonial feminist' is used broadly to describe writers whose work expresses a primary or substantial interest in addressing the implications of postcolonial legacies and related global disparities in the articulation of feminist perspectives and analyses.

2 This theorization of human rights, as integrally linked to transformative political engagement, is also influenced by works such as Kothari and Sethi (1989) and Sen (2004).

3 Public international law includes binding intergovernmental treaties and comments by treaty bodies, as well as nonbinding declarations and programmes of action produced by intergovernmental conferences.

4 Resolution 1325 recognizes the disproportionate and gender-specific impact of conflict on women and children. Additionally, it calls for women's 'full and equal' participation at all decision-making levels in 'prevention, management, and resolution of conflict', and for all participants in peacekeeping operations and peace-building processes to 'adopt a gender perspective'.

5 The writings and advocacy of Kimberlé Crenshaw (a law professor at the University of California, Los Angeles) were instrumental in introducing the feminist concept of intersectionality into global policy discussions, especially in the context of the 2001 World Conference Against Racism, Racial Discrimination, Xenophobia and Related Forms of Intolerance (WCAR) in Durban, South Africa.

6 Examples of such networks include the Association for Women's Rights in Development (AWID), Development Alternatives with Women for a New Era (DAWN), ISIS International and the Women's Global Network for Reproductive Rights (WGNRR).

7 For discussions of the backlash, see Sen and Corrêa (2000), Neuhold (2000) and CWGL and WEDO (2000).

Chapter 2 Human rights, gender and contested meanings

1 Generally, I use the term 'discourse' to mean the interplay of language, ideas and practice and related patterns in the exercise of power, which operate materially and symbolically along lines of gender, race, class and so on.

2 A human rights treaty is a formal quasi-legal agreement among states. It creates binding obligations on the part of states to protect and promote the human rights of individuals. Each human rights treaty creates mechanisms to monitor state compliance with the human rights standards it contains. This sometimes includes an individual complaints procedure, but always entails periodic reporting by states to the UN. Examples of human rights treaties are the International Covenant on Civil and Political Rights (1966); the International Covenant on Economic, Social and Cultural Rights (1966); the

International Convention on the Elimination of All Forms of Racial Discrimination (1965); the Convention on the Elimination of All Forms of Discrimination Against Women (1979); the Convention Against Torture and Other Cruel, Inhuman and Degrading Treatment (1984); the Convention on the Rights of the Child (1989); and the International Convention on the Protection of the Rights of All Migrant Workers and Members of Their Families (1990).

3 It must be emphasized that a treaty-monitoring committee is charged with reviewing the record of only those countries that have ratified the treaty in question. This provision reflects the imperative of state sovereignty in the international order.

4 The Commission on the Status of Women (CSW) was established in 1946. The principal global policy-making body on women's issues at the United Nations, the CSW has a mandate to prepare recommendations and reports on promoting women's rights in political, economic, civil, social and educational fields and to highlight urgent women's human rights problems requiring immediate attention. Following the FWCW (1995), the General Assembly mandated the Commission to review progress regularly on the critical areas of concern identified in the Beijing Platform for Action and to play a coordinating role in mainstreaming a gender perspective in United Nations activities. Forty-five UN member states serve as members of the CSW at any one time. They are elected by the Economic and Social Council of the UN (ECOSOC) for four-year terms according to the principle of equitable geographical distribution. For more information, visit the CSW website: www.un.org/womenwatch/daw/csw/index.html.

5 The UN Commission on Human Rights (UNCHR) – now replaced by the Human Rights Council (HRC) – evolved into the most influential human rights decision-making body in the UN system. It was established in 1946 by ECOSOC as a 'functional commission' reporting to ECOSOC and the General Assembly. The UNCHR had forty-three state members elected in regional groups by ECOSOC for four-year terms, and was responsible for broadly monitoring observance of existing human rights standards, recommending new standards, authorizing the investigation of human rights violations, and receiving complaints of human rights violations. In operation since 2006, the HRC carries over all of the UNCHR's mandates and responsibilities. It is the main UN forum for dialogue and cooperation on human rights. Its declared role is to help Member States to meet their human rights obligations through dialogue, capacity building and technical assistance, and to make recommendations to the General Assembly for further development of international law in the field of human rights. It has forty-seven members who are elected by the General Assembly by absolute majority for three-year terms in accordance with equitable geographical representation. In a fresh departure aimed at improving the credibility of the body, Member States of the Council are subject to a new universal human rights review mechanism during their term of membership and the General Assembly can suspend the rights and privileges of any Council Member that it decides has persistently committed gross and systematic violations of human rights during its term of membership. For more information, visit the HRC website at: www.un.org.

6 The first World Conference on Human Rights took place with little input from NGOs twenty-five years earlier in Tehran, Iran. The UN designated 1968 as the International Year for Human Rights to mark the twentieth anniversary of the Universal Declaration on Human Rights. It convened an International Conference on Human Rights in Tehran. The conference produced the Tehran Proclamation, which emphasized the principle of non-discrimination, condemned apartheid as a 'crime against humanity' and urged governments to ratify the International Covenant on Civil and Political Rights and the International Covenant on Economic, Social and Cultural Rights adopted by the UN two years earlier.

7 There is a vast literature on the negative impacts of the twentieth-century welfare state on individual freedoms and the quality of democracy and citizenship, including excellent feminist critiques, which must be taken on board when advocating for a more proactive state role in protecting and promoting all human rights.

8 A question is 'justiciable' if it is capable of being decided by legal principles or in a court of law.

9 For discussions problematizing dominant interpretations of the 'rule of law', especially in relation to the nexus of human rights discourse and the Third World, see Rajagopal (2003).

10 Legal systems where national constitutions and laws trump international standards and laws.

11 There is now a very large literature that problematizes assertions that economic, social and cultural rights are not justiciable and, therefore, not enforceable. For an overview of these debates, see Mapulanga-Hulston (2002).

Chapter 3 Women's human rights as equality and non-discrimination

1 I use the term 'Third World feminism' in keeping with the work of Chandra Mohanty (1988, 2003).

2 Malik reversed his sustained emphasis on individual rights when it came to the discussions of Article 16 on the family. He unsuccessfully proposed that 'the family' should be recognized in the declaration as a site of 'inalienable rights antecedent to all positive law' (Morsink 1991, 236). Malik also attempted, again unsuccessfully, to include the phrase 'from the moment of conception' in Article 8 addressing the right to life.

3 See 'Dr. Peng-chun Chang' on the website of the Franklin and Eleanor Roosevelt Institute: www.udhr.org/history/Biographies/biopcc.htm.

4 UN Doc. E/CN.4/AC.2/SR.5.

5 The Convention on the Granting of Political Rights to Women was adopted by the Inter-American Conference in 1948 (Hevener 1983, 112).

6 It is also important to note that many of the countries that had granted full political rights to women by 1950 were in the South, while countries like Canada, Australia, Switzerland and Portugal still maintained significant restrictions on women's participation. (For more information, see the website of the Inter-Parliamentary Union (IPU): www.ipu.org.)

7 More recently, the ILO has introduced a revised maternity protection convention (2000) as well as a number of other conventions that are particularly relevant to women, for example underpinning the rights of workers with family responsibilities (1981), part-time workers (1994) and home workers (1996).

8 There are different levels of NGO accreditation within the UN system. Organizations seeking direct access to intergovernmental meetings must go through a complex review process and meet specific criteria in order to gain consultative status with ECOSOC.

9 About 450 representatives from 131 accredited NGOs were permitted to attend the UN Conference as observers. Of the NGOs, 22 were women's organizations.

10 The majority of participants were from Europe and the USA (6,396) with the remainder from Asia and the Pacific (836), Latin America (357), Africa (245), the Middle East (47) and the Caribbean (41).

11 The NGO International Women's Rights Action Watch Asia Pacific (IWRAW Asia Pacific) provides a list of states that have entered reservations to the articles of CEDAW from which they claim exemptions at: www.iwraw-ap.org/convention/reservations_parties.htm.

12 An optional protocol is a separate treaty linked to a primary human rights treaty. It establishes procedures whereby treaty-monitoring bodies can receive complaints from individuals or groups whose rights have been violated, or instigate inquiries into particular human rights issues in the jurisdiction of a State Party with the consent of the government involved.

13 These included the Women in Law Project of the International Human Rights Law Group, the Maastricht Centre for Human Rights, and Amnesty International, among others.

14 Optional Protocol to the Convention on the Elimination of All Forms of Discrimination against Women, GA Res. 4, UN GAOR, 54th Session, Supp. No. 49, UN Doc. A/RES/54/4 (1999).

15 In this case, within the Optional Protocol working group, this included Cuba, China, India and Egypt.

16 Full reports on all complaints and procedures conducted under CEDAW's Optional Protocol are available at the CEDAW website: www.un.org/womenwatch/daw/cedaw/protocol/text.htm.

17 NGOs were centrally involved in bringing the two complaints against Austria concerning failures to protect women in situations of domestic violence culminating in murder (Nos. 5/2005 and 6/2005) and the complaint of forced sterilization in Hungary (No. 4/2004).

Chapter 4 Violence and reproductive health as human rights issues

1 The title 'Global Campaign for Women's Human Rights' was coined by a loose coalition of women's NGOs and networks from different regions that worked together in the run-up to the 1993 World Conference on Human Rights in Vienna. The initial purpose of the campaign was to ensure that women and gender concerns were included in the proceedings of the forthcoming conference. Campaign leaders were brought together to plan activities primarily under the auspices of the Center for Women's Global Leadership (CWGL) at Rutgers University. (See note 5 below for a list of participants.)

2 See the Human and Constitutional Rights Resources web page of the Columbia University Law School at: www.hrcr.org/chart/civil+political/personal_security.html.

3 The series of UN conferences included the UN Conference on Environment and Development (Rio de Janeiro, 1992), the World Conference on Human Rights (Vienna, 1993), the International Conference on Population and Development (Cairo, 1994), the Social Summit (Copenhagen, 1995), the Fourth World Conference on Women (Beijing, 1995) and the Second UN Conference on Human Settlements (Istanbul, 1996).

4 For a discussion of this meeting, see Chiarotti (2007). The methodology behind this activism is described in Suarez (1995).

5 The CWGL played a major coordinating role in the Global Campaign for Women's Human Rights (1991–5). As a US centre in the New York City area, the CWGL enjoys a relatively privileged position and greater access to a range of resources essential to effective women's human rights advocacy. It would be inaccurate, however, on this basis, to characterize the work of the CWGL, particularly its role in the Global Campaign, simply as a 'Northern' or US endeavour. Under the leadership of founder/director Charlotte Bunch, the CWGL promoted and facilitated extensive, regionally balanced North–South dialogue, consultation and networking that determined the direction and content of campaign activities. In particular, throughout the 1990s, the CWGL convened annual global women's leadership institutes and regular strategic planning meetings and co-convened many women's NGO caucuses at UN venues.

These involved hundreds of women from dozens of countries, organizations and networks too numerous to mention. A number of international feminist networks have been particularly active partners with the CWGL in the coordination of the Global Campaign and subsequent advocacy activities, including Development Alternatives with Women for a New Era (DAWN), the International Women's Health Coalition (IWHC), the International Women's Rights Action Watch Asia Pacific (IWRAW Asia Pacific), the International Women's Tribune Center (IWTC), ISIS International (Chile), the Women's Environment and Development Organization (WEDO), WiLDAF and WLUML.

6 The 16 Days campaign runs from 25 November (Latin American International Day against Violence against Women) to 10 December (International Human Rights Day), underlining that VAW is a human rights issue. The idea to initiate the 16 Days came out of the first annual Women's Global Leadership Institute (WGLI) convened by the Center for Women's Global Leadership (CWGL) in June 1991. The two-week residential institute brought together approximately twenty women from around the world who were established or emerging leaders on women's rights and gender equality issues in their countries. Many came from grassroots groups or women's or human rights NGOs, while others worked in service provision, the media, academia, legal practice and so on. As Coordinator of International Campaigns at the Center for Women's Global Leadership at the time, I had the responsibility for launching the first 16 Days campaign in November 1991 and for building momentum around the campaign in subsequent years. In the pre-Internet era, the tremendous efforts of a small number of student interns working at the CWGL in the early 1990s were vital to its successful take-off, especially Linda Posluszny, Raahi Reddy, Andrea Romani-Pitanguy and Tamara Xavier. While the CWGL still plays a nominal coordinating role, the 16 Days is now firmly established as a global campaign owned by women's groups and networks everywhere who work to eliminate VAW.

7 The petition drive proved so popular that its central coordinator, the Center for Women's Global Leadership, continued to gather signatures calling for actions to implement the Vienna commitments to women's human rights, and to carry these forward to subsequent UN conferences, especially the Fourth World Conference on Women (FWCW) in Beijing in 1995. Between 1993 and 1995, Amnesty International formally backed the petition and distributed it worldwide. In addition, it attracted a corporate sponsor, The Body Shop, which distributed the petition throughout its stores. As a result, the number of signatures gathered exceeded one million by the time of the FWCW in September 1995.

8 Petchesky notes that, in addition to the CWGL, other US-based international feminist organizations (such as WEDO and IWHC) have been subject to similar criticism for dominating strategic leadership vis-à-vis insider or high-level transnational feminist policy advocacy processes. Regarding the global reproductive health and rights movement, Petchesky offers a constructive response that problematizes such claims of Northern dominance in that movement and which apply equally to similar criticisms made of the Global Campaign for Women's Human Rights. Specifically, she highlights that: (1) most of those deeply involved in NGO efforts to draft alternative feminist language at the 1990s UN conferences were Southern women; (2) some of the most influential leaders of Northern-based NGOs have used their power and resources to open up political space for women from the South; (3) some of the most vocal critics of Northern NGO dominance are themselves Northern NGOs who refuse to engage with 'insider' UN processes; and (d) many Southern critics of Northern dominance are elite academics in prestigious Northern institutions who speak on behalf of subjected women from the South with whom they have no contact (Petchesky 2003, 66).

9 *The Vienna Tribunal: Women's Rights are Human Rights!* is a video documentary of the event distributed in the United States by Women Make Movies.
10 This discussion is informed by my experiences as Coordinator of the Vienna Tribunal.
11 This was especially important given that, less than 100 miles away, the war in the Former Yugoslavia was ongoing, along with the growing awareness of the existence of 'rape camps'.
12 It is noteworthy in this context that the 2003 Protocol to the African Charter on Human and Peoples' Rights on the Rights of Women in Africa is the first human rights instrument in the world to contain a provision recognizing women's right to abortion (Article 14(2)(c)).
13 Most notably, the following were key participants in many planning meetings and activities of the Global Campaign, as well as leaders in the transnational reproductive health and rights movement: Lynn Freedman, Director of the Averting Maternal Death and Disability (AMDD) Program and the Law and Policy Project, Columbia University, USA; Ros Petchesky, Professor of Women's Studies and Political Science and coordinator of the International Reproductive Rights Research Action Group (IRRRAG), Hunter College, USA; Jacqueline Pitanguy, Director of CEPIA (Citizenship, Research and Action), Brazil, a major partner organization of the IWHC; Nahid Toubia, a physician originally from Sudan, and founder/Director of the UK-based research and advocacy network Rainbo, which works to eliminate female genital mutilation and promote health and rights for African women; and Mona Zulficar, lawyer and Director of the NGO Women's Health Improvement Association, Egypt.
14 See, in particular, the proceedings of an International Conference on International Protection of Reproductive Rights, *American University Law Review* 44(4) (1995).
15 For a 'feminist report card on the Cairo Programme of Action', summarizing the gains achieved and gaps remaining, see Petchesky (2003, 44–5).

Chapter 5 Women's human rights in conflict and post-conflict transformation

An earlier version of chapter 5 was published as 'Seeking Gender Justice in Post-conflict Transitions: Towards a Transformative Women's Human Rights Approach', *International Journal of Law in Context* 3 (2007): 155–72.
1 The same definitions appear in Article 5 of the Charter of the International Military Tribunal for the Far East (IMTFE).
2 In the judgment of the International Military Tribunal for the Far East, rape is mentioned as a recurring element of conventional war crimes committed by Japanese forces under the direction of the men charged. In particular, the metaphorical 'rape of Nanking' involved actual rapes of more than 20,000 women and is documented in some detail in the judgment documents. Responsibility for rapes, however, is only mentioned in the verdicts of two out of twenty-eight war criminals prosecuted and does not form the primary basis of any indictment (www.ibiblio.org/hyperwar/PTO/IMTFE/).
3 Several leading women's human rights advocates who were instrumental in the Global Campaign for Women's Human Rights in the early 1990s also played key roles in advancing the work of the ICC NGO Women's Caucus for Gender Justice and linking it to a wider network of women's organizations internationally. Most notably, this included Sunila Abeysekera (Sri Lanka) of the Women's Media Collective and human rights NGO INFORM in Sri Lanka; Rhonda Copelon (US), founder/Director of the International Women's Human Rights Clinic, City University of New York; and Indai Lourdes Sajor (Philippines), formerly Co-Convener of the Women's International War Crimes Tribunal on Japan's Military Sexual Slavery (Tokyo Tribunal) (2000) and

Director of the Women's Caucus, and currently United Nations Mission in Ethiopia and Eritrea (UNMEE) Human Rights Officer.

4 This included coordinating regional meetings in Africa, South Asia and Central America, as well as a major popular hearing on crimes against women in recent conflict situations, featuring testimonies from survivors of conflicts in twenty-five countries across Asia, Africa, the Middle East and Europe. For more information on these activities, as well as technical details on ICC lobbying efforts, see ICC Women News (September 2000) at: http://iccwomen.addr.com/reports/nl200009.htm.

5 The Hague, 22 February 2001 (JL/P.I.S/566-e). Available online at: www.un.org-icty-foca/trialc2/judgement/index.htm.

6 For a discussion of these issues in the context of informal popular tribunals, see Reilly and Posluszny (2006).

7 See also Cockburn (2005).

8 Formed in June 2000, the NGO Working Group included the Hague Appeal for Peace, International Alert, the International Women's Tribune Center (IWTC), the ICC Women's Caucus, the Women's Commission for Refugee Women and Children, and WILPF (Hill et al., 2003). Over time, the campaign to implement Resolution 1325 continues to gain support among a wide range of peace, development and human rights NGOs around the world. For more details, see the Women Peace and Security NGO Web Ring at: www.peacewomen.org/web_ring.html.

9 Of all UN forums, the Security Council has been particularly inaccessible to NGO participation and input. However, since 1993 a procedure known as the 'Arria Formula' has been in place, which allows for special open sessions of the Security Council to which NGO guests can be invited to share their views on particular topics.

10 For more information, visit the PeaceWomen project website at: www.peacewomen.org.

11 Schola Harushiyakira spoke at an event in Derry, Northern Ireland, on 15 March 2007. The event was organized by the Irish development NGO Trocaire as part of its annual speakers' series. In 2007 the series focused on gender equality and implementation of the UN SCR 1325.

12 In the case of CEDAW, International Women's Rights Action Watch Asia Pacific provides comprehensive information as well as international training and capacity-building programmes to assist non-governmental groups from every region to participate in monitoring and reviewing their country's compliance with CEDAW. WILPF and UNIFEM play a similar role towards the implementation of SCR 1325.

Chapter 6   Development, globalization and women's human rights

1 For a comprehensive discussion of the strengths and limitations of the ICESCR as an advocacy tool, see Elson and Gideon (2004).

2 The Ethical Globalization Initiative aims to 'put human rights standards at the heart of global governance and policy-making and to ensure that the needs of the poorest and most vulnerable are addressed on the global stage'. For more details, visit the organization's website: www.realizingrights.org/.

3 The Montreal Principles were produced by the Working Group on Women's Human Rights of the Economic, Social and Cultural Rights Network (ESCR-Net). Established in 2000, ESCR-Net is a network of 139 organizations from around the world. It seeks to strengthen the field of all human rights, with a special focus on economic, social and cultural rights. Members of ESCR-Net that have also played a leading role in the Global Campaign for Women's Human Rights include BAOBAB for Women's Human Rights

(Nigeria) and Women in Law and Development in Africa (WiLDAF). The Montreal Principles on Women's Economic, Social and Cultural Rights can be accessed at: www. escr-net.org/actions/actions_show.htm?doc_id=426624.

4 The first World Social Forum (WSF) was held in Porto Alegre, Brazil, in 2001. It is now an annual meeting convened in different locations by members of the 'anti-globalization' movement. Participants meet to formulate and exchange ideas and to strategize around actions to challenge the detrimental impacts of globalization. Significantly, it meets in January parallel to the World Economic Forum in Davos, Switzerland.

5 See note 3.

6 For example, for analyses of gender, globalization, and trade and related issues, visit the websites of Women in Development Europe (www.eurosur.org/wide/home.htm) and Development Alternatives with Women for a New Era (DAWN) (www.dawnorg. org/index.html).

7 See, for example, 'United Nations 2005 World Summit Outcomes: Gains on Gender Equality, Mixed Results on Poverty, Peace, and Human Rights', a report prepared by a coalition of women's NGOs – the Center for Women's Global Leadership (CWGL), Development Alternatives with Women for a New Era (DAWN), Family Care International, United Methodist UN Office, and the Women's Environment and Development Organization (WEDO) – and published by the Gender Monitoring Group of the World Summit: CWGL, DAWN and WEDO, 12 October 2005 (www. cwgl.rutgers.edu/globalcenter/policy/millsummit/reportbackOct12.pdf).

8 MDG3 has one official target (No. 4) to 'eliminate gender disparity in primary education, preferably by 2005, and in all levels of education no later than 2015'. The indicators to be used in monitoring progress on MDG3 are the ratio of girls to boys in all levels of education, the ratio of literate women to men in the fifteen–twenty-four age category, the share of women in non-agricultural wage employment; and the proportion of seats held by women in elected parliaments.

9 See especially the articles on gender stereotyping (Article 5), marriage and family life (Article 16) and political and public life (Article 7).

10 There is one official target (Target 6) attached to MDG5: to reduce the maternal mortality rate by 75 per cent over the period 1990–2015. The two official indicators identified at UN level to measure progress are the maternal mortality rate (Indicator 16) and the proportion of births attended by skilled health professionals (Indicator 17).

11 The Human Rights Committee reviews and monitors states' compliance with the International Covenant on Civil and Political Rights (ICCPR) and issues recommendations or comments on how states can improve their implementation of the treaty's provisions.

Chapter 7 Fundamentalisms and women's human rights

1 See 'In Response to Global Gag Rule, Britain Pledges Money for Safe Abortion Services', Feminist Majority Foundation, 7 February 2006. Available online at: www.feminist. org/news/newsbyte/uswirestory.asp?id=9509.

2 See 'Case Challenging Manila Contraception Ban Dismissed', Center for Reproductive Rights, 15 August 2008. Available online at www.reproductiverights.org/worldwide. html.

3 Established in 1984, WLUML links progressive women's organizations, activists and researchers from more than 70 countries that share a common concern about the detrimental impact of Muslim laws in women's lives, as well as anti-Muslim discrimination and racism affecting Muslim minorities around the world. For more information, see the WLUML website: www.wluml.org.

4 In particular, see various essays in Imam et al. (2004), which feature the proceedings of a meeting of WLUML members held in November 2002.

5 http://riverbendblog.blogspot.com.

6 Doris Buss (2004) identifies the following organizations as playing a leading role in US Christian Right campaigns at the United Nations: the Catholic Family and Human Rights Institute, the World Family Policy Center, the Howard Center and the World Congress of Families. Anick Druelle's report (2000) also underlines the dominant role of North American (including Canadian) Judeo-Christian organizations in driving right-wing fundamentalist politics in UN forums.

7 The OIC is an international organization with a permanent delegation to the United Nations. It has fifty-seven member states, mainly from Africa, Asia and the Middle East, and five observer states, including Russia and Bosnia and Herzegovina.

Bibliography

5WWC (n.d.) '1975 World Conference on Women: Mexico City, June 19 – July 2 1975'. Available online at: www.5wwc.org/conference_background/1975_WCW.html.

Abeysekera, Sunila (1995) 'Organizing for Peace in the Midst of War: Experiences of Women in Sri Lanka', in Margaret Schuler (ed.), *From Basic Needs to Basic Rights: Women's Claim to Human Rights*. Washington, DC: Women, Law, and Development International.

(2001) 'Paying the Price for Ignoring Women's Calls against Fundamentalism'. Available online at: www.wluml.org/english/newsfulltxt.shtml?cmd%5B157%5D=x-157-3422.

(2004) 'Development and Women's Human Rights', in *Seeking Accountability on Women's Human Rights: Women Debate the UN Millennium Development Goals*. New York: Women's International Coalition for Economic Justice.

(2006) 'Engendering Transitional Justice', in T. Dam Truong, S. Wieringa and A. Chhachhi (eds.), *Engendering Human Security: Feminist Perspectives*. London: Zed Books.

Acar, Feride (2004) 'Statement at the Occasion of the 25th Anniversary of the Adoption of the Convention on the Elimination of All Forms of Discrimination Against Women by the General Assembly of the United Nations', New York: United Nations, 13 October.

Ackerly, Brooke, and Susan Moller Okin (1999) 'Feminist Social Criticism and the International Movement for Women's Human Rights', in Ian Shapiro and Casiano Hacker-Cordon (eds.), *Democracy's Edges*. Cambridge: Cambridge University Press.

Afkhami, Mahnaz (1995) 'Identity and Culture: Women as Subjects and Agents of Change', in Margaret Schuler (ed.), *From Basic Needs to Basic Rights: Women's Claim to Human Rights*. Washington, DC: Women, Law, and Development International.

Agarwal, Bina (1994) 'Positioning the Western Feminist Agenda: A Comment', *Indian Journal of Gender Studies* 1(2): 249–55.

Allan, Virginia R., Margaret E. Galey and Mildred E. Persinger (1995) 'World Conference of International Women's Year', in Anne Winslow (ed.), *Women, Politics, and the United Nations*. Westport, Conn.: Greenwood Press.

Alston, P. (2005) 'Ships Passing in the Night: The Current State of the Human Rights and Development Debate Seen through the Lens of the Millennium Development Goals', *Human Rights Quarterly* 27: 755–829.

Alvarez, Sonia (1990) *Engendering Democracy in Brazil*. Princeton: Princeton University Press.

American University Law Review (1995) 44(4). Proceedings of the Conference on the International Protection of Reproductive Rights, American University, 10–11 November, 1994.

Amin, Sajeda, and Sana Hossain (1994–5) 'Women's Reproductive Rights and the Politics of Fundamentalism: A View from Bangladesh', *American University Law Review* 44: 1319–43.

Amnesty International (1991) *Women in the Frontline: Human Rights Violations against Women*. New York: Amnesty International Publications.

    (2004) 'Women, HIV/AIDS and Human Rights'. Available online at: http://web.amnesty.org/library/pdf/ACT770842004ENGLISH/$File/ACT7708404.pdf.

Anderlini, Saram Naraghi, Camille Pampele Conway and Lisa Kays (n.d.) 'Transitional Justice and Reconciliation'. London: International Alert. Available online at: www.international-alert.org/pdfs/TK11_justice_reconciliation.pdf.

An-Na'im, Abdullahi (1992) 'Toward a Cross-Cultural Approach to Defining International Standards of Human Rights: The Meaning of Cruel, Inhuman, or Degrading Treatment or Punishment,' in An-Na'im (ed.), *Human Rights in Cross-Cultural Perspectives: A Quest for Consensus*. Philadelphia: University of Pennsylvania Press.

Antrobus, Peggy (2002) 'Feminism as Transformational Politics: Toward Possibilities for Another World', *Development* 45(2): 46–52.

    (2004a) *The Global Women's Movement: Origins, Issues, Strategies*. London: Zed Books.

    (2004b) 'MDGs – The Most Distracting Gimmick', in *Seeking Accountability on Women's Human Rights: Women Debate the Millennium Development Goals*. New York: Women's International Coalition for Economic Justice.

Archibugi, Daniele (ed.) (2003) *Debating Cosmopolitics*. New York: Verso.

Archibugi, Daniele, David Held and Martin Kohler (eds.) (1998) *Re-imagining Political Community*. Stanford, Calif.: Stanford University Press.

Askin, Kelly Dawn (1997) *War Crimes against Women: Prosecution in International War Crimes Tribunals*. The Hague: Martinus Nijhoff.

Banda, Fareda (2005) *Women, Law and Human Rights: An African Perspective*. Oxford: Hart Publishing.

Barton, Carol (2004) 'Introduction', in *Seeking Accountability on Women's Human Rights: Women Debate the UN Millennium Development Goals*. New York: Women's International Coalition for Economic Justice.

Basu, A. (ed.) (1995) *The Challenge of Local Feminisms: Women's Movements in Global Perspective*. Boulder, Colo.: Westview Press.

Beetham, David (1999) 'Human Rights as a Model for Cosmopolitan Democracy', in Beetham (ed.), *Democracy and Human Rights*. Cambridge: Polity.

Bell, Christine, and Catherine O'Rourke (2007) 'Does Feminism Need a Theory of Transitional Justice? An Introductory Essay', *The International Journal of Transitional Justice* 1: 23–44.

Bell, Christine, Colm Campbell and Fionnuala Ní Aoláin (2004) 'Justice Discourses in Transition', *Social and Legal Studies* 13: 305–28.

Benhabib, Seyla (1992) *Situating the Self: Gender, Community and Postmodernism in Contemporary Ethics*. London: Routledge.

Bos, Pascale (2006) 'Feminists Interpreting the Politics of Wartime Rape: Berlin 1945; Yugoslavia, 1992–1993', *Signs* 31: 995–1025.

Boserup, Ester (1970) *Woman's Role in Economic Development*. London: George Allen and Unwin.

Boyle, Kevin (1995) 'Stock-taking on Human Rights: The World Conference on Human Rights, Vienna, 1993', in David Beetham (ed.), *Politics and Human Rights*. Oxford: Blackwell.

Bronner, Stephen (2004) *Reclaiming the Enlightenment: Toward a Politics of Radical Engagement*. New York: Columbia University Press.

Brownlie, Ian (ed.) (1992) *Basic Documents on Human Rights*. 3rd edition. Oxford: Oxford University Press.

Bruce, Margaret K. (1998) 'Personal Notes on an Important Anniversary', *UN Chronicle* 35 (Winter).

Budlender, Debbie, and Guy Hewitt (2004) *Engendering Budgets: A Practitioners' Guide to Understanding and Implementing Gender-Responsive Budgets*. London: Commonwealth Secretariat.

Bunch, Charlotte (1987) 'Global Feminism', in *Passionate Politics: Feminist Theory in Action*. New York: St Martin's Press.

(1990) 'Women's Rights as Human Rights: Towards a Re-vision of Human Rights', *Human Rights Quarterly* 12: 486–98.

(2001) 'Why the World Conference against Racism Is Critical to Women's Human Rights Advocacy'. Paper presented to the UN Commission on the Status of Women.

(2004) 'International Women's Day: Where Are We in 2004?' Paper presented to the US Committee for UNIFEM.

Bunch, Charlotte, and Susana Fried (1996) 'Beijing 95: Moving Women's Human Rights from Margin to Center', *Signs* 22 (1): 200–4.

Bunch, Charlotte, and Niamh Reilly (1994) *Demanding Accountability: The Global Campaign and Vienna Tribunal for Women's Human Rights*. New York: UNIFEM.

(1995) 'The Global Campaign: Violence Against Women Violates Human

Rights', in Margaret Schuler (ed.), *From Basic Needs to Basic Rights: Women's Claim to Human Rights*. Washington, DC: Women, Law, and Development International.

Buss, D. (2004) 'The Christian Right, Globalization and the "Natural Family"', in M. Tétreault and R. Denemark (eds.), *Gods, Guns, and Globalization: Religious Radicalism and International Political Economy*. Boulder, Colo.: Lynne Rienner.

Butegwa, Florence (ed.) (1993) *The World Conference on Human Rights: The WiLDAF Experience*. Harare: Women in Law and Development in Africa.

(1994) 'Using the African Charter on Human and People's Rights to Secure Women's Access to Land in Africa', in Rebecca J. Cook (ed.), *Human Rights of Women: National and International Perspectives*. Philadelphia: University of Pennsylvania Press.

Carrillo, Roxanna (1991) 'Violence against Women: An Obstacle to Development', in C. Bunch and R. Carrillo, *Gender Violence: A Human Rights and Development Issue*. New Brunswick, NJ: Center for Women's Global Leadership.

CESCR (2005) *Substantive Issues Arising in the Implementation of the International Covenant on Economic, Social and Cultural Rights*. General Comment No. 16. Geneva: United Nations Committee on Economic, Social and Cultural Rights, 11 August (E/C.12/2005/4).

Charlesworth, Hilary (1994) 'What Are Women's International Human Rights?' in Rebecca J. Cook (ed.), *Human Rights of Women: National and International Perspectives*. Philadelphia: University of Pennsylvania Press.

Charlesworth, Hilary and Christine Chinkin (2002) 'Sex, Gender, and September 11', *American Journal of International Law* 96(3): 600–5.

Chiarotti, Susana (2007) 'Women and Human Rights: The Convergences and Divergences of Two Social Movements', *Women's Health Journal*, July.

Chinkin, Christine (1994) 'Rape and Sexual Abuse of Women in International Law', *European Journal of International Law* 5(1): 326–41.

(2001) 'Women's International Tribunal on Japanese Military Sexual Slavery', *American Journal of International Law* 95(2): 335–41.

Chinkin, Christine, and Hilary Charlesworth (2006) 'Building Women into Peace: The International Legal Framework', *Third World Quarterly* 27: 937–57.

Chinkin, Christine, and Kate Paradine (2001) 'Vision and Reality: Democracy and Citizenship of Women in the Dayton Peace Accords', *Yale Journal of International Law* 26: 103–78.

Cockburn, Cynthia (2005) 'War against Women: A Feminist Response to Genocide in Gujarat'. Available online at: http://cynthiacockburn.typepad.com//Gujaratblog.pdf.

(2007) *From Where We Stand: War, Women's Activism and Feminist Analysis*. London: Zed Books.

Cockburn, Cynthia, and Dubravka Zarkov (eds.) (2002) *The Postwar Moment: Militaries, Masculinities, and International Peacekeeping*. London: Lawrence and Wishart.

Cohn, Carol (1987) 'Sex and Death in the Rational World of Defense Intellectuals', *Signs* 12: 687–718.

(2004) 'Feminist Peacemaking', *Women's Review of Books*, Feb. Available online at: www.wellesley.edu/womensreview/archive/2004/02/highlt. html.

Cohn, Carol, and Sara Ruddick (2004) 'A Feminist Ethical Perspective on Weapons of Mass Destruction', in Sohail H. Hashmi and Steven P. Lee (eds.), *Ethics and Weapons of Mass Destruction: Religious and Secular Perspectives*. Cambridge: Cambridge University Press.

Collins, Patricia Hill (2000) 'It's All in the Family: Intersections of Gender, Race and Nation', in Uma Narayan and Sandra Harding (eds.), *Decentering the Center: Philosophy for a Multicultural, Postcolonial and Feminist World*. Bloomington: Indiana University Press.

Cook, Rebecca J. (1994a) 'State Accountability Under the Convention on the Elimination of All Forms of Discrimination Against Women', in Cook (ed.), *Human Rights of Women: National and International Perspectives*. Philadelphia: University of Pennsylvania Press.

(1994b) 'State Responsibility for Violations of Women's Human Rights', *Harvard Human Rights Journal* 7: 125–75.

(ed.) (1994c) *Human Rights of Women: National and International Perspectives*. Philadelphia: University of Pennsylvania Press.

Cook, Rebecca J., Bernard M. Dickens and Mahmoud F. Fathalla (2003) *Reproductive Health and Human Rights: Integrating Medicine, Ethics, and Law*. New York: Clarendon Press.

Coomaraswamy, Radhika (2003) *Integration of the Human Rights of Women and the Gender Perspective: Violence Against Women*. Report of the Special Rapporteur on Violence Against Women. Geneva: United Nations Commission on Human Rights, 6 January (E/CN.4/2003/75).

Coomaraswamy, Radhika, and Dilrukshi Fonseka (eds.) (2004) *Peace Work: Women, Armed Conflict and Negotiation*. New Delhi: Women Unlimited.

Copelon, Rhonda (1994) 'Surfacing Gender: Reconceptualising Crimes of Gender in Times of War', in Rebecca J. Cook (ed.), *Human Rights of Women: International Perspectives*. Philadelphia: University of Pennsylvania Press.

(2000) 'Gender Crimes as War Crimes: Integrating Crimes against Women into International Criminal Law', *McGill Law Journal* 46: 217–40.

(2003) 'International Human Rights Dimensions of Intimate Violence: Another Strand in the Dialectic of Feminist Law Making', *Journal of Gender, Social Policy and the Law* 11(3): 865–76.

Cornwall, Andrea, and Maxine Molyneux (2006) 'The Politics of Rights

– Dilemmas for Feminist Praxis: An Introduction', *Third World Quarterly* 27(7): 1175–91.

Cornwall, Andrea, and Celestine Nyamu-Musembi (2004) 'Putting the "Rights-based Approach" to Development into Perspective', *Third World Quarterly* 25(8): 1415–37.

Corrêa, Sonia (1994) *Population and Reproductive Rights: Feminist Perspectives from the South*. London: Zed Books.

(2005) 'Holding Ground: The Challenges for Sexual and Reproductive Rights and Health: In Dialogue with Sonia Corrêa', *Development* 48(4): 11–15.

Crawford, James, and Susan Marks (1998) 'The Global Democracy Deficit: An Essay in International Law and Its Limits', in Daniele Archibugi, David Held and Martin Köhler (eds.), *Re-imagining Political Community*. Stanford, Calif.: Stanford University Press.

Crenshaw, Kimberlé (1997) 'Intersectionality and Identity Politics: Learning from Violence against Women of Color', in Mary Lyndon Shanley and Uma Narayan (eds.), *Reconstructing Political Theory*. London: Polity.

(2000) 'Gender-Related Aspects of Race Discrimination'. Background paper for Expert Meeting on Gender and Racial Discrimination, 21–24 November, Zagreb, Croatia (EM/GRD/2000/WP.1).

CRLP (2005) 'Reproductive Rights'. Center for Reproductive Law and Policy.

Crossette, Barbara (2005) 'Reproductive Health and the Millennium Development Goals: The Missing Link', *Studies in Family Planning* 36(1): 71–9.

CRR (2006) 'The Teen Endangerment Act (H.R. 748; S.8,396,403): Harming Young Women Who Seek Abortions', Center for Reproductive Rights, January. Available online at: www.reproductiverights.org/pub_fac_ccpa.html.

CWGL (1993) *International Campaign for Women's Human Rights: 1992–1993 Report*. New Brunswick, NJ: Center for Women's Global Leadership.

(1995) *From Vienna to Beijing: The Cairo Hearing on Reproductive Health and Human Rights*. New Brunswick, NJ: Center for Women's Global Leadership.

(2005) 'Beijing +10: 49th Session of the Commission on the Status of Women (CSW), 28 February to 11 March 2005'. Available online at: www.cwgl.rutgers.edu/globalcenter/policy/b10/index.html.

CWGL and WEDO (2000) 'Beijing +5 Review Process', Center for Women's Global Leadership and Women's Environment and Development Organization, July. Available online at: www.cwgl.rutgers.edu/global-center/policy/beijing5reflections.html.

Dawkins, Darren (2002) 'Human Right Norms and Networks in Authoritarian Chile', in Sanjeev Khagram, James V. Riker and Kathryn Sikkink (eds.), *Restructuring World Politics: Transnational Social Movements, Networks, and Norms*. Minneapolis: University of Minnesota Press.

Dickensen, Donna (1997) 'Counting Women In: Globalization, Democratization and the Women's Movement', in Anthony McGrew (ed.), *The Transformation of Democracy*. Cambridge: Polity.

Donnelly, Jack (1989) *Universal Human Rights in Theory and Practice*. Ithaca: Cornell University Press.

Druelle, Anick (2000) 'Right-Wing Anti-Feminist Groups at the United Nations', Institut de recherche et d'études féministes, Université du Québec à Montréal. Available online at: http://netfemmes.cdeacf.ca/documents/Anti-Feminist%20Groups-USLetter.pdf.

Dutt, Mallika (2000) 'Some Reflections on United States Women of Color and the United Nations Fourth World Conference on Women and NGO Forum in Beijing, China', in Bonnie Smith (ed.), *Global Feminisms since 1945*. New York: Routledge.

Dyzenhaus, David (2003) 'Transitional Justice', *International Journal of Constitutional Law* 1(1): 163–75.

Edwards, Michael, and John Gaventa (eds.) (2001) *Global Civic Action*. Boulder, Colo.: Lynne Rienner.

Elson, Diane (2006) '"Women's Rights Are Human Rights": Campaigns and Concepts', in Lydia Morris (ed.), *Rights: Sociological Perspectives*. London: Routledge.

Elson, Diane, and Jasmine Gideon (2004) 'Organising for Women's Economic and Social Rights: How Useful Is the International Covenant on Economic, Social and Cultural Rights?' *Journal of Interdisciplinary Gender Studies* 8 (1/2): 14–30.

Enloe, Cynthia (1990) *Bananas, Beaches and Bases: Making Feminist Sense of International Politics*. Berkeley: University of California Press.

(2000) *Maneuvers: The International Politics of Militarizing Women's Lives*. Berkeley: University of California Press.

Ertürk, Yakin (2005) *Integration of the Human Rights of Women and the Gender Perspective: Violence against Women*. Report of the Special Rapporteur on Violence against Women, its Causes and Consequences. Geneva: United Nations Commission on Human Rights, 10 February (E/CN.4/2005/72/Add.3).

(2007) *Implementation of General Assembly Resolution 60/251 of 15 March 2006 Entitled Human Rights Council*. Report of the Special Rapporteur on Violence against Women, its Causes and Consequences. Geneva: Office of the High Commissioner for Human Rights, Human Rights Council, 7 February (A/HRC/4/34/Add.4).

Evans, Tony (1997) 'Democratization and Human Rights', in Anthony McGrew (ed.), *The Transformation of Democracy? Globalization and Territorial Democracy*. Cambridge: Polity.

Ewelukwa, U. U. (2003) 'Small Victories, but the War Rages On', *Human Rights Dialogue* 2(10): 25.

Falk, Richard (2004) *The Declining World Order*. New York: Routledge.

Fathalla, M. F. (2005) 'The Reproductive Health Community: A Valuable Asset for Achieving the MDGs', *Studies in Family Planning* 36: 135–7.

Fekete, Liz (2004) 'Anti-Muslim Racism and the European Security State', *Race & Class* 46(1): 3–29.

Fraser, Arvonne (2001) 'Becoming Human: The Origins and Development of Women's Human Rights', in Marjorie Agosín (ed.), *Women, Gender, and Human Rights: A Global Perspective*. New Brunswick, NJ: Rutgers University Press.

Fraser, Arvonne, and Irene Tinker (eds.) (2004) *Developing Power: How Women Transformed International Development*. New York: The Feminist Press at CUNY.

Freedman, Lynn P. (1996) 'The Challenge of Fundamentalisms', *Reproductive Health Matters* 18: 55–69.

(2003) 'Strategic Advocacy and Maternal Mortality: Moving Targets and the Millennium Development Goals', *Gender and Development* 11(1): 97–108.

Freedman, Lynn P., et al. (2005) *Who's Got the Power? Transforming Health Systems for Women and Children*. London: UN Millennium Project Task Force on Child Health and Maternal Health. Available online at: www.unmillenniumproject.org/documents/maternalchild-frontmatter.pdf.

Friedman, Elisabeth (1995) 'Women's Human Rights: The Emergence of a Movement', in Julie Peters and Andrea Wolper (eds.), *Women's Rights, Human Rights: International Feminist Perspectives*. New York: Routledge.

(2003) 'Gendering the Agenda: The Impact of the Transnational Women's Rights Movement at the UN Conferences of the 1990s', *Women's Studies International Forum* 26(4): 313–31.

Germain, Adrienne, and Ruth Dixon-Mueller (2005) 'Reproductive Health and the MDGs: Is the Glass Half Full or Half Empty?' *Studies in Family Planning* 36(2): 137–40.

Gideon, Jasmine (2006) 'Accessing Economic and Social Rights under Neoliberalism: Gender and Rights in Chile', *Third World Quarterly* 27(7): 1269–83.

Glendon, Mary Ann (2001) *A World Made New: Eleanor Roosevelt and the Universal Declaration of Human Rights*. New York: Random House.

Goetz, Anne Marie, and Shireen Hassim (eds.) (2003) *No Shortcuts to Power: African Women in Politics and Policy Making*. London: Zed Books.

Goldberg, Pamela (1993) 'Anyplace but Home: Asylum in the United States for Women Fleeing Intimate Violence', *Cornell International Law Journal* 26: 565–604.

Goldberg, Suzanne B. (1993) 'Give Me Liberty or Give Me Death: Political Asylum and the Global Persecution of Lesbians and Gay Men', *Cornell International Law Journal* 26: 605–23.

Gómez Isa, Felipe (2003) 'The Optional Protocol for the Convention on the Elimination of All Forms of Discrimination against Women: Strengthening the Protection Mechanisms of Women's Human Rights', *Arizona Journal of International and Comparative Law* 20(2): 291–321.

Gould, Carol (2004) *Globalizing Democracy and Human Rights*. Cambridge: Cambridge University Press.

Grenfell, Laura (2004) 'Paths to Transitional Justice for Afghan Women', *Nordic Journal of International Law* 73: 505–34.

Grewal, Inderpal (1999) '"Women's Rights as Human Rights": Feminist Practices, Global Feminism and Human Rights Regimes in Transnationality', *Citizenship Studies* 3(3): 337–54.

Guhathakurta, Meghna (2003) 'Minorities, Women and Peace', *Journal of Social Studies* 100: 88–99.

Habermas, Jürgen (2001) *The Postnational Constellation*. Cambridge: Polity.

Haslegrave, M. (2004) 'Implementing the ICPD Programme of Action: What a Difference a Decade Makes', *Reproductive Health Matters* 12(23): 12–18.

Heise, Lori (1989) 'International Dimensions of Crimes Against Women', *Response to the Victimization of Women and Children* 12(1): 3–11.

Heise, Lori, Jacqueline Pitanguy and Adrienne Germain (1994) *Violence against Women: The Hidden Health Burden.* Washington, DC: The World Bank.

Held, David (1995) *Democracy and Global Order: From the Modern State to Cosmopolitan Governance*. Cambridge: Polity.

(2002) 'Cosmopolitanism: Ideas, Realities and Deficits', in David Held and Anthony McGrew (eds.), *Governing Globalization: Power, Authority and Global Governance*. Cambridge: Polity.

(2005) 'Globalization, International Law and Human Rights'. Lecture presented on 20 September at the Human Rights Center, University of Connecticut.

Hevener, Natalie Kaufman (1983) *International Law and the Status of Women*. Boulder, Colo.: Westview Press.

Hill, Felicity (2001) 'Women's Participation in Security and Peace Policy Making'. Paper presented on 5 March at Columbia University. Available online at: www.wilpf.int.ch/publications/2001scr1325.htm.

Hill, Felicity, Mikele Aboitiz and Sara Peohlman-Doumbouya (2003) 'Nongovernmental Organizations' Role in the Build-up and Implementation of Security Council Resolution 1325', *Signs* 28: 1255–69.

Hom, Sharon K. (1992) 'Female Infanticide in China: The Human Rights Specter and Thoughts Toward (An)other Vision', *Columbia Human Rights Law Review* 22(2): 249–314.

hooks, bell (1984) *Feminist Theory from Margin to Center*. Boston: South End Press.

Hosken, Fran P. (1981) 'Toward a Definition of Women's Human Rights', *Human Rights Quarterly* 3(2): 1–10.

Human Rights Watch (1993) *A Modern Form of Slavery: Trafficking of Burmese Women and Girls into Brothels in Thailand*. New York: Human Rights Watch. Available online at: www.hrw.org/legacy/reports/1993/thailand/.
(1994) *A Matter of Power: State Control of Women's Virginity (Turkey)*. New York: Human Rights Watch. Available online at: www.hrw.org/legacy/reports/1994/turkey/TURKEY.pdf.

Human Rights Watch and Fédération Internationale des Ligues des Droits de l'Homme (1996) *Shattered Lives: Sexual Violence during the Rwandan Genocide and its Aftermath*. New York: Human Rights Watch. Available online at: www.hrw.org/reports/1996/Rwanda.htm.

Human Rights Watch and Helsinki Watch (1993) *War Crimes in Bosnia-Hercegovina*. Volume II. New York: Human Rights Watch.

Humphrey, John P. (1983) 'The Memoirs of John P. Humphrey', *Human Rights Quarterly* 5: 387–439.

Huntington, Samuel P. (1993) 'The Clash of Civilizations?' *Foreign Affairs* 72 (Summer): 22–49.

ICTJ (2007) *Truth Commissions and Gender: Principles, Policies and Procedures*. New York: International Center for Transitional Justice.

Imam, Ayesha (2003) 'Working within Nigeria's Sharia Courts', *Human Rights Dialogue* 2(10): 21–4.

Imam, Ayesha, Jenny Morgan and Nira Yuval-Davis (eds.) (2004) *Warning Signs of Fundamentalisms*. London: Women Living under Muslim Laws.

Imam, Ayesha, and Nira Yuval-Davis (2004) 'Introduction', in Imam, Jenny Morgan and Nira Yuval-Davis (eds.), *Warning Signs of Fundamentalisms*. London: Women Living under Muslim Laws.

International Labour Organization (ILO) (2002) 'The Importance of Considering Gender Issues in Migration'. International Labour Organization. Available online at: www-ilo-mirror.cornell.edu/public/english/protection/migrant/projects/gender/.

ISRRC (2004) 'Statement of the International Sexual and Reproductive Rights Coalition to the 37th Session of the Commission on Population and Development'. Available online at: www.plannedparenthoodnj.org/library/files/101_ngostateme.doc.

Jaggar, Alison (2000) 'Globalizing Feminist Ethics', in Uma Narayan and Sandra Harding (eds.), *Decentering the Center*. Bloomington: Indiana University Press.

Joachim, Jutta (1999) 'Shaping the Human Rights Agenda: The Case of Violence against Women', in Mary Meyer and Elisabeth Prugl (eds.), *Gender Politics in Global Governance*. New York: Rowman and Littlefield.

Keck, Margaret E., and Kathryn Sikkink (1998) *Activists Beyond Borders: Advocacy Networks in International Politics*. Ithaca: Cornell University Press.

Kelleher, P., and M. O'Connor (1999) *Safety and Sanctions: Domestic Violence and the Enforcement of Law in Ireland*. Dublin: Women's Aid.

Kerr, Joanna (2001) 'International Trends in Gender Equality Work'. Occasional Paper 1. Toronto Association for Women's Rights in Development, November. Available online at: www.awid.org/eng/Issues-and-Analysis/ Library/International-trends-in-gender-equality-work.

Kesic, Vesna (2003) 'Muslim Women, Croatian Women, Serbian Women, Albanian Women', in Dusan Bjelic and Obrad Savic (eds.), *Balkan as Metaphor: Between Globalisation and Fragmentation*. Boston: Massachusetts Institute of Technology Press.

Khagram, Sanjeev, James V. Riker and Kathryn Sikkink (2002) *Transnational Social Movements, Networks and Norms*. Minneapolis: University of Minnesota Press.

Klausen, Jytte (2005) *The Islamic Challenge: Politics and Religion in Western Europe*. Oxford: Oxford University Press.

Kothari, Smitu, and Harsh Sethi (1989) *Rethinking Human Rights*. New York: New Horizons Press.

Lash, Joseph P. (1972) *Eleanor: The Years Alone*. New York: New American Library.

Lentin, Ronit (ed.) (1998) *Gender and Catastrophe*. New York: St Martin's Press.

Linklater, Andrew (1998) *The Transformation of Political Community*. Columbia: University of South Carolina Press.

McGrew, Anthony (1997) 'Globalization and Territorial Democracy: An Introduction', in McGrew (ed.), *The Transformation of Democracy? Globalization and Territorial Democracy*. Cambridge: Polity Press.

McNeill, David (2007) 'Japanese Prime Minister Plays Nationalist Card', *Irish Times*, 31 March.

Mapulanga-Hulston, J. K. (2002) 'Examining the Justiciability of Economic, Social and Cultural Rights', *International Journal of Human Rights* 6(4): 29–48.

Matua, Makau (2002) *Human Rights: A Political and Cultural Critique*. Philadelphia: University of Pennsylvania Press.

Matus Madrid, Verónica (1995) 'The Women's Movement and the Struggle for Rights: The Chilean Experience', in Margaret Schuler (ed.), *From Basic Needs to Basic Rights: Women's Claim to Human Rights*. Washington, DC: Women, Law, and Development International.

Menon, Ritu, and Kamla Bhasin (1998) *Borders and Boundaries: Women in India's Partition*. New Brunswick, NJ: Rutgers University Press.

Merry, Sally Engle (2006) *Human Rights and Gender Violence: Translating International Law into Local Justice*. Chicago: University of Chicago Press.

Mertus, Julie (2004) 'Shouting from the Bottom of the Well: The Impact of International Trials for Wartime Rape on Women's Agency', *International Journal of Feminist Politics* 6(1): 110–28.

Meyer, Mary K., and Elisabeth Prügl (eds.) (1999) *Gender Politics in Global Governance*. New York: Rowman & Littlefield.

Mitter, Swasti (1986) *Common Fate, Common Bond: Women in the Global Economy*. London: Pluto.

Moghadam, Valentine (2002) 'Islamic Feminism and Its Discontents: Toward a Resolution of the Debate', *Signs* 27(4): 1135–71.

(2005) *Globalizing Women: Transnational Feminist Networks*. Baltimore: Johns Hopkins University Press.

Mohanty, Chandra Talpade (1988) 'Under Western Eyes: Feminist Scholarship and Colonial Discourses'. *Feminist Review* 30: 65–88. (Originally published in 1986 in *Boundary 2* 12(3): 333–58.)

(2003) 'Under Western Eyes Revisited: Feminist Solidarity in Anti-Capitalist Struggles', in Mohanty, *Feminism Without Borders: Decolonizing Theory, Practicing Solidarity*. Durham, NC: Duke University Press.

Molyneux, Maxine, and Shahra Razavi (2006) *Beijing Plus 10: Ambivalent Record on Gender Justice*. Geneva: UN Research Institute for Social Development.

Morales, Flor (2004) 'Indigenous Women and Environmental Sustainability', in *Seeking Accountability on Women's Human Rights: Women Debate the UN Millennium Development Goals*. New York: Women's International Coalition for Economic Justice.

Morsink, Johannes (1991) 'Women's Rights in the Universal Declaration', *Human Rights Quarterly* 13: 229–56.

Mukhtar, Albaqir A. (2003) 'Working within Sharia Takes You Only So Far', *Human Rights Dialogue* 2(10): 26.

Nainar, Vahida (1999) 'The ICC Process Moving Forward', *Women's Human Rights in Conflict Situations Newsletter*, 1 August (Montreal: Rights & Democracy (International Centre for Human Rights and Democratic Development). Available online at: www.dd-rd.ca/site/publications/index. php?id=1322&page=2&subsection=catalogue.

Nankani, Sandhya (n.d.) 'Right-Wing Forces Mobilize to Challenge Beijing Platform'. Available online at: www.womenswire.net/right-wing.htm.

Narayan, Uma (2000) 'Essence of Culture and a Sense of History: A Feminist Critique of Cultural Essentialism', in Narayan and Sandra Harding (eds.), *Decentering the Center: Philosophy for a Multicultural, Postcolonial and Feminist World*. Bloomington: Indiana University Press.

Neuhold, Brita (2000) 'Women 2000: Gender Equality Development and Peace for the 21st Century'. WIDE briefing paper for the UN General Assembly Special Session. Available online at: http://62.149.193.10/wide/ download/B+5%20Briefing.pdf?id=124.

Neumann, Franz (1957) *The Democratic and the Authoritarian State: Essays in Political and Legal Power*. New York: The Free Press.

Ní Aoláin, Fionnuala (1997) 'Radical Rules: The Effects of Evidentiary and Procedural Rules in the Regulation of Sexual Violence in War', *Albany Law Review* 60: 883–905.

(2006) 'Political Violence and Gender during Times of Transition', *Columbia Journal of Gender and Law* 15: 829–49.

Ní Aoláin, Fionnuala, and Catherine Turner (2007) 'Gender, Truth and Transition', *UCLA Women's Law Journal* 16: 229–79.

Nikolic-Ritanovic, Vesna (1998) 'War, Nationalism and Mothers in the Former Yugoslavia', in Ann Lorentzen and Jennifer Turpin (eds.), *The Women and War Reader*. New York: New York University Press.

Nussbaum, Martha (1999) *Sex and Social Justice*. Oxford: Oxford University Press.

(2001) *Women and Human Development: The Capabilities Approach*. Cambridge: Cambridge University Press.

O'Brien, Robert, Anne Marie Goetz, Jan Aart Scholte and Marc Williams (2000) *Contesting Global Governance: Multilateral Economic Institutions and Global Social Movements*. Cambridge: Cambridge University Press.

Obando, Ana Elena (2004) 'Sexual Rights and the Commission on Human Rights'. Toronto: Association for Woman's Rights in Development. Available online at: www.awid.org/eng/Issues-and-Analysis/Library/ Sexual-Rights-and-the-Commission-on-Human-Rights.

Okin, Susan Moller (1981) 'Liberty and Welfare: Some Issues in Human Rights Theory', in Roland J. Pennock and John W. Chapman (eds.), *Human Rights*. New York: New York University Press.

(1999) *Is Multiculturalism Bad for Women?* Princeton: Princeton University Press.

(2000) 'Feminism, Women's Human Rights, and Cultural Differences', in Uma Narayan and Sandra Harding (eds.), *Decentering the Center*. Bloomington: Indiana University Press.

Othman, Norani (2006) 'Muslim Women and the Challenge of Islamic Fundamentalism/Extremism: An Overview of Southeast Asian Muslim Women's Struggle for Human Rights and Gender Equality', *Women's Studies International Forum* 29(4): 339–53.

Pateman, Carole (1988) *The Sexual Contract*. Cambridge: Polity.

Petchesky, Rosalind P. (2000) 'Reproductive and Sexual Rights: Charting the Course of Feminist NGOs'. Geneva 2000 Occasional Paper 8. Geneva: United Nations Research Institute for Social Development.

(2003) *Global Prescriptions: Gendering Health and Human Rights*. London: Zed Books.

Peters, Julie, and Andrea Wolper (eds.) (1995) *Women's Rights, Human Rights: International Feminist Perspectives*. New York: Routledge.

Phillips, Anne (2007) *Multiculturalism Without Culture*. Princeton: Princeton University Press.

Picciotto, Sol (1997) 'International Law: The Legitimation of Power in World Affairs', in Paddy Ireland and Per Laleng (eds.), *The Critical Lawyers' Handbook 2*. London: Pluto Press.

Pietilä, Hilkka, and Jeanne Vickers (1990) *Making Women Matter: The Role of the United Nations*. London: Zed Books.

Pogge, Thomas (2005) 'Real World Justice', *Journal of Ethics* 9(1–2): 29–53.

Porter, Elizabeth (2003) 'Women, Political Decision-making and Peace-building in Conflict Regions', *Global Change, Peace and Security* 15(3): 245–62.

Portugal, Ana Maria (2004) 'ISIS International: A Latin American Perspective', in Arvonne Fraser and Irene Tinker (eds.), *Developing Power: How Women Transformed International Development*. New York: The Feminist Press at CUNY.

Rajagopal, B. (2003) *International Law from Below: Development, Social Movements and Third World Resistance*. Boston: Massachusetts Institute of Technology Press.

Rao, Arati (1995) 'The Politics of Gender and Culture in International Human Rights Discourse', in Julie Peters and Andrea Wolper (eds.), *Women's Rights, Human Rights: International Feminist Perspectives*. New York: Routledge.

Reilly, Niamh (ed.) (1996) *Without Reservation: The Beijing Tribunal on Accountability for Women's Human Rights*. New Brunswick, NJ: Center for Women's Global Leadership.

(2007a) 'Cosmopolitan Feminism and Human Rights', *Hypatia* 22(4): 180–98.

(2007b) 'Seeking Gender Justice in Post-conflict Transitions: Towards a Transformative Women's Human Rights Approach', *International Journal of Law in Context* 3: 155–72.

Reilly, Niamh, and Linda Posluszny (2006) *Women Testify: A Planning Guide for Popular Tribunals and Hearings*. New Brunswick, NJ: Center for Women's Global Leadership. Available online at: www.cwgl.rutgers.edu/global-center/womentestify/index.htm.

Reiss, Hans (ed.) (1970) *Kant's Political Writings*. Cambridge: Cambridge University Press.

Riverbend (2003). Blog post. 1 August. Available online at: http://riverbend-blog.blogspot.com/2003_08_01_riverbendblog_archive.html.

Robertson, A. H., and J. G. Merrills (eds.) (1996) *Human Rights in the World: An Introduction to the Study of the International Production of Human Rights*. 4th edn. Manchester: Manchester University Press.

Robinson, Fiona (2003) 'Human Rights and the Global Politics of Resistance: Feminist Perspectives', *Review of International Studies* 29: 161–80.

Romany, Celina (1995) 'On Surrendering Privilege: Diversity in Feminist Redefinition of Human Rights Law', in Margaret Schuler (ed.), *From Basic Needs to Basic Rights: Women's Claim to Human Rights*. Washington, DC: Women, Law, and Development International.

Ross, Fiona (2003) *Bearing Witness: Woman and the Truth and Reconciliation Commission in South Africa*. London: Pluto Press.

Roth, K. (1994) 'Domestic Violence as an International Human Rights Issue', in Rebecca Cook (ed.), *Human Rights of Women: National and International Perspectives*. Philadelphia: University of Pennsylvania Press.

Rubio-Marin, Ruth (ed.) (2006) *What Happened to the Women? Gender and Reparations for Human Rights Violations*. New York: Social Science Research Council.

Saghal, Gita (2004) 'Two Cheers for Multiculturalism', in Ayesha Imam, Jenny Morgan and Nira Yuval-Davis (eds.), *Warning Signs of Fundamentalisms*. London: Women Living under Muslim Laws.

Said, Edward (1978) *Orientalism*. New York: Random House.

Schuler, Margaret A. (ed.) (1995) *From Basic Needs to Basic Rights: Women's Claim to Human Rights*. Washington, DC: Women, Law, and Development International.

Scott, Joan Wallach (2007) *The Politics of the Veil*. Princeton, NJ: Princeton University Press.

Sen, Amartya (1990) 'More Than 100 Million Women Are Missing', *New York Review of Books*, 20 December.

(1999) *Development as Freedom*. Oxford: Oxford University Press.

(2004) 'Elements of a Theory of Human Rights', *Philosophy and Public Affairs*. 82(4): 315–56.

Sen, Gita, and Sonia Onufer Corrêa (2000) 'Gender Justice and Economic Justice: Reflections on the Five-Year Reviews of the UN Conferences of the 1990s'. Paper prepared for UNIFEM in preparation for the Five-Year Review of the Beijing Platform for Action. Available online at: http://web.archive.org/web/20050310212617/http://www.dawn.org.fj/global/health/gender-justice.html.

Sen, Gita, and Caren Grown (1987) *Development, Crisis, and Alternative Visions: Third World Women's Perspectives*. New York: Monthly Review Press.

Shaheed, Farida (1989) 'Women, Religion and Social Change in Pakistan: A Proposed Framework for Research – Draft. An International Centre for Ethnic Studies Project (1988–1989)'. Dossier 5–6, December 1988 – May 1989. London: Women Living under Muslim Laws. Available online at: www.wluml.org/english/pubs/rtf/dossiers/dossier5-6/D5-6-10-pakistan.rtf.

(1995) 'Linking Dreams: The Network of Women Living under Muslim Laws', in Margaret A. Schuler (ed.), *From Basic Needs to Basic Rights: Women's Claim to Human Rights*. Washington, DC: Women, Law, and Development International.

(2001) 'Constructing Identities: Culture, Women's Agency and the Muslim World'. Dossier 23–34, July. London: Women Living under Muslim Laws. Available online at: www.wluml.org/english/pubs/rtf/dossiers/dossier23-24/D23-24-03-construct-id.rtf.

(2008) 'Gender, Religion and the Quest for Justice in Pakistan' (Draft working document). United Nations Research Institute for Social Development.

Smart, Carol (1989) *Feminism and the Power of Law*. New York: Routledge.

Sparr, Pamela (ed.) (1994) *Mortgaging Women's Lives: Feminist Critiques of Structural Adjustment*. London: Zed Books.

Spelman, Elizabeth V. (1988) *Inessential Woman: Problems of Exclusion in Feminist Thought*. Boston, Mass.: Beacon Press.

Spivak, Gayatri (1988) 'Can the Subaltern Speak?' in Cary Nelson and Lawrence Grossberg (eds.), *Marxism and the Interpretation of Culture*. Urbana: University of Illinois Press.

Stephenson, Mary-Ann (2005) 'Bush versus Women's Rights', *Mail & Guardian Online*, 15 March. Available online at: www.mg.co.za/article/2005-03-15-bush-versus-womens-rights.

Streeten, Paul (2001) *Globalisation: Threat or Opportunity?* Copenhagen: Copenhagen Business School Press.

Suarez, Maria (1995) 'Popularizing Women's Human Rights at the Local Level: A Grassroots Methodology for Setting the International Agenda', in Julie Peters and Andrea Wolper (eds.), *Women's Rights, Human Rights: International Feminist Perspectives*. New York: Routledge.

Susskind, Yafit (2005) 'African Women Confront Bush's AIDS Policy', *Foreign Policy in Focus*, 2 December. Available online at: http://www.fpif.org/pdf/gac/0512confront.pdf.

Symington, Alison (2004) 'MDGs and International Law', in *Seeking Accountability on Women's Human Rights: Women Debate the UN Millennium Development Goals*. New York: Women's International Coalition for Economic Justice.

Thompson, Karen Brown (2002) 'Women's Rights Are Human Rights', in Sanjeev Khagram, James V. Riker and Kathryn Sikkink (eds.), *Restructuring World Politics: Transnational Social Movements, Networks, and Norms*. Minneapolis: University of Minnesota Press.

Tinker, Irene (1981) 'A Feminist View of Copenhagen', *Signs* 6(4): 771–90.

Tsikata, Dzodzi (2004) 'The Rights-based Approach to Development: Potential for Change or More of the Same?' *IDS Bulletin* 35(4): 130–3.

Turpin, Jennifer (1998) 'Many Faces: Women Confronting War', in Lois Lorentzen and Turpin (eds.), *The Women and War Reader*. New York: New York University Press.

UN (1953) *Report on the United Nations Commission on the Racial Situation in the Union of South Africa*. 8 GAOR, Suppl. No. 16 (A/2505 and Add. 1).

——— (1993) *Vienna Declaration and Programme of Action*. UN GAOR, World Conf. on Hum. Rts., 48th Sess., 22d plen. Mtg., part I, fl 5, United Nations Doc. A/CONF.157/23.

——— (1995) Beijing Declaration and Platform for Action, in *Report of the Fourth World Conference on Women, Beijing, China, 4–15 September*. United Nations Doc. A/Conf.177/20.

(2000) *Women Go Global: The United Nations and the International Women's Movement*. CD-ROM. United Nations.

(2006) *Ending Violence Against Women: From Words to Action. Report of the Secretary General*. New York: United Nations. Available online at: www.un.org/womenwatch/daw/public/VAW_Study/VAWstudyE.pdf.

UNIFEM (2004a) *Women, Peace and Security: UNIFEM Supporting Implementation of Security Council Resolution 1325*. New York: United Nations Development Fund for Women.

(2004b) *Women, Peace and Security: CEDAW and Security Council Resolution 1325: A Quick Guide*. New York: United Nations Development Fund for Women.

Urbinati, Nadia (2003) 'Can Cosmopolitical Democracy Be Democratic?' in Daniele Archibugi (ed.), *Debating Cosmopolitics*. New York: Verso.

Waylen, Georgina (2000) 'Gender and Democratic Politics: A Comparative Analysis of Consolidation in Chile and Argentina', *Journal of Latin American Studies* 32: 765–93.

Wilets, James D. (1997) 'Conceptualizing Private Violence against Sexual Minorities as Gendered Violence: An International and Comparative Law Perspective', *Albany Law Review* 60(3): 989–1050.

WILPF (2007) 'Challenges and Opportunities for Implementing 1325', *PeaceWomen E-News* 85, 31 January, Women's International League for Peace and Freedom. Available online at: www.peacewomen.org/news/1325News/Issue85.pdf.

Wilson, Richard A. (1997) 'Human Rights, Culture and Context: An Introduction', in Wilsons (ed.), *Human Rights, Culture and Context: Anthropological Perspectives*. London: Pluto Press.

Winslow, Anne (ed.) (1995) *Women, Politics, and the United Nations*. Westport, Conn.: Greenwood Press.

Winter, Bronwyn (2006) 'Religion, Culture and Women's Human Rights: Some General Political and Theoretical Considerations', *Women's Studies International Forum* 29(4): 381–93.

WLUML (1997) 'Plan of Action – Dhaka 1997'. London: Women Living under Muslim Laws. Available online at: www.wluml.org/english/pubs/rtf/poa/dhakapoa.rtf.

Women's International War Crimes Tribunal for the Trial of Japan's Military Sexual Slavery (2001) 'The Prosecutors and the Peoples of the Asia-Pacific Region v. Hirohito et al.' Case No. PT-2000-1-T. The Hague, Netherlands, 4 December. Available online at: www1.jca.apc.org/vaww-net-japan/english/womenstribunal2000/Judgement.pdf.

Young, Iris Marion (2000) *Inclusion and Democracy*. Oxford: Oxford University Press.

Yuval-Davis, Nira (1997) *Gender and Nation*. London: Sage.

(2006) 'Human/Women's Rights and Feminist Transversal Politics', in

Myra Marx Ferree and Aili Mari Tripp (eds.), *Global Feminism: Women's Transnational Activism, Organizing, and Human Rights*. New York: New York University Press.

Zakaria, Rafia (2006) 'Veil and a Warning', *Frontline* (India) 23(2), 28 January–10 February.

Index

9–11 *see* September 11 attacks
16 Days of Action against Gender
    Violence (1991–) viii, 75–6, 171
2005 World Summit 137, 174

abortion 13, 70, 84–7, 89, 137–8,
    141–2, 147, 156, 166, 172, 174
Acar, Ferida 65–6
accountability 6, 16, 19, 25, 30–1, 34,
    39–43, 72, 85–6, 90, 95–6, 102,
    105, 113, 121, 124, 127, 129–32,
    137–8, 165
Afghanistan 81, 96, 110, 122, 147
Afkhami, Mahnaz 154
Agarwal, Bina 9
Algeria 147
Amnesty International (AI) 13, 31, 33,
    64, 69, 73, 170–1
An-Na'im, Abdullahi Ahmed 34–5
Annan, Kofi 82
apartheid 24, 28, 40, 56, 58, 168
Argentina 75
Asia 13, 15, 48–9, 72, 74, 148, 152, 169,
    173, 175
Asia Pacific Forum on Women, Law
    and Development (APWLD)
    71
Association for Women's Rights in
    Development (AWID) 167
Australia 25, 56, 156, 169
Austria 65, 79, 170
Austrian Women's Shelter Network
    79

Bahrain 156
Bangkok 74
Bangladesh 78, 144, 147, 151–2, 177
BAOBAB for Women's Human
    Rights 153–4, 173
Begtrup, Bodil 50
Beijing Declaration (1995) 88
Beijing Platform for Action (BPA)
    (1995) 12, 21, 64, 88–9, 109–10,
    112, 115, 130, 134, 168
Beijing plus Five (2000) 89, 163
Beijing plus Ten (2005) 89, 163
Berlin Wall 28
Boserup, Ester 120
Brazil 48, 156, 172, 174
Bruce, Margaret 48, 50
Bunch, Charlotte viii, 8–9, 11, 57–8,
    170
Burundi 110–11

Cairo Hearing on Reproductive
    Health and Human Rights 85
Cairo Programme of Action – *see*
    ICPD Programme of Action
    (POA) (Cairo, 1994)
Canada 36, 56, 156, 169
Cape Verde 79
Caribbean 71, 169
Caribbean Association for Feminist
    Research and Action (CAFRA)
    71
Center for Reproductive Rights
    (CRR) 174

Center for Women's Global
    Leadership (CWGL) viii,
    73–4, 84–5, 89–90, 167, 170–1,
    174
Chang, Peng-chun 49, 169
Charter of Economic Rights and
    Duties of States (1974) 117
Chechnya 147
Children's Rights Convention – *see*
    UN Convention on the Rights of
    the Child (1989)
Children's Summit (2002) – *see* UN
    General Assembly Special
    Session (UNGASS) on Children
    (2002)
Chile 25, 53, 96, 142, 171
China, 25, 49, 106, 170
Christian fundamentalism – *see*
    fundamentalisms, Christian
Christian right (USA) 155–6, 175
classical liberalism – *see* liberalism,
    classical
Cold War 1, 26–9, 73, 118, 144
comfort women 15, 102, 105–6
Commission on Human Rights – *see*
    UN Commission on Human
    Rights (UNCHR)
Commission on the Status of Women
    – *see* UN Commission on the
    Status of Women (CSW)
Committee on the Elimination of
    Discrimination against Women
    61–6, 72, 113, 134–5
Convention against Discrimination in
    Education (1960) 52
Convention Concerning
    Discrimination in Respect of
    Employment and Occupation
    (1960) 52
Convention on the Consent to
    Marriage, Minimum Age for
    Marriage and Registration of
    Marriages (1962) 52

Convention on the Elimination of All
    Forms of Discrimination Against
    Women (CEDAW) (1979)
    11–12, 19, 44–7, 55, 58–67, 72,
    81, 88, 102, 112–15, 127, 130,
    134–5, 162, 168–70, 173
Convention on the Granting of
    Political Rights to Women
    (1948) 169
Convention on the Nationality of
    Married Women (1957) 51
Convention on the Political Rights of
    Women (1952) 51
Convention on the Rights of the
    Child (1989) 60, 168
Coomaraswamy, Radhika (SRVAW,
    1994–2003) 81–2
Copenhagen NGO Forum 57
Copenhagen Programme of Action
    56
cosmopolitan feminism – *see*
    feminism, cosmopolitan
cosmopolitanism 5–6, 11, 14, 24
Costa Rica 74–5
Crenshaw, Kimberlé 14–16, 167
cultural legitimacy thesis (CLT) 34–5,
    153
cultural relativism 16, 22, 30, 34–8,
    143, 148, 150
cultural rights – *see* rights, cultural

Darfur 40, 146
Declaration on the Elimination of
    Violence against Women – *see*
    UN Declaration on the
    Elimination of Violence against
    Women (DEVAW) (1993)
Declaration on the Right to
    Development (1986) 117
democracy 2, 6–7, 13, 17, 23–4, 26, 29,
    33, 39, 93, 97–8, 103, 107–8, 111,
    114, 136, 142–3, 146–8, 151–3,
    158–9, 164–5, 169

Democratic Republic of Congo 110
development
    right to 28, 117–18
    rights-based approaches to (RBA)
        17, 118–22, 124–5, 128, 130–2,
        138
Development Alternatives with
    Women for a New Era (DAWN)
    58, 84, 167, 171, 174
Donnelly, Jack 35–6
dowry-related abuse and killings 16,
    72, 80, 89
Dravu, Margaret 78

Ebadi, Shirin 166
Economic, Social and Cultural Rights
    Network (ESCR-Net) 127, 173–4
economic rights – *see* rights, social
    and economic
Egypt 59, 89, 147, 155, 157, 170, 172
Ertürk, Yakin (SRVAW, 2003–)
    81–2
Ethical Globalization Initiative – *see*
    Realizing Rights: The Ethical
    Globalization Initiative (EGI)
Europe 15–16, 24, 28, 47–8, 54, 56–7,
    71, 79, 140–1, 169, 173–4
European Union (EU) 156

female genital mutilation 15–6, 69, 72,
    80, 85, 138, 172
female infanticide – *see* infanticide,
    female
feminism
    cosmopolitan 4–18, 34, 38, 74,
        90–2, 131, 158–62, 165–6
    global 6–10, 13–17, 55, 160–1, 166
    radical 47, 67, 70, 85, 121
    transnational – *see* transnational
        feminist advocacy (TFA)
Feminist Encuentro for Latin America
    and the Caribbean (Bogotá,
    Colombia, 1981) 71

First World Conference on Women
    (Mexico City, 1975) – *see* UN
    World Conference on Women
    (Mexico City, 1975)
Foča case 103
Former Yugoslavia 94, 99, 102, 146,
    172
Fourth Geneva Convention 101
Fourth World Conference on
    Women (FWCW) (Beijing,
    1995) – *see* UN World
    Conference on Women (Beijing,
    1995)
France 25, 50
fundamentalisms
    Christian 13, 141–2, 145–7, 155,
        165
    Islamic 141
    religious 2, 13, 21, 39, 84–5, 112,
        140–60, 165, 174

G-77 countries 87
GABRIELA 71
gender, law and development
    (GLAD) 125
gender and development (GAD) 20,
    84–5, 118–21, 125–31, 139, 164–5
gender-based violence – *see* violence,
    gender-based
General Assembly – *see* UN General
    Assembly
Geneva 28, 62, 101, 103
Geneva Conventions 101, 103
genital mutilation, female – *see* female
    genital mutilation
Germany 24–5, 65, 101
Ghana 59, 87,
Global Campaign for Women's
    Human Rights 9–12, 15–17, 19,
    23, 46, 63–4, 68–77, 80, 83, 85,
    90, 94, 101–2, 105, 170–3
global feminism – *see* feminism,
    global

Global Tribunal on Violations of
   Women's Human Rights
   (Vienna, 1993) 75–9, 85, 172
globalization 1–2, 4–5, 7, 10, 13–14,
   18, 29, 35–7, 41, 43, 45, 84–5, 92,
   111–12, 116–39, 144–5, 157, 160,
   164, 166, 173–4
Gould, Carol 5
Guatemala 36, 96, 109

Haiti 166
Harushiyakira, Schola 111, 173
headscarf controversy 141, 143–4,
   149–50
health
   reproductive and sexual (RSH) 8,
      59, 69–92, 102, 127–8, 130–1,
      135–7, 139, 142, 155–7, 162–4,
      166, 170–2
   right to 63, 85, 88, 91, 127, 163
Held, David 5–6, 17
HERA: Health, Empowerment,
   Rights, and Accountability 86
HIV / AIDS 13, 82, 85, 110, 128, 136,
   141, 156
Hom, Sharon 7–8, 35
Home Work Convention (1996) 126,
   169
Hosken, Fran 69
Human Rights Commission 48,
   168
Human Rights Committee 26–7, 138,
   174
Human Rights Council (HRC)
   168
human rights law – *see* law, human
   rights
humanitarian law – *see* law,
   humanitarian
Hunt, Paul (UN Special Rapporteur
   on the Right to Health, 2002–8)
   88
Huntington, Samuel 142

ICC NGO Women's Caucus for
   Gender Justice 12, 102–4, 172–3
ICPD Programme of Action (POA)
   (Cairo, 1994) 21, 86–7, 128, 156,
   172
Ikramullah, Shaista 51
ILO Maternity Protection
   Convention (1952) 52, 169
ILO Part-Time Work Convention
   (1994) 126, 169
Imam, Ayesha 153–5
India 50, 75, 170
indivisibility of rights – *see* rights,
   indivisibility of
Indo-Pakistani War 99
Indonesia 106
infanticide, female 7, 16, 72, 117
Inter-Parliamentary Union (IPU)
   169
International Campaign on Abortion,
   Sterilisation and Contraception
   (ICASC) 84
International Conference on
   Population and Development
   (ICPD) (Cairo, 1994) 19, 74, 83,
   85–7, 92, 102, 127–8, 130, 135,
   139–40, 151, 155–7, 164, 170
International Convention on the
   Elimination of All Forms of
   Racial Discrimination (ICERD)
   (1965) 60–1, 112, 168
International Covenant on Civil and
   Political Rights (ICCPR) (1966)
   27, 70, 138, 167–8, 174
International Covenant on Economic,
   Social and Cultural Rights
   (ICESCR) (1966) 27, 88, 112, 115,
   117, 122, 135, 167–8, 173
International Criminal Court (ICC) 6,
   12, 15, 20, 31, 67, 94, 100–6,
   112–13, 163, 173
International Criminal Tribunal for
   Rwanda (ICTR) 102

International Criminal Tribunal for the Former Yugoslavia (ICTFY) 102

International Day against Violence against Women (25 November) 71, 171

International Initiative for Justice in Gujarat (2002) 105

International Labour Organization (ILO) 13, 52, 123, 126, 169

International Military Tribunal for the Far East (IMTFE) (1946–8) 100, 172

International Preparatory Committee (IPC) 74

International Sexual and Reproductive Rights Coalition (ISRRC) 87

International Women's Health Coalition (IWHC) 84, 171–2

International Women's Rights Action Watch (IWRAW) 58, 62, 73

International Women's Rights Action Watch Asia Pacific (IWRAW Asia Pacific) 62, 169, 171

International Women's Tribune Center (IWTC) 55, 73, 171, 173

International Women's Year (IWY) (1975) 53

International Women's Year Tribune (Mexico City, 1975) 54, 56–7

Iran 57, 89, 147, 154–5, 157, 166, 168

Iraq 2, 110, 122, 147, 150

ISIS International 58, 167, 171

Islam 13, 34, 88, 140–58, 165, 174

Islamic fundamentalism – *see* fundamentalisms, Islamic

Israel 2, 24, 56

Italy 79

Japan 15, 101, 105–6, 172

justice, transitional – *see* transitional justice

Kant, Immanuel 23–5

Katsina State Sharia Court of Appeal (Nigeria) 153

Kerr, Joanna 125

Kuala Lumpur 166

La Nuestra (Latin American women's human rights conference, San José, Costa Rica) 74

Latin America 48, 58, 71, 74, 142, 169, 171

law
  human rights 6, 23, 37, 40, 45, 49, 64, 66, 72, 87, 132–3, 155, 161, 170
  humanitarian 31, 80, 100, 105, 113, 158
  rule of 3–4, 17, 33, 38–9, 94, 97–8, 142–3, 151, 158–9, 165, 169
  Sharia 147, 152–4

Lawal, Amina 153

Lebanon 25, 49

Lefaucheux, Marie-Hélène 50

legalism 18, 30, 38–40

lesbian, gay, bi-sexual and trans-gendered (LGBT) people and movements 47, 50, 72, 156–8, 165

liberalism, classical 25

Libya 155

Logar, Rosa 79

Lourdes de Jesus, Maria 79

Lutz, Bertha 48

MADRE 166

Mahathir, Mohamad 152

Malaysia 62, 106, 144–7, 151–3, 156, 166

Malik, Charles 49, 169

Martha, Perveen 78

Mauritius 147

Mehta, Hansa 50

Menon, Lakshmi 50
Mexico 54–7, 59, 65–6, 83, 87
Middle East 110, 169, 173, 175
Millennium Declaration – *see*
    UN Millennium Declaration
    (2000)
Millennium Development Goals – *see*
    UN Millennium Development
    Goals (MDGs)
Millennium Project – *see* UN
    Millennium Project
Millennium Project Task Force on
    Maternal Health and Child
    Health – *see* UN Millennium
    Project Task Force on Maternal
    Health and Child Health
Moghadam, Valentine 154
Mohanty, Chandra 8, 13, 169
Montreal Principles 127, 173
Muslim 21, 71, 141 140–58, 165,
    174

Nairobi Forward-looking Strategies
    for the Advancement of Women
    (FLS) 57–8, 71
Nairobi NGO Forum 58
Narayan, Uma 7, 35
National Front (Malaysia) 152
Nepal 75
New International Economic Order
    (NIEO) 54, 120, 122
New York City 28, 62, 86, 166, 170,
    172
NGO International Women's
    Health Conference (Cairo, 1994)
    85
NGO Working Group on Women
    and International Peace and
    Security 109–10, 173
Nigeria 144, 147, 151, 153–4, 173
North America 15, 24, 71, 175
Nuremburg Charter (1945) 100
Nuremburg trials 100

Obama, Barack 141
Optional Protocol to the Convention
    on the Elimination of All Forms
    of Discrimination against
    Women (1999) 63–5, 67, 102, 170
Organisation of the Islamic
    Conference (OIC) 156, 175
Othman, Norani 146, 149, 152–4, 158

Pakistan 51, 99, 147, 155–6
Palestine 2, 24, 57–8
Pan-Malaysian Islamic Party 152
Panama 36
PeaceWomen project 12, 110, 173
Poland 59
popular tribunals 12, 17, 75–9, 85, 92,
    95, 99, 100, 102–6, 114, 172–3
Population Council 84
postmodernism 3–4, 8, 22, 38, 160
Programme of Concerted
    International Action for the
    Advancement of Women (UN
    Resolution 2716 (XXV), 1970) 53
public–private divide 3, 11, 19, 22, 24,
    30–2, 35, 45–7, 51, 61, 64, 70–1,
    73, 80, 82, 90, 98–99, 105, 107,
    111, 114, 131, 133–40, 143, 157,
    160, 165, 177

radical feminism – *see* feminism,
    radical
Rao, Arati 7, 35–6
Realizing Rights: The Ethical
    Globalization Initiative (EGI)
    127, 173
relativism, cultural – *see* cultural
    relativism
religious fundamentalism – *see*
    fundamentalism, religious
reproductive health – *see* health,
    reproductive and sexual (RSH)
reproductive rights – *see* rights,
    reproductive and sexual

rights-based approaches to
    development – *see* development,
    rights-based approaches to
    (RBA)
right to development – *see*
    development, right to
right to health – *see* health, right to
rights
    cultural 25–28, 30–1, 59, 61, 65, 88,
        112, 117, 127–8, 135, 167–9,
        173–4
    social and economic 22, 25–8, 33,
        38, 41, 45, 49, 52, 79, 91, 112,
        117–19, 122–4, 126–7, 131–2,
        135, 139, 164–5
    indivisibility of 1, 20, 26, 29, 38, 42,
        65–6, 76, 79, 80, 82, 85, 91–2,
        114–15, 118, 126–30, 136, 139,
        164–5
    reproductive and sexual 19, 80,
        83–8, 91, 126, 142, 151, 155–7,
        163, 167, 172, 174
Riverbend blog 150, 175
Robinson, Mary (UN High
    Commissioner for Human
    Rights, 1997–2002) 127
Romany, Celina 76
Rome Statute of the International
    Criminal Court (1998) 12, 31, 102
Roosevelt, Eleanor 48, 169
rule of law – *see* law, rule of
Rwanda 96, 99, 102, 146

Saghal, Gita 148–9
San Francisco, California 47–8
San José, Costa Rica 74
Saudi Arabia 156
second wave – *see* women's
    movements, second wave
Second World Conference on
    Women – *see* UN World
    Conference on Women
    (Copenhagen, 1980)

Security Council 12–13, 109–14,
    162–3, 173
Security Council Resolution (SCR)
    1325 (2000) 12, 20, 67, 94–5,
    108–14, 162–4, 167, 173
Sen, Amartya 72
September 11 attacks 17, 128, 142,
    144, 156, 158
sexual health – *see* health,
    reproductive and sexual (RSH)
sexual rights – *see* rights, reproductive
    and sexual
sexual slavery – *see* slavery, sexual
Shaheed, Farida 145
Sharia law – *see* law, Sharia
Shariah Criminal Offences Act
    (Malaysia) 153
Sierra Leone 109–10
slavery, sexual 15, 31, 57, 80, 102,
    105–6, 114, 172
social rights – *see* rights, social and
    economic
Social Summit – *see* World Summit
    for Social Development
    (Copenhagen, 1995)
Somalia 109–10
South Africa 24, 28, 36, 40, 87, 96, 147,
    167
sovereignty, state – *see* state
    sovereignty
Soviet Union – *see* USSR
Special Rapporteur on the Right to
    Health – *see* UN Special
    Rapporteur on the Right to
    Health
Special Rapporteur on Violence
    against Women – *see* UN Special
    Rapporteur on Violence against
    Women (SRVAW)
Sri Lanka 81, 110–11, 172
Sri Lanka – Liberation Tigers of
    Tamil Eelam (LTTE) Ceasefire
    Agreement (2002) 111

state sovereignty 26, 30, 39–40, 42, 48, 64, 122, 168
structural adjustment programmes (SAPs) 120–1, 153
Sudan 2, 85, 110, 147, 155, 172

Teen Endangerment Act 147
Thailand 73, 87
Third Committee of the General Assembly 25
Timor-Leste 96, 99, 106
Tokyo Tribunal – *see* Women's International War Crimes Tribunal on Japan's Military Sexual Slavery (Tokyo Tribunal) (2000)
trafficking in women 2, 11, 16, 29, 32, 55–6, 58, 73, 80, 82, 90, 101–2, 108, 117, 160
transitional justice 20, 94–9, 104, 106, 112
transnational feminist advocacy (TFA) 1–4, 7, 10, 15, 17–19, 45, 74, 82–3, 94, 101, 106, 113, 127, 139, 151, 159–61, 171
tribunals, popular – *see* popular tribunals
Truth and Reconciliation Commission (TRC) (South Africa) 96
Tsikata, Dzodzi 124–6
Tunis 74
Turkey 73, 81

UN 1956 Supplementary Convention on the Abolition of Slavery 52
UN Charter 40, 48, 50, 66, 128
UN Commission on Human Rights (UNCHR) 25, 28, 40, 50, 81, 88, 156, 168
UN Commission on Population and Development (CPD) 87

UN Commission on the Status of Women (CSW) 28, 48, 50–5, 59–61, 63, 89, 109, 157, 168
UN Committee on Economic, Social and Cultural Rights (CESCR) 135
UN Convention on the Rights of the Child (1989) 88, 112
UN Decade for Women (UNDW) (1976–85) 1, 7, 16, 45–7, 53–61, 67, 71–2, 116, 120, 162
UN Declaration on the Elimination of Discrimination against Women (1967) 53, 59
UN Declaration on the Elimination of Violence against Women (DEVAW) (1993) 12, 72, 80–1, 89
UN Development Fund for Women (UNIFEM) 55, 73, 110, 113, 126–7, 173
UN Division for the Advancement of Women (DAW) 54
UN Economic and Social Council (ECOSOC) 59–60, 63, 168–9
UN Educational, Scientific and Cultural Organisation (UNESCO) 52
UN General Assembly 12, 25–6, 51–3, 59–60, 65, 80, 89, 128, 156, 168, 170
UN General Assembly Special Session (UNGASS) 89, 156
UN General Assembly Special Session (UNGASS) on Children (2002) 156
UN High Commissioner for Human Rights 127
UN International Conference on Population (Mexico City, 1984) 83
UN International Research and Training Institute for the Advancement of Women (INSTRAW) 55

UN Millennium Declaration (2000)
    128–9
UN Millennium Development Goals
    (MDGs) 18, 20, 37, 87, 119,
    128–39, 164, 174
UN Millennium Project 128, 136–7
UN Millennium Project Task Force
    on Maternal Health and Child
    Health 136
UN Special Rapporteur on the Right
    to Health 88
UN Special Rapporteur on Violence
    against Women (SRVAW) 12,
    81–2
UN World Conference on Human
    Rights (Vienna, 1993) 16, 28–9,
    63, 73–85, 91–2, 101–2, 105, 112,
    118, 123, 127, 138–9, 155, 157,
    163–4, 170–2
UN World Conference on Women
    (Beijing, 1995) 16–17, 20, 63–4,
    75–6, 82–3, 85, 88–92, 102, 105,
    130, 139–40, 155–7, 164, 168,
    170–1
UN World Conference on Women
    (Copenhagen, 1980) 46, 55–7,
    59–60
UN World Conference on Women
    (Mexico City, 1975) 53–7, 59
UN World Conference on Women
    (Nairobi, 1985) 57–8, 72
United Kingdom 25–6, 48, 122, 147–8,
    166, 172
United Nations 1–2, 4, 6–7, 11–12,
    16–21, 23, 25–6, 28, 37, 39–48,
    50–1, 53–9, 63, 66–7, 71–7, 80–3,
    85–9, 95, 102, 109–11, 114,
    116–17, 119, 121, 123–4, 126–8,
    130, 135, 137, 140, 144, 155–7,
    160, 162–4, 167–75
United States 16–17, 24, 47–9, 54, 57,
    66, 69, 74, 87, 89–90, 122, 141–2,
    145, 147–8, 155–6, 169–72, 175

Universal Declaration of Human
    Rights (UDHR) (1948) 19, 25–6,
    29–30, 40, 44, 48–9, 51, 66, 81,
    122, 161, 168
USSR 25–6, 48–51, 59, 79

Vatican 87–8, 155–6
veils, Muslim women and – *see*
    headscarf controversy
Vienna Declaration and Programme
    of Action (VDPA) (1993) 12, 29,
    73, 75–6, 79–80, 112, 118, 136
Vienna Tribunal – *see* Global Tribunal
    on Violations of Women's
    Human Rights (Vienna, 1993)
violence
    against women (VAW) 2, 11–16,
        19, 30–1, 43, 47, 49, 56, 63, 65–7,
        69–92, 98–9, 101, 103, 108, 118,
        125–6, 133–4, 157, 160, 162, 164,
        171
    gender-based 12, 31, 61, 69, 71–3,
        80–2, 100, 117, 135

war on terror 2, 18, 29, 122, 144, 148
Westphalian world order 39
Women and Armed Conflict Caucus
    109
women in development (WID) 46,
    54, 120–1
Women in Law and Development in
    Africa (WiLDAF) 71, 74, 171,
    173
Women Living under Muslim Laws
    (WLUML) network 21, 71, 143,
    147, 149, 154, 171, 174–5
Women's Caucus for Gender Justice
    – *see* ICC NGO Women's
    Caucus for Gender Justice
Women's Coalition for the
    International Conference on
    Population and Development
    (ICPD) 86

Women's Convention – *see* Convention on the Elimination of All Forms of Discrimination Against Women (CEDAW) (1979)
Women's Environment and Development Organization (WEDO) 84, 167, 171, 174
Women's Global Network for Reproductive Rights (WGNRR) 83–4, 167
Women's International League for Peace and Freedom (WILPF) 109–10, 173
Women's International Network (WIN) News 69
Women's International War Crimes Tribunal on Japan's Military Sexual Slavery (Tokyo Tribunal) (2000) 105–6, 114, 172

women's movements, second wave 14, 46, 50, 53, 70
World Bank 84, 120, 127, 153
World Conference on Human Rights (Vienna, 1993) – *see* UN World Conference on Human Rights (Vienna, 1993)
World Plan of Action (Mexico City, 1975) 55
World Social Forum (WSF) 127, 174
World Summit for Social Development (Copenhagen, 1995) 170
World War II 15, 17, 39–40, 95, 99–101, 105, 120

Yuval-Davis, Nira 9–10

Zimbabwe 2, 156, 166